SUCCESSFUL
RECRUITMENT
AND SELECTION

SUCCESSFUL
RECRUITMENT
AND SELECTION

A Practical Guide for Managers

Margaret Dale

**KOGAN
PAGE**

YOURS TO HAVE AND TO HOLD

BUT NOT TO COPY

First published in 1995

Kogan Page Limited
120 Pentonville Road
London N1 9JN

© Margaret Dale, 1995

British Library Cataloguing in Publication Data

A CIP record for this book is available from the British Library.

ISBN 0 7494 1422 7

Typeset by JS Typesetting, Wellingborough, Northants.
Printed and bound in Great Britain by Biddles Ltd, Guildford and Kings Lynn.

Contents

Acknowledgements

Thanks are due to my colleagues in the Personnel Department and elsewhere in Sheffield Hallam University for their help and support. In particular I am grateful to Debbie Stevens and Professor Dianne Willcocks, whose trust has encouraged me to develop my practice, ideas and understanding, and Jennie Merriman who has kindly provided feedback and typographic corrections.

Ian Day of Barnes Kavelle has also helped to increase my understanding of the issues from the perspective of a consultant.

Roger's determined 'tunnel digging' sets all job seekers an example and his experiences have made me acutely aware of the effect recruiters can have on people. As ever, he has provided me with the moral support and TLC needed to complete a project of this size.

Margaret Dale
April 1995

1

Successful Recruitment and Selection: An Introduction

The primary purpose of the recruitment and selection process is to achieve one desired end — picking the right person for the job. This sounds obvious and as if it should be easy. If only this were so. The process is lengthy, complex and presents as many opportunities for making wrong or bad decisions as there are for making the right one. Research has shown that the 'best' selection method has a predictive validity coefficient of 0.6 — ie the method has an excellent chance of predicting that an individual candidate's subsequent performance will match the criteria. This means that there is also a strong chance that the appointee will *not* achieve the desired standard. The most commonly used method — a face-to-face interview — can only claim a coefficient of 0.2. This means that there is an excellent chance of not appointing the best candidate. Long odds, especially if the appointment is critical for the organisation's success or failure!

A poor or bad selection decision can have catastrophic consequences for an organisation. Even at a basic level a poor learner who is not in tune with the organisation's ethos and aims can damage production, customer satisfaction, relationships with suppliers and the overall quality of service. The new appointee can adversely affect the morale and commitment of co-workers and negate efforts to foster team working. For managers, whose performance is frequently assessed on the basis of their staff, a bad or poor selection decision can reflect very badly on their subsequent performance. Also, correcting bad decisions can be costly. Even if it is possible to dismiss the new appointee quickly the recruitment costs have already been incurred, and the cost and loss of labour during the time it takes to make another appointment and the learning time of the second newly appointed individual must be taken into account. If it is not possible to rectify a poor decision in this way, living with the consequences can have long-term repercussions that can not easily be costed. We all have had experience that demonstrates just how expensive they can be.

For an individual appointed to the wrong job, there is no easy way out. Trying to be effective in the wrong job can rapidly lead to a loss of self-esteem. It is easy for appointees to blame themselves and assume that they are not up to the job, that their skills are not adequate or that they overestimated their own level of capability when applying for the job. It is not easy to recognise (especially in the early days of an appointment) that the post was badly constructed, that the selection criteria were unrealistic or that the members of the appointment panel did not know what they were looking for. Finding a respectable way out can be more difficult for the individual than for the employer. Resignation is risky if unemployment is high and, in any case, the appointment mistake is usually taken as a reflection of the individual's level of competence. Living with the situation can lead to a loss of morale and self-confidence, thus lowering performance levels even more and making it harder for the individual to find another job.

Even when the odds of making the right decision are 50–50, it is possible to reduce further the risks of getting it wrong. The first step is to recognise that the end decision is, in fact, two way. The employer offers a contract of employment and the individual decides whether to accept or reject it. The factors influencing the decision are complex. The employer's decision is usually made as a result of an assessment of which candidate is the 'best person for the job' (whatever this means), while the individual's decision has to take account of the post in question, the effect it will have on subsequent jobs and the rest of his or her life. The decision needs to be seen from the different perspectives of the two main parties if the resultant contract is to be mutually beneficial.

The actions taken by the employer to ensure that the 'best' candidate is attracted and selected can be equated to an investment decision (and examples of the different types of action available will be described later). Rectifying a bad or poor decision can be time-consuming and costly; making a good decision can lead to the realisation of rewards and pay-offs that far outstrip initial expectations of the parties involved. An individual who fits with the organisation, its culture and other employees and is prepared and encouraged to develop and improve personal and organisational performance can bring unpredictable benefits. Picking the right person does not necessarily cost a lot of money. Moreover many of the actions that can be taken do not require highly developed skills of experienced professional practitioners. They do, however, require thought, planning and preparation.

WHAT IS TO COME

This book aims to provide practical insights, suggestions and examples of simple, cost-effective ways of improving every stage of the recruitment and selection process. While it is intended primarily for managers and personnel practitioners, it will also help those applying for jobs. It will be particularly useful for employers and potential employees who are entering the labour market for the first time. Most people involved in the appointment process are aware of the importance of making the right decision, and therefore it is likely to be a tense, stressful experience for all concerned. This book aims to reduce this stress by demystifying the process and, based on examples of known good and bad practice, by explaining the different stages and methods available.

Explanations of the underpinning theories are also given to help those currently involved in recruitment and selection to improve their practice. Other than in large organisations, or ones with high staff turnover, employing people is not an everyday activity. It is understandable that skills become rusty and busy managers and personnel professionals get out of touch with current thinking and practice. Checklists will accompany the examples and explanations to help readers chart their way through the different stages of the process.

This book does not claim to be an exclusive text book. References will be made to other work where appropriate and some suggestions made for further reading. Case law, tribunal decisions and the influences of European legislation are bringing about changes to employment law that are requiring different and new approaches to employment practice. Because these are changing constantly as judgments redefine and interpret statute, details will not be given. Rather than risk misleading the reader, some suggestions are given about general good practice and how to find out about the latest position.

Describing the job and the best person

Chapter 2 outlines how to build and describe the job. Often a collection of tasks are bundled together, the resultant package is called a job and a person is sought to fill it. It is generally assumed that these tasks will be carried out by one individual who will work full time to achieve a satisfactory standard of performance and the desired objectives. Job sharing possibilities sometimes are thought about but, more often, the consideration of part-time working is restricted to areas of work where large numbers of the same type of worker (frequently women or young people) are employed. In the case of more specialist jobs or senior manager posts, normally it is assumed the postholder needs to be employed to work full time, if not more.

Whether that job can realistically be performed by a single human being is even more rarely considered — until, that is, that human begins to fail in some way. But usually the human is faulted rather than the 'design' of the job. Chapter 2 offers ways of analysing the organisational requirements in a way that produces a useful description of the job that needs to be done. These methods include consideration of those factors that influence whether a job is do-able. Elements of the job that lead to satisfaction for the postholder and foster their development are also covered. The description of a job should not be a static record. It should be tight enough to provide an accurate outline of job purpose and its main responsibilities and objectives, but it should be broad enough to allow for change, growth and contraction.

The person specification

Once described, the job outline can be the basis for a person specification that defines the sort of individual best suited to perform the duties of the job. It should not, however, be a stereotypical picture — rather an indication of the attainment, experiences, skills and attributes that are needed to enable an individual to fill the role, perform the job and achieve the desired objectives. The person specification is the foundation (along with the job description) for any recruitment activity and establishes the competency standards against which candidates will eventually be assessed. It can also be used to inform the initial training of the person appointed and their subsequent development plan.

In addition, compilation of the job description and person specification can be used to check against bias and the inappropriate use of assumptions and stereotypes. Especially when filling a post occupied previously, it is easy to either build the characteristics of the previous postholder into the specification or to go to the opposite extreme. This practice can be dangerous because it can lead to the appointment of clones or the introduction of people who are so different that the organisation is not able to assimilate them. The compiler of the specification should be encouraged to look forward to what attainments, experiences, skills and attributes are needed for acceptable performance in the future. The creation of a vacancy, be it from the termination of an existing contract or the creation of a new post, provides the opportunity for drawing up a new job description or validating the existing one, and writing a new person specification that enables the question to be asked, 'What does the organisation really need now?'

Attracting candidates

Knowing what to look for makes the search for the right person somewhat easier. Recruitment is about attracting candidates who, in the context of the employing organisation, are qualified and able to carry out the job. We must explore where the power lies because, even in the case of search, it is the candidates who decide to indicate their interest in working for a particular organisation. How to get the right person's attention and interest is the challenge of recruitment. Ways of doing this, including some novel approaches, are suggested in Chapter 3. Because the process is very similar to selling a product or service, some ideas will be drawn from marketing. However, despite the attention given to press advertisements and the use of recruitment agencies, candidates are attracted for most jobs via other methods. The Equal Opportunities Commission and the Commission for Racial Equality have produced guidance on how to ensure that jobs are made available to suitably qualified people from all sections of the community, regardless of race, marital status and gender. Recently, increasing concern is being expressed about age discrimination. Ways of promoting vacancies fairly will be considered as part of the discussion of the different methods.

Making decisions

The human decision-making process is known to be flawed. This imperfection affects the ways in which recruiters and selectors make judgements about applicants and how potential applicants decide whether to submit and continue with their application. As these decisions are central to each stage of the recruitment and selection process, in Chapter 4 some of the more common biases and sources of error are described.

The main influence on how decisions are made is the information available to the person concerned and the media used to communicate that information. The initial medium is the advertisement or other public announcement and this is then supplemented by supporting details such as information packs. These tend to be used mainly by larger employers who recruit significant numbers of employees, but more widespread use could be beneficial to employers and employees in ways unrelated to merely attracting candidates. The information given helps applicants and influences the way in which they frame their applications. This, in turn, influences the recruiter when making shortlisting decisions. Research also suggests that the more (quality) information given to the ultimate postholder before the start of the appointment, the more successful that appointment is likely to be. Creating an accurate impression of the organisation and job in the minds of candidates contributes to induction and initial training.

Submitting an application

There are a number of means by which candidates are expected to express their interest, and each sector tends to have its own preferences that can influence how an uninitiated candidate's application will be received. This simple lack of knowledge of what is expected, which may have nothing to do with their ability to perform the job, can inhibit people moving between industrial sectors. This barrier can work to the detriment of individuals and the economy as a whole as it prevents the development of generic competencies and the transfer of skills and approaches. The different methods in common use are explored in Chapter 5 in order to explain how different expectations can best be met and applications assessed in terms of best fit against the person specification and job requirements instead of conformity to sectorially specific norms. The exploration should prove useful to employers and those appointing applicants from other sectors, and it should also help applicants decide how best to present their applications.

Assessing applications

Assessment of the application is normally the first stage of selection — a process of discrimination aimed at picking the 'best' candidate — and it is at this stage where prejudices and stereotypes begin to show up. Interestingly, very little research has been conducted into decisions made during shortlisting. This opportunity therefore is used to consider what might be taking place in shortlisters' minds. Suggestions will be made to explain what is happening to help both selectors and those putting themselves forward for selection to understand better the possible factors influencing the processes. This will lead to some proposals to improve current practice and make subconscious, hidden decisions more transparent.

Selection events

The selection event is usually the first time when applicants and potential employers formally meet in person. As discussed in Chapter 6, the interview is by far the most common selection method used, and it continues to be the preferred method of selecting staff despite much evidence to the effect that as a tool for predicting likely performance it is weak. Some organisations have rejected the interview and have experimented with other ways of assessing applicants' skills and attributes that have better predictive validity. Some of these have attracted controversy of their own and have been the subject of heated debate at professional conferences and in the press. There is a popular belief that these methods are high cost and do not necessarily justify the expenditure.

Even when an appointment decision is seen merely in mechanistic terms, recruitment activity is costly and the investment made in an individual by the time an appointment is made can be substantial. When the human aspects are added, the decision takes on a different perspective. If the appointment is critical in terms of organisational success (and even a lowly paid receptionist can have a major impact on levels of customer satisfaction), the decision to appoint becomes of major importance. It is, therefore, worth spending more than half an hour having a chat in order to make sure the right and best person is appointed.

Some of the more common approaches are discussed in Chapter 6, plus practical ways of implementing them. References will be made to less well-known techniques that should be of help to managers and personnel specialists wishing to reduce the odds of making a poor decision. The chapter will also help those facing selection events to prepare themselves for what may be a new experience. A well-run selection event, even if the application is not successful, can be very helpful for the individual applicant. A period of reflection is needed for the completion of the application, which can be linked to a critical appraisal of skills. These will be assessed against a predetermined profile, and sensitively supplied, feedback may then be given in a way that can be of benefit for an individual's development.

The impact on applicants

Sadly, selection events have been known to damage some individuals. It is rare for an employer to look at the recruitment and selection process from the perspective of the individual applicant. Putting oneself forward for the sort of critical appraisal carried out during selection is stressful and requires the individual to make an investment of energy and emotion. The applicant has to engage in a period of self-examination and has to create several different scenarios of the future that could involve major changes for themselves, partners and families. It is right that selection events should be challenging and testing but they should not be destructive. What is the point in putting candidates through gruelling, traumatic activities to see if they are 'up to it' when 'it' is not a true requirement of the job? Some of the ways in which an organisation engages with and affects applicants and candidates are discussed in Chapter 7. Much can be done to improve the interaction and reduce unnecessary stress without removing the challenge and thorough examination of skills and attributes.

After the event, successful and unsuccessful candidates deserve some information in return for the efforts they will have expended in applying for the job. Giving feedback ineptly can also lead to unnecessary damage being done to an individual's self-esteem and it can give grounds for complaint where otherwise there would have been none. An employer needs to remember that an individual may have the right to take a case to an Industrial Tribunal if they believe they have been treated unfairly. This is not an excuse for failing to give feedback; nor is it justification from wrapping up helpful but critical information in generalities. Rather it is a reason for making sure that feedback is provided in a constructive manner, providing enough information to help the individual learn while leaving their self-confidence intact.

Once the selection events have been held, those with the responsibility for the appointment have to make the decision. No matter how sophisticated the techniques used during selection, the human beings involved can not absolve themselves from responsibility for the final decision. But the decision to appoint is not just one way. The selected candidate has some say in the matter and there are other questions to be discussed in addition to 'Do you want the job — yes or no?'. Because changes in employment practices have resulted in more individually negotiated contracts, the offer of employment is increasingly taking the form of a negotiation. These, especially at senior levels, include more than discussions on pay and hours of work. Without going into the detail of the legalities of contracts, some consideration is given in Chapter 8 to what can form part of the offer of employment.

Induction and inclusion

Just after the final selection decisions have been made, the period of negotiation begins. During this stage the details of the employment contract are settled, including agreement on the explicit and implicit terms. Frequently employers do not realise the importance of these discussions. The understandings of both parties create further expectations and interpretations about the job, the standards required and the conditions surrounding the work. Misinformation and misleading discussions can cause problems later on. Also, the appointed person will be clarifying details of their reward package and such personal details as housing, relocation reimbursements and the like.

Nevertheless, despite all the efforts to get the appointment right, occasionally wrong decisions are made. Remedying such as situation can be time-consuming, painful and costly if handled badly. We do not often acknowledge errors, partly because it is not easy to rectify them. Consequently, some simple steps are outlined to suggest ways in which remedial action can be taken. It is important to allow both the employer and the newly appointed employee to get out of the situation and to admit a genuine error of judgement has been made without either party losing too much face.

Increasingly, access to training and development is being seen as a part of an individual's broader reward package. All employees have the right to expect to be adequately trained to carry out their duties to the required standard. Even those with considerable experience need some initial training in order to orientate them to the new organisation's ways of working and to induct them into its culture. The early days of employment (the induction period) can be critical to the long-term success of the appointment. This phase is not often seen as part of the recruitment and selection process, yet how the new employee is treated during recruitment, selection and induction can make or break the achievement of the expected outcomes from the employment. If induction goes wrong, all the effort put in and money spent on the appointment of the individual can be squandered. There is a temptation to see the newly appointed person as being perfect, but even outstanding candidates will need help to fit into the organisation and to improve on the weaker aspects of their overall match to the requirements of the job. Ways of improving the induction phase of employment are described in Chapter 9 and some guidance is given on what and what not should be expected of someone new into a job.

The person appointed also has the right of access to training and longer-term development to help them equip themselves for the changes the future is guaranteed to bring. The period just after appointment presents ample opportunities for the creation of an individual development plan. By this time, an individual's skills will have been appraised against a carefully considered job description and person specification and he or she will have been compared with other suitably qualified individuals. Even in the euphoria of success, the individual will be as open as they are ever likely to be for constructive feedback and positive guidance.

Evaluation

Finally, ways of evaluating the success of the recruitment and selection process are described in Chapter 10. Even if the post has not been filled, the process should have contributed to the organisation's operations in some way. Every exposure to the outside world has an impact on an organisation's image, and bringing people in for the purposes of selection says something publicly about the way the employer treats people. Therefore, it is worth using an appointment as part of the overall marketing and promotion effort of the organisation, and a successful appointment process can produce useful lessons for next time a post needs to be filled. Market testing the skills and attributes thought to be needed against those available can be salutary. It also helps to assess the value and performance levels of existing staff. There is always a temptation to see those outside as being 'better' than one's current employees, but sometimes this is an illusion.

If the recruitment and selection process has been expensive, it may be necessary to justify the cost. The utility of the process can be calculated and the result used to demonstrate longer-term value to the organisation. If an appointment is viewed in parallel with other forms of investment it becomes possible for recruitment and selection to demonstrate its role in strategic planning and claim its successes. Once an appointment has been made, it is easy to forget the effort that went into getting it right, and a thorough evaluation can help to ensure that responsibility and praise are fairly attributed.

This book is intended as an aid to those wishing to understand the recruitment and selection process better, and wanting to make improvements. Its contents are based on experience of applying for jobs, comparing these experiences to those of others, running recruitment and selection activities and reflecting on these and the reports of others. Going through a recruitment and selection process can have a major impact on all the individuals involved, as well as on the employing organisation. Even if the very best methods are used, the ways in which they are applied can result in good appointments or disastrous mistakes. The process can be stressful for everyone concerned and contains a lot of risk. Because it is complex and lengthy, it provides plenty of opportunities for getting things wrong. Yet, getting it right need not be difficult or costly. In fact, making use of good practice can actually reduce cost as well as increase the chances of picking the right person for the job.

2

Describing the Job

Appointing the right person for the job is much more than simply making the right decision after an interview. Several stages have to occur before the final decision can be made. To start the process leading to the selection of the right person, suitably qualified and experienced applicants must be attracted, but what 'suitably qualified and experienced' means has to be determined. If this definition is not communicated clearly, people will not know whether to apply — and if there is doubt, the chances are they will not apply; in these circumstances it will not be possible to compare candidates. What will applicants be assessed against and how will the best person be recognised? Most recruiters are aware of the need to identify desirable and essential qualifications and experience, but specifying the qualification and experience required is only one part of describing the most suitable candidate. The job that person is to do needs to be described.

The compilation and use of job descriptions and person specifications will probably be familiar to those who have some experience of recruitment and selection. However, to be fully useful their contents need to be written in such a way that they can be used for factual and comparative assessment. This means that skills, traits and aptitudes should be described precisely, and indicators included so assessments can be based on evidence.

Often, the job is a gathering of tasks that need to be done or that have traditionally been done by previous postholders. The way in which a job is constructed can lead to effective or ineffective performance by the postholder. It is immaterial whether the person appointed to perform those tasks is the most qualified and experienced individual. If the job is badly constructed the person's chances of success are relatively small. From reading advertisements and recruitment literature, it seems as though very little systematic job design is carried out. This is a shame because the way in which a job is built up affects both the performance of and the satisfaction obtained by the postholder. A well-designed job can motivate an individual and provide opportunities for their personal and career development. It can also enable the employing organisation to look forward. Good job design starts with an initial analysis of what the organisation requires, but this analysis should be more than looking at past successful performance. It should be linked closely to the needs of the business operations of the organisation and what will be required in the future to maintain success, achieve new objectives and improve performance. Simple ways of carrying out this analysis (which should also take account of what can reasonably be expected of the postholder) will be described in this chapter.

The first stage of analysing need presents the opportunity for past assumptions and historic models to be challenged. We tend to build up pictures of the type of people we think are best suited to certain jobs and position in the organisation. These pictures are limited by our own past experiences of people and images of likely future success. It is certain that these images are flawed as their foundations are based on incomplete information, prejudices and false assumptions. Drawing up job descriptions and person specifications based on the requirements of a job to be done in the future can avoid some of the traditional stereotypes. The discussion of how this can be achieved needs to take into account the implications of equal opportunities legislation. Statutes and case law that place obligations on employers at the moment tend to be minimalist; they say what should not be done rather than indicating what could be done to correct historic unfairness. There are positive, legal ways of addressing previous discrimination. Some practical suggestions will be made about the positive action approaches that can be taken in the early stages of the recruitment and selection process.

DESIGNING THE JOB

Most recruitment begins with the job description. Really, this should be the second step rather than the first. The first should be the design of the job. A job is more than a collection of tasks; it should be a role with meaning and purpose in the context of the organisation and the part of the organisation in which it is located. It should also be do-able by a human being. There are a number of ways to prevent a job from being do-able. Its design can be so poor that the individual occupying it cannot hope to succeed; the component tasks may be disjointed and unrelated (too many duties or too few and the job may not make sense); it can be so unrewarding that most postholders are just demotivated; or it can require a range of skills too wide for any one individual to possess.

Scientific management

The traditional approach to job design is rooted in 'Taylorism'. Frederick Taylor (1991) was the father of what is called 'scientific management' and one of the first to set down principles that could be used generally to divide tasks and organise labour. His approach was developed in the late 19th century for the heavy industries of North America. His goal was to increase the productivity of the labourer and he believed in the notion of 'economic man' (ie an individual desires to maximise the benefit to himself and so will increase his efforts to do so). Taylor's ideas laid the foundations for the division and organisation of work and various payment by results schemes.

Taylor's approach was based on the belief that there was only one way to do a job — the right way. This led to the study of work and the establishment of rule books that codified working methods. Taylor went on to recommend that an individual worker's skills be assessed so that worker and job could be matched. The worker would be paid for the results of his skill and effort but would work under the control of a functional foreman. The foreman's legitimate authority would be built on his expertise and work would be organised into functional groups. Functional grouping came from the ideas of the 18th century economist, Adam Smith, who suggested that tight division of labour would have three advantages:

- The simplification of routines would improve the dexterity of the worker.
- The 'routinisation' of operations would reduce time delays as the worker could be deployed on one task and so would not have to change tools or materials.
- Specialist machines could be used to aid production.

Ted was a successful entrepreneur. He had a history of buying small companies in difficulty, streamlining their operations and taking them from the brink of bankruptcy back to full viability. The approach he adopted had been the same for each company. He examined the organisation as a flow process and broke the systems into their component stages. He then considered how to simplify each stage in a way that would enable it to lead from the previous phase smoothly into the next.

In most companies he had found that the staff tended to follow whatever was being processed from start to finish. His experience had shown that this was extremely inefficient. The staff were not good at anything in particular and could not take a pride in their work. Ted believed that it was far better to encourage staff to specialise on a single aspect, develop their skills in that area of work and get a sense of a job well done. This approach led to other problems, such as disputes between groups of workers, and there was a tendency for one group to blame another if mistakes were made. However, the improvements to profitability of the operations meant that it was possible to employ good quality supervisors who were able to put a stop to any silliness.

By the time Ted retired he had created a conglomeration of small and medium-sized companies, was chairman of the local chamber of commerce and had received an OBE.

Evidence of Adam Smith's thinking can still be seen in current approaches to the organisation of work. The assembly line is still the basis of mass production; the application of precise rules can be found in fast food outlets to ensure standardisation of product; and the computer control of plant and equipment has been introduced to reduce the chances of human error (as well as reducing the risk of accident and eliminating boring jobs).

Even though many work practices still make use of 19th century thinking about people's behaviour at work and the sources of their motivation, the underpinning beliefs have been challenged. The biggest flaw with Taylorism is that people are not economic and rational; motives other than personal profit drive people to work productively. Taylor's principles were developed in the context of the North American steel mills, which were staffed largely by immigrant workers. Many of these people were ill-educated, nearly illiterate and at starvation level — unsurprisingly, the need to eat dominated their thinking and their motivation at work. Since then, other motivators and drives have been identified and have been used to inform the less traditional thinking behind job design.

Human relations school

After World War I, other factors were identified as sources of motivation that affected levels of performance. The 'science' of management and its study was being influenced by the related work of psychologists and sociologists. Various investigations into productivity set the foundations for the modern approaches to the construction, organisation and management of work. The rational economic approach was largely discredited and was replaced by the human relations school. It is beyond the scope of this book to explore the details of these approaches, but interested readers will find ample coverage in texts such as Handy (1985) or Child (1984).

In the field of motivation and job satisfaction, two major theories have stood the test of time. Both have been widely criticised and efforts have been made to discount them. Nevertheless, the approaches of Maslow and Hertzberg have appeal and practical application. Their work is simple and understandable because it is grounded in a reality that can be recognised by managers and other people in the workplace. Also, later work tends to complement rather than contradict their ideas.

Abraham Maslow (1954) was a theoretical psychologist who hypothesised about the factors that motivate individuals. His work was put forward in the early 1950s as an untested idea. Nevertheless, it was accepted and has remained current largely because of its intuitive appeal. Maslow suggested that human motives can be arranged in a five-step hierarchy of priorities (see Figure 2.1). The basic assumption Maslow made to underpin his hypothesis was that as one base need was satisfied the individual would be motivated to satisfy the next. However, he did not see a satisfied need as a motivator. Maslow's work differed considerably from that of Taylor. Maslow recognised that human beings were driven by a number of factors — not just money — and that when ultimately the needs in deficit were satisfied, individuals would be motivated by the wish to be themselves.

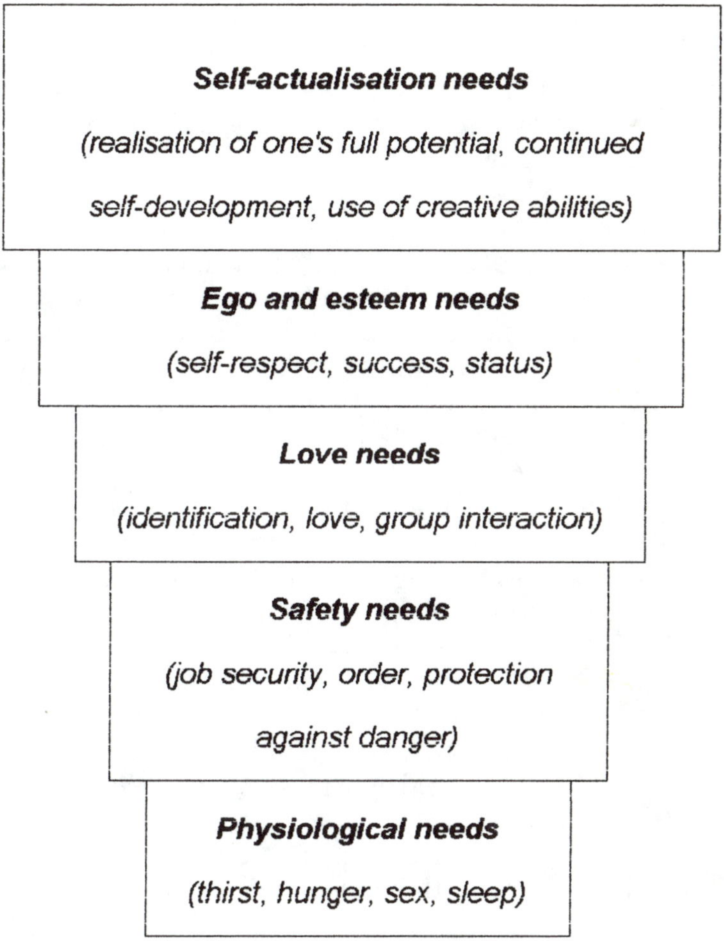

Figure 2.1 Maslow's hierarchy of needs

The company was set up by three friends — Ian, Mary and Rhand. They had studied for their professional qualifications together but had drifted apart for a few years. They met again, by accident, at a conference. When they had caught up with each other's histories, it became clear that none of them were happy working for the large organisations that currently employed them. They decided to establish a consultancy that would allow them to be their own bosses and to do the sort of work that really interested them.

Rhand was a little worried. She had recently taken on a large mortgage and was struggling to make ends meet. Giving up her large salary would be a big step for her. Still she was prepared to give it a go.

Ian had similar but different concerns. He had a young family and was concerned about his longer-term security. His current employer had very generous pension and health provisions and had made guarantees against redundancy. He felt that he would have to take out substantial insurance to make sure his family was safeguarded if the firm was not successful.

Mary was worried about leaving her current colleagues. She was part of a close-knit group of friends at her present company. Leaving them would be sad, but Ian assured her that if they were real friends, they would stay in touch.

Within two years they had established the business as a successful company. Its reputation was spreading and the number of clients was increasing to such an extent that the three friends were considering expanding and taking on extra staff. They all agreed that the risks had been worth taking. The potential now available for them to develop their own talents was far greater than it would have been if they had stayed with their previous employers. With hindsight, they wondered what had concerned them.

The 'self-actualised' person is perhaps now tarnished by the stereotype of the free love hippies of the 1960s. Really, it is a concept that attempts to portray an individual who is able to focus on developing, realising and using their best abilities rather than someone who is trying to live up to expectations. Maslow also recognised that individuals were motivated by different factors in different circumstances for different reasons. He was aware of that the hierarchy was more than the simple straight-line progression shown in Figure 2.1.

The other frequently quoted research in this area was carried out by

Frederick Hertzberg and his associates (1959). Dissatisfied by previous work, Hertzberg and his team set out to question workers about the factors that led to their satisfaction and dissatisfaction at work. On the basis of hundreds of questionnaires and interviews, clusters of factors were isolated. These were separated into those incidents that led to increased satisfaction and those that did not, and these two groupings were labelled as hygiene factors and motivators (see Table 2.1). The latter term was used to describe those factors that would lead a worker to increase effort. The former factors, however, would only serve to maintain the level of motivation if they were right. More importantly, if they were wrong they would demotivate a worker.

Table 2.1 Hertzberg's hygiene factors and motivators

Hygiene factors	*Motivators*
(main source of bad feelings when wrong; slight increase in performance when right)	*(increased satisfaction when right; slight decrease in performance when wrong)*
Company policy and administration	Achievement
Supervision	Recognition
Relationship with supervisor	Work itself
Work conditions	Responsibility
Salary	Advancement
Relationship with peers	Growth
Status	
Security	

Thomas was the personnel manager for a production company in the west of England. He was proud of his company's reputation for being a good employer. Whenever a vacancy arose, which was rare, he was flooded with applications. He was devastated when the accounts staff went on strike. The reason for the walk-out was a trivial dispute that had occurred between the office supervisor and Robert. Robert was one of the longest serving members of staff and was known as being reliable, even if he did not act on his own initiative very often. The cause of the argument was not clear but the office supervisor ended it by shouting a verbal warning to him across the office. The union convenor seized the opportunity and called on the other union members to walk out.

Thomas was faced with a situation where both the convenor and the supervisor had broken the rules, and there was a group of staff who were extremely angry with everyone. He called the two combatants together and demanded they apologise to each other. The convenor and supervisor both undertook to stay within agreed procedures in future. But still the staff were angry and Thomas was puzzled about why they were so ready to walk out and risk their jobs when their conditions of employment were so good. He decided to investigate because he was concerned about a similar thing happening again.

He called in a consultant to undertake a confidential staff attitude survey. The results demonstrated that the staff thought that the company, as an employer, was OK, but that the supervisor was extremely unpopular. The staff felt that the office was overcrowded, their equipment poor quality and that they were denied training opportunities. The supervisor, a number of people said, did not listen to staff views about the running of the office; she was too busy on her own pet projects.

Thomas talked to the supervisor, who had only been with the company for two years. It transpired that she did not know the company's policy on access to training and development. She believed that, because she did not have a discrete budget, she could not fund any staff training and therefore had been telling staff they could not attend any courses until she had sorted out the funding. This had taken low priority because she had been more concerned with the specification for a new system (and this too had been the reason why she had told the staff that there was no point in considering any changes to the office layout). But she had not told the staff about the new system. It soon came clear to Thomas that the real reason for the walk-out had been the supervisor's failure to communicate properly with her staff. She agreed to introduce a monthly

> briefing session and to make sure that the staff both knew about developments and had the opportunity to voice their views.

Some common areas can be identified between Maslow's hierarchy and Hertzberg's approach, especially the importance of relationships and the need for achievement and growth. In fact, it was this emphasis on relationships that led to these and associated theories being labelled as the human relations school.

Complementary work in the UK carried out by the Tavistock Institute demonstrated that the division of work into functional specialisms led to the isolation of work groups from each other, increased inter-group conflict and reduced productivity. Thus the links between the technology of work and social relationships was formed.

Work design

During the 1960s and 1970s most of the experiments in work design concentrated on finding ways of making work more meaningful as a method of motivating workers to improve their productivity as well as increasing their satisfaction. Initiatives such as quality of working life, quality circles, autonomous work groups, job enlargement, enrichment and rotation programmes are those most frequently reported. However, these tend to be more concerned with techniques rather than finding a model that can be generally applied. Maslow and Hertzberg, even though flawed, provide guidance to a manager on ways of organising and managing work.

The contribution made by the research of Hackman and Oldham (1980) into job characteristics is also useful. They identified three critical states — the core job dimensions, critical psychological states and personal and work outcomes — that are likely to affect motivation and job satisfaction. The features of the job are linked (as shown in Figure 2.2) to the likely impact they are thought to have on the individual's state of mind. How the individual experiences the job (its component parts and in its entirety) affects the outcomes he or she obtains from their work, which in turn influences the level of their overall job satisfaction.

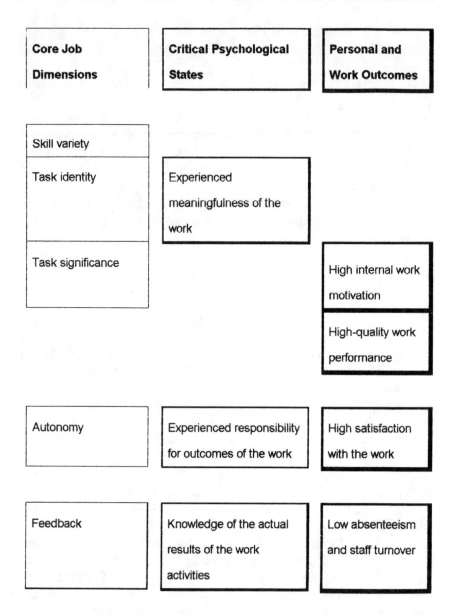

Figure 2.2   Goal-setting and work characteristics

'Management by objectives' (MbO) was being developed at about the same time as a technique to link individual responsibilities into the overall aims of the organisation through a process of joint goal-setting, monitoring and evaluation of achievement. Based on principles similar to goal-setting theory, both identify the importance of clear, shared objectives, claiming that hard (but achievable) goals result in higher performance. The need for goals to be specific rather than vague, and the realisation that incentives had no effect unless they were linked to specific goals were also recognised as being essential parts of any MbO/goal-setting process. The line manager, it is argued, plays a critical role in the attainment or non-attainment of those goals. Even though MbO was rejected as being prescriptive and the process of setting and agreeing goals too problematic, its application did have some successes.

The need to achieve was one of the three drivers identified in the 1950s by McClelland (1953). When linked with expectancy theory, there is some theoretical basis to claim that when people know what is expected of them and they know what rewards or punishments achievement or non-achievement will bring, they are likely to direct their efforts accordingly. McClelland's work has recently regained attention because it was his research that was used to aid the search for competent performance. He argued that the needs of individuals are more complex than those previously suggested by Maslow. He proposed that many needs are socially acquired rather than being inherent, and vary according to culture. He defined three types of socially acquired need — achievement, power and affiliation. These were used when the McBer Consultancy team was asked by the American Management Association to identify the difference between an average and superior performer, ultimately they became the competency statements described by Boyatzis (1982).

Some other interesting work has been done by Alban-Metcalfe and Nicholson (1984) and Nicholson and West (1988) which supports the American findings. It shows that work preferences, listed below, are common between members of both genders and generally affect levels of performance:

1. work content — challenging work to do;
2. the quality of senior management;
3. work where individual accomplishment is appreciated and recognition given for achievement;
4. opportunity to improve knowledge and skills;
5. a job where workers can be creative in doing things their own way;
6. opportunities for advancement;
7. working with people who are friendly and congenial;
8. opportunity to influence organisational policies;
9. job security;
10. belonging to an organisation that is highly regarded; and

11.   opportunity for high earnings.

The economic difficulties of the 1970s and 1980s have hampered the updating of many of these theories. Moreover, as most of the work was done in the United States many regarded the findings as inappropriate and not transferable across cultures. In addition, most of the primary research was carried out at a time of continuous economic growth and expansion. Nevertheless, the experiments and hypotheses should not be rejected simply because of the changes in economic conditions. People, to a certain extent, remain constant. The longevity of the earlier research has shown the potential of these ideas and has indicated how they may be used to improve the design of jobs and the organisation of work.

Return of Taylorism

More recently, organisations' need to survive has become more important than the design of the employees' jobs. The need to balance accounts and pay bills has taken over from quality of working life improvements, and sources of motivation were reduced from hygiene factors and self-actualisation by the very real prospect of redundancy and unemployment. Many of the ideas put forward by those belonging to the human resource and needs schools of thought in the 1960s and 1970s were forgotten as monetarism became the focus of attention during the recovery of the 1980s. The notions of Taylor again came to the fore. As the recession reversed and employment prospects expanded (in both the US and the UK), the amount of money in the economy increased and pay once again was believed to be the main motivator. The introduction of so-called private sector business methods into the public sector demonstrated this thinking, even though many of the approaches copied by public sector managers as examples of good practice and the right way to tackle the new problems were, in fact, techniques that had been replaced in the more forward-looking organisations. The most controversial of these have been performance-related and merit pay. Dainty (1987) asked 'is progress over' when he summarised the main areas of research. He concluded that little had been done to move the earlier experiments into practice.

This lack of progress, the return to the belief in the 'rational economic man' and functional specialism can be seen in modern definitions of job design. For example, Armstrong (1991) describes the process as, 'deciding on the contents of a job, its duties and responsibilities and the relationships that exist between the job holder and his/her superiors, subordinates and colleagues'. Torrington and Hall (1991) describe it as, 'the specification of the contents, methods and relationships of jobs in order to satisfy technological and organisational requirements as well as the social and personal requirements of the job holder'. Both definitions imply a top down focus based on the division of labour into functional component parts. It must be recognised that these approaches perform well when work can be broken into routine tasks that are not prone to change.

Similar thinking has informed the approach used by the National Council for Vocational Qualifications to identify occupational competence statements. Functional analysis has been used to identify the key purpose of each occupational role and to break it down into units and component elements. This approach has been much criticised for being reductionist and atomistic, and failing to portray the job as an holistic entity. An individual may be assessed as being competent across all the elements yet be unable to perform the job competently. The competence approach, on the other hand, has helped some organisations to think more carefully about the ways in which tasks are gathered together to make up jobs that have a meaning and provide satisfaction for the postholder.

Kakabadse, Ludlow and Vinnicombe (1987) say:

> There are two main approaches (to work design): scientific management and the job characteristics model. Under the principles of scientific management, it is considered that work can be broken down into manageable tasks.... In the job characteristics model ... the person needs to have knowledge of his results and the person needs to feel the responsibility for the results of his work, so that he is aware of his accountability for work outcomes.... By combining the key elements of needs, incentives and expectancy theory, it is possible to develop strategies for increasing the levels of motivation of individuals.

These key elements are more complex than suggested. Rather than being combined, they should be viewed as interactive — each affecting the other in a way that sometimes makes it difficult for the individual concerned to separate out the important and less important factors. Consequently, the design of jobs needs to take a broad approach that enables these factors to be reflected in their construction.

ALTERNATIVES TO TRADITIONAL JOB DESIGN

Most modern organisations are trying to move away from traditional bureaucratic methods and rigid hierarchies based on expertise and longevity. Moreover, the expectations of the workforce have changed. Periods of unemployment, the removal of trade unions as buffers against bad employment practices and weak management and the increased availability of performance-linked rewards mean that people are no longer prepared to be treated as units of production. However, the most recent recession has shown how frail money and pay-related benefits are. Even though the threat of unemployment is a constant reality for many, there is a growing wish for rewards to be paid in other ways. Opportunities to develop skills, increase employability and transferability and to improve job satisfaction are becoming more important.

The trends towards flatter structures, decentralisation of decision making to the lowest levels in the hierarchy, the increased employment of professional or knowledge workers and the wish to involve staff in their work requires that jobs now need to be designed in ways that facilitate change. The changes in career paths and patterns of employment have also led to different approaches to working practice. Workers no longer expect jobs for life and their career paths may be disjointed: the notion of portfolio careers is gaining acceptance. Charles Handy's latest work (1989 and 1991) has drawn attention to the types of job that may be expected in the foreseeable future. Workers and managers alike expect to have the opportunities to apply their intelligence and develop their skills and abilities. The ways in which jobs are designed can facilitate growth or inhibit it.

The links between the design of work, motivation, job satisfaction and performance levels have now been well accepted, but the relationships between these factors tend to be portrayed in simple straight-line terms. People are not rational creatures behaving according to predictions. They differ and behave unpredictably, even when conditions are static. In times of change and turbulence human behaviour can be either totally predictable or random and irrational. As conditions of constant change are endemic to most people's working lives, the traditional approaches to work design now need to be refined into more sophisticated models.

The traditional approaches to the design of work, as indicated earlier, are based on assumed factors of motivation and job satisfaction. They now provide normative theories rather than practical guidance for those wishing or needing to take a more radical approach. Even though the work of

Maslow, Hertzberg, Hackman, Oldham and the others has been the subject of valid criticism, they still offer some ideas. Sadly, with the return of the belief that performance-related pay is the main source of motivation, job design has not progressed. Recent models are variations on themes already stated rather than the development of new thinking. Even though other sources of job satisfaction have been recognised, the importance of monetary rewards cannot be denied. Pay is still a main reason for people to work and beliefs about its importance are varied; influenced by changes in employment levels and social conditions. However, the role of money tends to be seen as the only motivator, while other needs and sources of satisfaction are ignored.

Figure 2.3 has been developed to show how some of the previous ideas can be combined into a more holistic approach. The separate elements of the factors are intertwined and so should not be seen in isolation from each

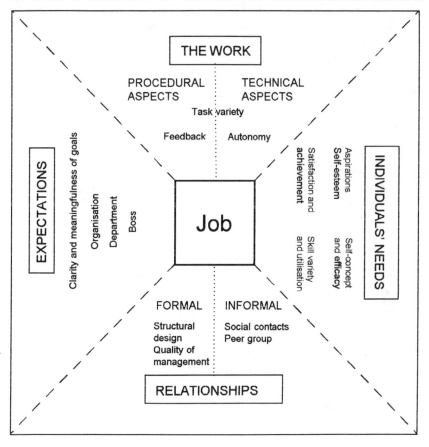

Figure 2.3   Job design — a more holistic approach

other. Rather, they interact and influence each other, contributing jointly to the overall quality of the job, the achievability of its purpose and its contribution to job satisfaction and organisational performance.

Expectations

The clarity and meaningfulness of the goals of the organisation, the section in which the postholder is to be located, the requirements of the boss and the definition of the job are fundamental to effective performance. No one can do a job that has any result or reward if the reasons for doing it are unclear.

Why is this job being created, *what* is its objective and *how* does it contribute to the achievement of overall goals must be the first questions asked when constructing a job. All too often the approach taken in practice is different. The tasks to be carried out are identified and get bundled together, and a person is appointed to complete them without any consideration being given to whether these tasks need to be done at all. Even worse, an organisation is designed top down, focusing on the need to create the hierarchy to control the organisation rather than examining its function and then determining the jobs needed to provide and support the organisation's primary purpose. Even if all the jobs identified do need to be performed, how often are they seen as a whole role which:

- makes sense;
- has a purpose which makes a contribution that has an obvious meaning to the organisation;
- requires complementary skills to enable it to be occupied by a flawed human being;
- gives scope for growth and skill enhancement; and
- will give the occupier satisfaction and a sense of achievement.

The work

It can be helpful to break down a job into two separate but complementary parts. The *technical aspects* of any job are those which concern the tools and techniques used to carry out the tasks and require knowledge and skills for their effective use. The *procedural aspects* are the internal arrangements used by a particular organisation, such as administrative rules and internal processes. For example, the task of decision making can require the use of tools such as the Delphi technique or decision trees, and the skills needed to use these would be common regardless of the organisation in which the individual was employed. The procedural aspects, however, would require knowledge of the organisation's committee structures, the allocation of responsibilities for making a decision and the distribution of power. The ways in which these two aspects interact and combine will affect how the job is to be performed.

Over-routinised jobs or separation of the components result in obscure work that is performed without any context. Lack of meaning can lead eventually to either the misdirection of effort or to learnt incapacity. Learnt incapacity occurs when a worker discovers the minimum level of acceptable performance. It is often found when the results of effort or lack of its effect are not clear and a worker is able to say, 'Not my fault/job'. The way of avoiding this is to ensure that each job includes areas of work that are linked to some direct output and that each worker has a valid and meaningful part to play in its achievement. This is now known as 'single point responsibility'. Accountability expressed this way also provides a worker with feedback, which is needed if individuals are to assess the value of their own contribution in relation to their peers and the achievement of overall goals. It is also a valuable source of information to aid an individual's development.

All of these factors, which can be built into a job, affect the ability of the individual to perform. However, performance rarely takes place in isolation. The context and conditions under which the job is carried out also impact the postholder as do the relationships that are developed during the working day.

Relationships

A number of the theories on motivation and job satisfaction emphasise the importance of the relationship between the postholder and significant others. Relationships are formed with peers and their expectations are influenced by the culture of the work group, its norms and accepted standards, and the informal groupings and friendships. The formal relationships are found in the structures and reporting relationships — up, down and across the organisation. The way in which information flows, the systems used and the quality of communication channels affect individuals' perceptions, understanding of organisational goals and availability of feedback, and have a direct impact on individual achievement.

Individuals' needs

Maslow's hierarchy of needs acknowledges the importance of monetary rewards. Hertzberg argued that if the salary was wrong it would demotivate, while if it were right it would only maintain performance levels, not increase them. Expectancy theory confirms this by suggesting the available rewards must be in a 'currency' that the individual values, and if this be money, so be it. The increase in consumerism and the advent of performance-related rewards has focused employees' attention more on to the value and worth of their pay packet. Even so, pay should not be regarded as the only source of motivation and incentive. People look for other factors when seeking a rewarding job.

The variety of skills needed to perform a job adds to its intrinsic interest. Routinising work as recommended by scientific management was seen as a way of increasing productivity, not job satisfaction. Since then, efforts have been made to vary assembly line tasks as a means of increasing motivation and thus productivity. As well as wanting to use a range of skills, individuals, it is generally believed, want jobs that allow them to make full use of their existing skills. If possible, chances to develop and add to those skills are also sought. However, any one individual's range of talents is inevitably limited. Expecting one person to operate across too wide a range of skills is unreasonable, and it will likely result in failure in some areas as well as being demotivating.

The belief that the sought-for rewards are equitably available is also important. Individuals need to be able to see the link between their expenditure of effort and the achievement of the agreed objectives and outcomes, but they also need to believe that the distribution of rewards between themselves and others in the organisation is fair. This link influences an individual's perception of their own abilities and sense of self-esteem. Someone will not make an effort or see themselves in a good light if the results of their hard work and application of skills and knowledge are not recognised or recognisable.

The term 'self-efficacy' means the sense of power and influence an individual feels over their own destiny. The loss of self-efficacy leads to a sense of hopelessness. Anyone in this condition can be seen as being lethargic and low in energy; levels of performance are also low and a sense of achievement or the ability to achieve is absent. A job can be built to give an individual some control over factors such as speed and quantity of work, the achievability of objectives and goals, the availability of the desired rewards and the chance to use and develop skills.

The individual's aspirations and the reality of the job should also have some harmony. While objectives should be stretching, if they are too high their very inaccessibility can be demotivating. Similarly, if they do not fit with the hopes and desires an individual holds for the future, this mismatch can lead to a loss of interest and drive. Having to work hard at tasks that are not taking you where you want to go hardly encourages a worker to get out of bed in the morning. But the chance to work on a job that clearly is leading in the direction an individual desires to move is both stretching and satisfying.

Bearing these features in mind when setting up or re-analysing a job, enables the manager to establish firm foundations and leads naturally into the formal description of purpose and responsibilities. The checklist in Table 2.2 is designed to help ensure that these have been considered.

Table 2.2   Analysing the job: a checklist

Questions	*Answers and considerations*
Job purpose	
Is the purpose of the job clearly and unequivocally expressed?	'To be responsible for the efficient organisation and the effective operation of a client centred service'.
Is its contribution to the organisation's objectives evident?	Key tasks: To contribute to the organisation's management by being a full and active member of the executive team.
	To ensure the Department's operations and expenditure are in accordance with business plans and resources used economically.
	To plan, enable and evaluate the personal and professional development of the department's staff.
Is its contribution to the work of the department in which the job is located obvious?	Words such as 'liaise', 'facilitate' and 'provide for' are vague enough to enable the point of responsibility to be obscured.
Is the postholder responsible for the successful completion of the whole job?	For example, a member of a team can find it difficult to recognise their 'unique contribution' or the input their efforts have made on the end product.

Questions	*Answers and considerations*
Do the internal systems help the postholder to do the job?	An administrative system designed years ago to satisfy a superseded need can prevent the now needed responsive and flexible approach to customer service.

Skill range

Does the job cover a reasonable but not too extensive range of different tasks?	A job which requires highly developed interpersonal skills as well as those expecting large amounts of detail and high levels of accuracy needs an extraordinary individual.
Do the opportunities exist for the postholder to use the knowledge and skills associated with effective performance of the job?	Over-recruiting well-qualified trainees for dead end jobs leads to frustration and high turnover. If the recruits can't leave, rebellion is likely to brew. Similarly people without the underpinning knowledge or required skills may underperform because organisational expectations are unrealistically high.
Can the individual make full use of their skills and develop their skill base?	If the best qualified, most experienced applicant was appointed for the job (someone who could hit the ground running), how long will it be before they run off...

Relationships

Are the formal relationships clearly specified and related to the achievement of the objectives?	Normally up–down reporting relationships are outlined in job descriptions. It is also worth specifying the significant others and the nature of the relationship. This is especially important in matrix organisations when roles have cross-organisational or department responsibilities.
Is there opportunity to develop working relationships within and across the department's boundaries?	Myopia and parochialism are two of the most serious chronic illnesses found in large organisations. Secondments, cross-working and shared projects can be designed into jobs. Involvement in training and development and policy development are two such examples.
Are colleagues available with whom the postholder can discuss professional issues?	Professional debate and discussion are valuable ways of developing skills and extending thinking. Specialist posts can be isolated and insulated. Building in developmental duties can help ensure that 'professional stagnation' does not creep up on the postholder.

Questions	*Answers and considerations*

Job outcomes

Can the postholder see the results of their efforts?	Jobs in supporting roles such as an office junior or secretary often have no direct output of their own; most of their work contributes to the jobs of others. Everyone likes to have their effort acknowledged.
Can the results of the postholder's efforts be recognised?	Has the job been divided laterally or horizontally? For example, a receptionist may take in customer complaints and pass them on to the 'right' department for a response. Alternatively the receptionist may be responsible for receiving and replying to complaints.
Does the postholder have the opportunity to influence their own levels of performance and achievement of the objectives?	Setting a salesperson taxing targets which result in high levels of pay for the individual and high sales levels for the company is fine for everyone, providing the salesperson can ensure that production, delivery and invoicing deadlines are met.

Rewards

Are the rewards appropriate and obtainable?	If the reward for hard work is even more difficult and complex work, am I likely to work hard? If the performance-related element of my pay is 10% and I need to work 50% harder than my colleagues to obtain it, am I likely to work harder than the others?
Are the rewards linked directly with the performance of the postholder?	If it is not clear what I have to do to be promoted, what chance will I have of being promoted?

JOB DESCRIPTIONS

The Trade Union Reform and Employment Rights Act 1994 requires that every employee who works for more than eight hours per week shall have, after four weeks continuous employment, a statement that includes the title of the job which the employee is employed to do or a brief description of the work for which the employee is employed. The inclusion of a job description with a contract of employment could be evidence that the job description is intended to be a contractual arrangement. What should that description include and what should it look like? Armstrong (1991) says of job descriptions, 'They provide basic information about the job under the headings of the job title, reporting relationships, overall purpose and principal accountabilities and tasks or duties.'

This definition encompasses a huge range of possible formats — from a brief paragraph to a lengthy document outlining every possible task a postholder could ever be expected to perform. The latter was most common in organisations firmly wedded to the principles of bureaucracy. (A bureaucracy is defined as an organisation with a tightly structured hierarchy, staffed by trained experts, with clearly defined functions, roles and relationships and reliant on written records.) Job descriptions of this type do have the advantage of being comprehensive. To draw them up, a thorough analysis of the job has to be carried out, and this too gives them a strength. They are highly prescriptive and so are most suitable for organisations that operate in stable conditions. They have an endurance that means that they are able to withstand the passage of time. They can also aid other personnel functions in addition to recruitment and selection, such as grading and job evaluation, and can contribute to assessment of performance when it is deemed desirable to be precise in judgement.

However, their very precision can also be their weakness in that they tend not to accommodate change. Slow evolution can be dealt with — the job description can be modified by subtraction and addition — but rapid, radical change is more problematic. The rigidity of such job descriptions cannot respond to situations that require responses different from 'more or less than'. Frequently, new job descriptions have to be prepared when different tasks and objectives are to be taken on by postholders. This need to redefine jobs can in itself pose industrial relations and managerial problems additional to those created by the changing situation.

Other problems are associated with the use of job descriptions that are too prescriptive. For example, demarcation disputes characterised by statements such as 'It's not in my job description' or 'It's not my responsibility' can be created between staff groups. Other common responses to change includes requests for pay grades to be reassessed, lengthy disputes about the wording of alterations to the written document or demands for precise indications defining the full meaning of a new situation.

Role outlines

The more modern version of the job description is a role outline, which describes the purpose of the job or role. The briefest version is a written paragraph that sketches out the purpose of the job and indicates, broadly, the main areas of responsibility. An example is given in the panel. The strength of this approach is the flexibility born from ambiguity. The meaning of the outline can be negotiated and renegotiated when needs be, and this can be on-going should the circumstances warrant it. However, ambiguity also provides scope for dispute. Many senior executives have parted company with their employing organisation because of different interpretations of their role and the meaning in practice of degrees of responsibility and accountability. The compromise between the precision of the bureaucratic approach and the thumb-nail sketch of the role outline is a job description that outlines the purpose of the post and its key areas of responsibility.

ROLE OUTLINE

The works manager will be responsible for the day-to-day management of the Engineering Works of XYZ Company, its efficient, effective and safe operation and the management of the staff. The postholder will be expected to be part of the Company's management team and implement the planning, operational and personnel policies and practices, as agreed.

A job description written more precisely usually provides a statement outlining the key contribution the job will make to the organisation's goals. It is also common to find a specification of reporting lines and relationships. This is followed by a summary of main tasks or key objectives. Written in the active case, the tasks or objectives help to assess performance and assign accountability, and they can also indicate the relative importance of the different areas of work. An example is given in the 'Job description' panel.

JOB DESCRIPTION

Post title: Works manager
Responsible to: Managing director
Responsible for: Senior engineers
                       Works supervisors
Purpose: To agree and implement an operational
                       plan for the XYZ Works which ensures
                       efficient, effective and safe production
                       and develops working methods and the
                       skills of staff
Main duties: As follows

1. PLANNING

(a)   Propose and agree operational plans designed to achieve XYZ's business plan.
(b)   Monitor the implementation of the plan to ensure that necessary action can be taken and future plans adjusted as necessary.
(c)   Assess the reaction of customers and ensure that their feedback is used for planning and modification of current operations.

2. OPERATIONS

(a)   Implement the plan as agreed.
(b)   Monitor and adjust operations to ensure that working methods remain efficient and effective.
(c)   Ensure compliance with health and safety legislation and that safety procedures are followed.
(d)   Monitor the implementation of the plans and the achievement of agreed objectives.
(e)   Take remedial action as required to ensure that operations remain effective.

3. DEVELOPMENT

(a)   Review working methods and organisation continuously.

(b)   Instigate changes within the scope of the operational plan.

(c)   Negotiate other changes as needed.

(d)   Facilitate the participation of the workforce in review mechanisms.

4. STAFF

(a)   Instigate and operate an appraisal system to review the performance of all staff.

(b)   Agree personal objectives and review performance of engineers and supervisors.

(c)   Agree, implement and evaluate development plans for all staff.

(d)   Establish communication systems that ensure that staff are kept fully up to date and allow them to participate appropriately in decision making.

5. SELF-MANAGEMENT

(a)   Prioritises and manages own workload.

(b)   Engages in personal and professional development.

(c)   Reviews own performance and participates in appraisal activities.

(d)   Contributes as part of the senior management team to the overall management of the XYZ Company.

It will be noticed in this example that the main duties are not listed — rather the contents are grouped together in clusters. This enables areas of work that are related in practice to be drawn together to demonstrate their relationships. Other methods of ordering the contents can include listing in priority or sequential order, or reflecting the frequency of each task.

Often the post is named before the job description is drawn up, although it can be argued that this should be done at the end. Once the purpose and main areas of responsibility have been defined and the relationships are clear, the label to be attached to the post should be obvious. Giving the job a name too early can tempt the definer to fit the purpose and main duties to the title. Really, the title should be a simple indication of what the job is about. Long hierarchies in bureaucracies can lead to some lovely names that tell the uninitiated absolutely nothing. For example, what does a senior principal assistant do? Who is assisted, who is junior and, if there is a principal, are there secondaries?

The purpose of producing a job description is not to catalogue every possible task or routine a postholder may be required to carry out. It is to create a working description of the job the postholder will occupy for a period of time. It should be useful for the employee and help him or her to carry out the terms of their contract and help the line manager and others in the organisation decide whether the performance is to the standard agreed. While it should be an accurate representation of the job, it should also be flexible enough to adjust to the most likely changes to be encountered. This does not mean it should be a catch all, and nor can it be expected to last for ever. There will be times when a job description becomes out dated and therefore should be discarded.

To conclude, a job description should indicate:

- the post title;
- reporting relationships (to whom the post is accountable and who is accountable to the postholder);
- the purpose of the post and its scope; and
- the main areas of responsibility, limits of authority, key objectives or standards of performance.

At one time it was advised that the phrase 'and any other duties that may be assigned or agreed' be included in a job description, but the current thinking seems to concern the quality of the contents rather than an attempt to be comprehensive. Providing the description is accurate (ie produced as a result of analysis and design), is realistic and contains scope for change, there should be no need to try to be all inclusive. A job description is just that — not a prescription.

PERSON SPECIFICATION

Once the job description has been drafted, it is possible to start work on a person specification. There are several traditional ways to compile a person specification, each as good as the others. The increasing use of competence statements is also having an effect on describing the 'ideal' postholder. Torrington and Hall (1991) say that a person specification is 'a statement, derived from the job analysis process and the job description, of the characteristics that an individual would need to possess in order to fulfil the requirements of a job.' The use of the word 'characteristics' presents the first of many issues that are encountered during the compilation of a specification.

The most common formula used to write person specifications is 'Rodger's seven-point plan'. This model is often quoted in personnel textbooks such as Torrington and Hall (op cit), and was used as a basis for Table 2.3. The main attraction of using a pro-forma like this is that it provides a list of headings to ensure that all essential features of the ideal postholder are included. The main danger is that it is completed without thought. It is too easy to put down the characteristics of the previous postholder, describe (as a stereotype) the dream person or replicate (as a clone) an idealised but historic image of previous successful employees.

Drawing up a person specification provides an opportunity to look into the future. Various questions can be posed that enable the compiler to think critically about the features that will be needed for the achievement of the main purpose, the successful completion of the tasks and competent performance in the job. By projecting one's thinking a year forward the most likely areas of difficulty and critical work tasks can be considered and included. Thus, the person specification can be an aid to effective appointing while facilitating the creation of an initial development plan for the new postholder. Table 2.3 (based on Rodger's seven points) poses questions designed to prevent an automatic response.

Table 2.3   Compiling a person specification

Points	Questions	Comments
Attainment	What educational requirements and specialist knowledge are *really* needed for successful completion of the task?	A degree provides an indication of level of study or a subject degree to indicate detailed knowledge.
Experience	What roles and tasks should have been occupied to ensure the postholder is adequately equipped? These can be gained in and out of work.	Budget management, for example, happens at home and work. Organising people can include line management experience and experience of organising voluntary groups.

Points	Questions	Comments
Abilities	What skills need to be deployed for the competent performance of the tasks?	Skills or abilities can be learnt and developed from experience, feedback and practice, such as communication, interpersonal and some mental abilities.
Aptitudes	Where will the postholder's strengths lie; what particular talents do they need to possess?	An aptitude is a personal inclination or preference such as team working, a self-starter, innovator or can pay attention to detail.
Interests	What interest relevant to the work will suggest possession of sought-after skills and aptitudes?	Someone preferring their own company will cite activities that reflect their preference (eg listening to music, reading). More social individuals will give examples that bring them into contact with others.
Circumstances	How will out of work activities effect the adequate completion of the tasks?	Active membership of a professional or community body may be a plus or a minus.
Physical make-up	The use of this question is debatable unless there are some *real* reasons for its inclusion.	Ascertainment of genuine occupational or physical qualifications (eg when membership of a specified sex or ethnic group is needed for the provision of personal services to members of the same group) are legally permissible.

Contents

A good person specification does what the term implies — it specifies the sort of person needed to perform, adequately and competently, the whole of the job. It should not be an historic document, looking back at past requirements, but rather it should pitch into the future and predict the characteristics likely to be required. If it is drawn up in this way it should be flexible enough to allow for change and development of the job and the organisation in which it is located. Questions such as 'What would lead me to say, in a year's time, the person appointed has been successful or unsuccessful?' or 'What would the person be doing to make me think the appointment was the right decision?' can help to elicit the critical measures in behavioural terms. Alternatively, the questions 'Which problems, if resolved, would make the most impact on the organisation?' and 'What skills and background do we need to tackle these problems?' focuses on the critical incidents and skills required.

There can be a danger, however, of describing a super or even supra human being. A superhuman is one who is perfect in every respect and performs to the utmost of expectations, above and beyond what is normally found in any one person. This tendency is seen when the person specification expects the postholder to be competent across a range of skills that could not realistically be possessed by one individual. (For example, it would be unrealistic to expect an individual to have obtained a higher degree, have had substantial work experience and be aged under 30.) This tendency to specify a superhuman can also be found in the description of types of work experience and the range of skills and aptitudes. A person who is inclined to work alone on detailed tasks that require close attention and thoroughness is unlikely to be inclined towards team work. Similarly, it is not easy for one individual to gain experience of the public and private sectors, or of manufacturing, financial services and retailing. This may be nothing to do with the person's abilities and employability, but with the prejudices of employers in the different sectors. A person specification, while being ambitious and forward looking, needs to remain in the zone of reasonableness.

Even if it does, finding the person to match the specification perfectly is highly unlikely. The recruitment and selection process can only hope to result in the best fit. The ultimate match may require some adjustments on both sides. Some organisations do this by deciding which features are essential and so must be matched, and which others are just desirable. The latter can either be done without or obtained in other ways, including acquisition from other sources or the development of the person appointed. In any case, a forward-looking person specification will allow for growth.

Language

The final point to be taken into account when drawing up a person specification concerns the language used to express the elements. A person specification is an outline of the person being sought. It should not be a stereotype — ie the image constructed to represent a member of a group and containing the most commonly found or expected features. These include appearance, behaviour and psychological make-up, and extend to assumptions about background, intelligence and likely responses. Language is the vehicle used for the conveyance of these assumptions and encodes value systems. More will be said about this topic later, because the way in which language is used during the recruitment and selection process can lead to indirect discrimination.

Moreover, the contents of a person specification can very easily transmit requirements and values that are no longer relevant to the organisation, simply because the words used do not reflect the current situation. For example, the head of a new business unit resigned 18 months after the unit opened. The person specification had originally been written for the start-up and contained requirements such as 'experience of new business developments, ability to act on initiative, lead staff through change, negotiate new contracts.' The start-up phase had been successful and the business moved to another phase. Even thought the specification was only 18 months old, appointing to it again would be wrong. The current requirements should be more concerned with 'experience of managing a successful operation, consolidating developments, assuring and enhancing customer satisfaction, finding other customers for existing products.' A very different person!

Biases

Some interesting work has been done into the gender and other biases that can be inbuilt, unwittingly, into person specifications. These will be discussed later. The person specification set out in Table 2.4 focuses more on job requirements than personal characteristics.

Table 2.4   Person specification for works manager

Factor	Requirements
Attainment	HND or equivalent in relevant subject
	Formal training in management skills
	Training in HASAW matters

Factor	Requirements
Experience	Staff management
	Creation and implementation of plans
	Work in an organisation that used TQM or other quality systems
Skills	Communication
	Leadership
	Planning and organising skills
Aptitudes	Committed to quality and customer satisfaction
	Facilitator of other achievements
	Safe worker
	Monitors achievement and follows through to ensure adequate progress
	Consultative and participative
Interests	Own development
	Continuous improvement
	Other people
Circumstances	Able to be flexible

Regardless of the format, a person specification should portray the features of the person equipped to do the job in question. (There have been occasions when the person specification has been drawn up to portray the individual the manager and others would like to work with, rather than the type of person best suited for the job.) It follows, therefore, that the job in question needs to be described in terms that allow the outline of the person to be made explicit. The use of behavioural language helps to avoid stereotypes, assumptions and unrelated values. Questions, such as those described earlier in this section, help to make what could otherwise be waffly, imprecise terms, explicit.

The person specification should aim to indicate what is expected of the successful postholder in terms of prerequisite attainments, experiences, knowledge and skills, aptitudes and inclinations. It should not merely describe the individual who will be the best on the day. It should form the basis for the longer-term development of the person appointed and establish the benchmark criteria for assessing performance subsequently.

SUMMARY

This chapter has briefly examined the history of job design and has suggested that the main approaches found in scientific management, the human relations school and needs theories can be combined to take a different, more holistic approach. The reason for integrating the different factors and demands of a job is to ensure that:

- the job is constructed in relation to organisational need;
- the expectations of the postholder and the organisation are explicit and understood;
- the formal and informal working relationships are acknowledged;
- the skills needed for its effective performance are complementary; and
- the job provides for the needs and growth of the individual.

Once the job has been designed, it is possible to describe its purpose and the main duties and responsibilities expected of the postholder. The format suggested will meet the needs of legislation while providing a flexible working tool to guide the postholder and manager. The job description also forms the basis for the person specification.

The person specification is the place to challenge stereotypes and ensure that the post is filled by someone who will be able to develop to meet the challenges of the future as well as do the job as it stands now to an acceptable standard. The person specification and job description together supply the information needed to start the recruitment phase of the process. The following chapter describes the various ways they can be used. The person specification also forms the basis for decision making in shortlisting and later selection activities. Ways of doing this are discussed in subsequent chapters.

3

Attracting the Right Person

Recruitment is generally seen as another form of advertising. All that needs to be done when a post has to be filled by someone from outside the organisation is to place an advertisement in a suitable place. This could be a newspaper or trade journal, Job Centre, a local shop or (despite being strongly condemned as discriminatory since the Sex Discrimination Act 1974) word-of-mouth advertising. Recruitment advertising is big business. Two surveys describing how individuals obtained their latest jobs, reported in the magazine *Personnel Today* in 1994, paint similar pictures (see Table 3.1).

Table 3.1   How individuals obtained their latest jobs, 1994

Method	Survey 1	Survey 2
Someone already working for the organisation	30%	
Personal contact		16%
Replying to an advertisement	26%	21%
Replying to a consultancy advertisement		19%
Direct application (speculative letters)	17%	12%
Job Centre	8%	
An agency	7%	
Other	13%	5%
Direct approach by headhunters		18%
Direct approach by the company		9%

The recessions of the 1970s and 1990s have fundamentally changed the labour market. Skill shortages and the reluctance of organisations to commit themselves to permanent contracts of employment have played havoc with the historic approaches to recruitment. Even though unemployment levels have been high, the 'normal forces' of the labour market no longer function as before. The skills, experience and people sought are in the wrong place forming the wrong profile, so employers are finding that the balance of power is switching. Large groups of workers whose skills used to be highly valued are not able to find employers who want them. At the same time, people whose skills are in demand are increasingly saying 'No' to offers of employment. They are clearer about their expectations and requirements from a job and from an employer, and they are also aware that the final decision is not the decision to offer an appointment but the decision to accept the offer.

Consequently, the normal approaches to recruitment need to be reviewed and their effectiveness assessed against different criteria. For example, a typical newspaper advertisement can generate hundreds of applications from people, desperate for work, but none of whom possess the essential skills needed for effective performance in the job. Alternatively, an apparently desirable, easy to fill post can attract only a few applications. Which are the best advertisements? As with many other aspects of human resource management, different ways of recruiting suitably skilled, experienced or able individuals are being developed to cope with these new conditions. Since the late 1980s newspaper advertising has declined and, as a result, advertising agencies have altered their portfolio from simply designing and placing advertisements and advising on media to running campaigns, engaging in search and using alternative outlets to attract the right people for their clients.

The second part of this chapter explores some of the different recruitment methods available and gives examples of how they may be best used. The traditional approaches are mentioned but, because these can easily be looked up in personnel textbooks, more attention will be given to 'other' methods. Alternative and some unusual ways of attracting applicants are described, including the use of radio, mailshots, recruitment events, targeting, plus some 'off-the-wall' ideas. The marketing concept as it applies to recruitment is outlined at the start, and is then discussed as part of a guide to the design and operation of recruitment methods. If the vacancy to be filled is seen as a product, service or other form of goods, the techniques drawn from marketing will be relevant. The main aims of both functions are the same:

- reaching the right people at the right time;
- interesting them in what is being offered; and
- tempting them to react in an appropriate fashion (in this case, by submitting an application).

MARKETING THE JOB

If the marketing concept is to help recruitment, a new way of looking at the employment contract is needed. It can no longer be regarded as a binding lifelong agreement under which the employer holds all the cards. When skilled and experienced employees are scarce and their contracts are temporary or for a fixed term, the master–servant relationship is an invalid concept. Valued skills are too marketable so, if employees feel exploited and undervalued, it is easy to lose them to competitors. Skilled staff also leave for other reasons, such as self-employment, career changes, further study and decisions to follow other avenues in different roles. The employment contract, especially in areas where skills are in high demand, is now more a contract between two equal partners.

Who do you want to attract?

Continuing the marketing analogy, the job description and person specification are redefined to become the profile of the target audience or segment of the labour market. The job description outlines the purpose of the post and indicates what the person to be appointed will be doing. The person specification describes the essential (and in some cases the desirable) attainment, experience, skills and aptitudes. However, care needs to be taken because drawing up a profile can tempt the unwary manager to stereotype and project unreasonable expectations of the ideal person to be appointed. A way to avoid this trap is to think about skill, knowledge and aptitudes as inputs, and the outcomes of performance as the achievement of the objectives. The following questions may be helpful:

- What will the postholder need to know in order to do the job satisfactorily?
- What skills will be used?
- How will that knowledge and those skills have been gained?
- What type of experiences will the successful postholder have had?
- Could these have been gained in ways other than paid employment such as ...?
- What sort of job would the postholder need to prefer (eg one that is predictable, one that changes frequently, one that is clearly defined or one that is ambiguous)?
- What sort of working arrangements would the postholder prefer (eg

alone, with others, in positions of responsibility, operating routine systems or developing opportunities)?

- What would the postholder expect from the job?
- What sort of organisation would the postholder want to work for?

Where are they and what are they doing now?

Once a profile of the potential employee has been developed, it is possible to start thinking about where the people in the target market segment are likely to be. This thinking explains why some organisations advertise in parts of the country other than where they are based. (For example, a company in Leicester looking for people with heavy engineering skills would be advised to search in South Yorkshire or Wales. Manchester would be a good location to seek people with electronic component experience.) It is worth remembering though that the very people being sought may not be looking for a job. The consequences of this will be discussed later.

There are various sources of information that help a recruiter explore the labour market more thoroughly. Local Training and Enterprise Councils (TECs) carry out labour market research and the Department of Employment (through the *Employment Gazette* and other publications such as the *Skills and Enterprise Network* mailings) publishes information about skill shortages and employment patterns in various regions and segments of the market. Local authorities will have information about their own areas and careers services collect information that will help the seekers of job-seekers. Job Centres are also providing an increasing range of services for employers.

The information gathered about the sources of the required knowledge, skills and experience and what is happening in that particular segment of the labour market, will help the recruiter make critical decisions about how best to target the people being sought. These decisions not only help to determine the method of contacting the people; they will inform how best to promote the employing organisation, and how to support the recruitment process.

What do potential employees already know about the organisation?

The employing organisation's existing image constrains what can be said as part of a recruitment campaign. While the fair trading legislation does not cover job advertisements, it would be a foolish organisation that tried to falsify its position to prospective employees. That is a good way of obtaining high staff turnover and recruitment costs. Newly appointed employees find out the reality fairly quickly and, if they cannot leave, they easily become disillusioned, possibly having a negative impact on the morale and productivity of their colleagues.

Often, organisations are not aware of their real image so they spend time and money telling the outside world what is already known. Alternatively, organisations take for granted that they and their employment benefits (such as pensions, sickness schemes, parental leave, etc) are common knowledge and neglect to sell themselves to potential employees. It is easy to become blind to the ways in which others see us and, therefore, it may be worth finding out what the employer's public face looks like. Market research can help to test out how much information there is in the public domain, and this can help the recruiter to decide how much more or less information needs to be given and what action needs to be taken to create the sort of image the employing organisation wishes to portray.

Market research to explore what the market already knows about the organisation will help to determine what needs to be communicated. Obviously, once the initial research has been done, carrying out a comprehensive investigation every time a post requires filling is unnecessary; it would be expensive and probably add only detail to the existing picture. Certain assumptions can be safely made and some simple checks carried out to confirm their accuracy. The scope and size of any research project also depends on the scale and size of the organisation. A small local estate agency wishing to appoint a receptionist will know their reputation from existing data showing the level of responses to normal 'house for sale' advertising. On the other hand, a large, multinational holding company may be almost unknown to the general public and so will need to augment recruitment activity with descriptions of the organisation.

What do you want potential applicants to know?

Depending on the results of the market research and the existing information about the employer's public profile, the recruiter can decide how much more information should be given out to attract potential applicants. The reason for sending out information at the first stage of recruitment is to encourage suitably qualified and experienced individuals to express their interest in the job to be filled — in other words, to sell the vacancy. The message being sent out by the organisation needs to be appealing, but also accurate. If the advertisement paints a false image, potential applicants will quickly find out the truth.

Place, product, presentation and price

Getting the desired message to the desired group is only one aspect of marketing. We often think of the concept as being solely concerned with promotion and publicity, but the other part of the function is to ensure that the product is actually delivered to the consumer. For this the consumer has to be in the right *place*, must want the *product*, must be attracted by the *presentation* and be prepared to pay the *price*. The 'four Ps' will be discussed in the following sections in the context of examining ways in which the vacancy can be sold to potential applicants.

The choice of medium (place)

There are many different places where the message may be located that can contribute to or detract from it. Media choice for recruitment purposes was traditionally a decision between newspapers but, increasingly, other channels of communication are now becoming available. Each medium has its own market segment that needs to be taken into account unless the recruiter approaches potential applicants directly. To illustrate the options available to a recruiter, examples of some of the most frequently used channels are listed below with an indication of the profile of their likely audience:

- **Newspapers**. Different daily and Sunday papers are aimed at specific market segments and have their own distinct characteristics. Some carry more job advertisements than others. At the moment *The Guardian* carries most advertisements and is reputedly read mainly by the liberal to left-wing middle classes; the *Sun* contains very few job advertisements and is bought generally by members of the working class. Trade journals are bought by those active or wanting to be active in the particular occupational area. A new outlet for advertisements is developing in some women's journals.
- **The Job Centres and the Department of Employment**. These outlets target mainly those out of employment.
- **Radio**. This is a growing medium and, in the main, it is local stations that carry job adverts. Sometimes local TV stations also publicise vacancies.
- **Recruitment agencies**. These outlets promote themselves and the vacancies they are filling on behalf of their clients through a number of media, including notice and sandwich boards, press adverts, high street offices, trade handbooks, direct selling and active search for

positions. People seeking work either approach the agency direct or respond to an invitation to do so. Agencies tend to specialise in certain types of occupational categories, level of jobs or industrial sectors.

Recruitment, in some ways, is a very traditional activity and the choice of medium for the message is influenced by a large number of other factors that have nothing to do with the organisation or its vacancy. These traditions limit the scope for innovation because the aim is to ensure that the message gets into the right market-place. There is little point in advertising in *The Times* for a domestic worker for a local residential home, nor is there any reason for expecting a good response to an advertisement for a financial analyst placed in *Construction News*. People looking for jobs will hunt in the outlets known to carry vacancy announcements, and those looking for applicants will advertise in outlets known to be used by job-seekers. This traditionalism undermines some of the attempts to distribute the message more widely.

The job (product)

If the job vacancy is to be seen as a product, the way in which it is packaged and presented to its potential consumers will influence the way in which they perceive it. The accountants Price Waterhouse conducted some research into the elements of job advertisements that attract job-seekers' attention. It was found that job-seekers look first for a job title (or heading), a location and a salary that matches their requirements. If these catch the reader's attention, there is a chance that he or she will read the rest of the advertisement.

Designing and writing newspaper advertisements has become such a skilled task that in-house efforts can look extremely amateurish. Also, because the cost of placing press adverts is high, many small employers find other ways of recruiting staff. However, press adverts can be one of the most effective ways of finding suitable applicants quickly, and they also provide opportunities for contributing to the general promotion of the employing organisation.

There are some general principles that can help to maximise the use of an advertisement. In particular, 'image' — the job-seeker first sees the whole advert. This may be a flier, a sandwich board, a poster, a letter or a newspaper advertisement and, in the latter case, the job is competing with many others. Advert designers know the importance to the eye of white space (surrounding the text), and the following was one of the most creative and imaginative adverts ever devised.

If you can fill this space, ring 0345 9876

An imaginative use of white space

The advertisement appeared in a newspaper specialising in creative and media posts. Can you imagine the impact it made on a page full of text? Most advertisers of job vacancies cannot get away with this minimalistic approach and need to use other ways to attract attention. The border style and use of logo, the typeface and layout all contribute to the image being presented and they need to be complementary. Otherwise the end-products can look a mess.

Presentation

The importance of post title, location and salary has already been mentioned, but it is surprising the number of advertisements that do not give those basic details. Salary, especially, is a big secret, reserved for the initiated few only. Some advertisements, particularly those that try to attract attention by using snappy slogans, hide the job title in the text. The following example shows how enthusiasm can get in the way of selling the job.

WE ARE LOOKING FOR THE VERY BEST IN THE WORLD.

ARE YOU THAT PERSON?

We have a *REALLY* exciting opportunity for a skilled and able **special person**. If you have managed a busy shop, provided a high standard of quality service and trained new staff you will have had the experience we want. We want a **strong personality**, a **good communicator** and an **energetic leader**. If you are ready to go *places* and are looking for some *new challenges* with a *successful* and *adventurous* company ring me ***NOW***.

Peter Smith on 0133-23 67 58 99

But what job is being advertised?

Location can also be used to advantage. For example, an advert was placed by a large national organisation for graduate management trainees. The organisation's main base is just outside a small market town, midway between two cities. One of the cities is a popular tourist venue and is generally regarded as being a very pleasant place to live, while the other (the nearest to the organisation's base) is an industrial centre, generally seen as a dump. Guess which city was given in the address?

Other advertisements try to cram everything into a very small space. Some basic information about the organisation, the job and the sought for qualities need to be included, but just how much is needed is a value judgement. It depends on the medium to be used and, in part, on how much is already known about the organisation and the type of job. Market research helps to decide what and how much to include. It seems from scanning advertisements that these decisions are not often consciously made. Many seem to be overloaded with information that could be provided in other ways or at other times. This indiscriminate use of words leads to dense, small print in newspapers; it can be an overkill that does not tempt people to read on, and actually achieves the reverse of what was intended.

The purpose of an advertisement for a job vacancy is to interest possible candidates. They should have enough information on which to base their initial decision — that is, whether to find out more. This first stage is critical. It is the occasion when many potentially good applicants might choose not to go further because the initial advertisement does not appeal to them. Contrast the following two advertisements to see how the same job can be portrayed in totally different ways.

TUTORS TO DEVELOP JOB-SEEKING SKILLS
c £18,000
South Yorkshire, The Midlands and South Wales

Experienced trainers are needed by one of the country's largest providers of programmes for the unemployed. You will need good presentation skills and experience of working on government funded projects. You will also need to understand the difficulties facing those looking for jobs in areas of high unemployment. Interviews will be held in various locations around the country. For more information telephone A.J. Smethurst to whom applications should be sent.

HELPING THE UNEMPLOYED
115, WESTLEY ROAD, KINGSVILLE, KG3 5JP
0345 9876

Trainer advertisement — version one

Could you help others find their future?

A leading provider of training opportunities aimed at the unemployed seeks to appoint experienced trainers. Those appointed will be expected to deliver programmes aimed at the development of job search skills. To do this effectively you will already possess well developed presentational and communication skills. You should also be able to relate well to individuals who have experienced the disadvantages caused by high levels of prolonged unemployment.

The appointed person will be based in South Yorkshire, the Midlands or South Wales, depending on personal preference and circumstances. Interviews will be conducted locally. The salary paid will be in the region of £18,000 and will be accompanied by attractive benefits.

Applications should be sent to A.J. Smethurst at Helping the Unemployed, 115 Westley Road, Kingsville KG3 5JP. Mr Smethurst will be pleased to discuss the post and may be contacted on 0345 9876

Trainer advertisement — version two

These two advertisements could easily take the form of a flier, poster, an enclosure with a letter, or an advertisement in a newspaper or journal. They illustrate how phraseology, tone and layout can affect the picture of the job. This, naturally, will influence readers' decisions, their immediate view of the job and the employing organisation, and will condition their approach to the latter stages of the application (if the decision were to proceed). Research has shown that we all form our impressions early and on the basis of a limited amount of information. Subsequent information obtained is used to confirm that impression and disproving information is discounted. It is therefore important to the long-term success of a post that the initial impression, given via the advertisement, is attractive and accurate.

The language used is also important. The previous two examples illustrate differences in tone, while the following two show how different words and expressions can be used to build gender-specific stereotypes. It is well known that the use of gender labels (man, women) are not permitted in press advertisements except under certain circumstances. (Although, despite the fact that the legislation was enacted in 1974, it is still possible to find advertisements looking for 'foremen' or 'managers who have experience of hands-on man management'.) Discrimination can occur in less obvious, often unconscious, ways. Some research was conducted to find out if people could identify the characteristics of the candidates most likely to succeed when applying for five jobs. The jobs were exactly the same except that the descriptions of the desired applicants were written in gender-laden ways.

TRAINEE MANAGERS WANTED
BY LEADING RETAILER

We want to appoint trainee managers to be based in our stores located across the country. We are looking for self-starting individuals who have the confidence to set the pace of change. We are dynamic and thrusting and take an aggressive stance to the competition in our market. We want people who are prepared to work hard to keep up with us and who are determined to forge ahead in their careers.

If you have these talents and wish to join our challenging training scheme, please call 081-234-5678

Gender stereotyping — version one

TRAINEE MANAGERS WANTED
BY LEADING RETAILER

We want to appoint trainee managers to join our staff teams located in stores across the country. We are looking for capable individuals who can guide and enable staff through change. We are an energetic organisation, enthusiastic to take on challenges and meet competition. We want people who are committed to enhancing the quality of our services to our customers and staff.

If you are interested in using your talents and wish to develop along with us, please call 081-234-5678

Gender stereotyping — version two

The research discovered that potential applicants could detect bias (intended or otherwise) in advertisements. What happens is that the image portrayed is compared by individuals to their own self-image and their images of others. If the self-image matches, the individual assesses their chances of success as being good, and therefore the likelihood of their applying for the job in question would be higher. If the images do not match, the individual is unlikely to apply. Other research suggests that women are less likely than men to apply for jobs with high salaries because they tend to undervalue themselves. Similarly, members of ethnic minority groups are not likely to seek employment in organisations that evidently only want applications from one particular ethnic group. The evidence used to form this judgement may be anecdotal or impressionistic; nevertheless, it may be strong enough to dissuade well-qualified applicants from responding to the advertisement. While legislation concerns itself with blatant discrimination and exclusion, the above examples demonstrate how stereotypical images are reinforced and communicated.

The cost of applying (price)

Applying for jobs does not obviously cost an applicant money. Or does it? One of the major difficulties facing those out of paid employment is the amount of money it takes to submit large numbers of applications. The information about vacancies (ie buying newspapers and trade journals) is expensive. Producing letters of application, CVs and making telephone calls all incur cost. Above all, it takes time. Standard CVs used for all jobs may be cost-efficient, but is this approach cost-effective? Employers are intolerant and can detect the all-purpose letter of application and CV. A typical response is: 'If this person can't be bothered to think about my job and customise her application, she cannot want it that much.' While this is an understandable reaction to standardised applications, it also demonstrates a failure to understand the reality of applying for jobs.

Customising an application to suit a particular job requires time and thought. Some organisations expect more from applicants than others. Typically an applicant is asked for a CV, with the expectation that they will tailor their submission to suit the requirements of the job and organisation. Application forms are also widely used. Primarily designed to meet the needs of the selectors, some employers do consider the ease of completion. However, filling in an application form takes time, thought and effort. Sometimes employers ask applicants to do other things to augment their submission, including the completion of supplementary questionnaires, the submission of an 'essay' or compilation of a portfolio of evidence. They all expect applicants to invest energy, time and commitment very early on in the recruitment process.

Hidden costs

Organisations also expect applicants to invest in other ways. The effort needed to get hold of additional information, obtain application forms and meet deadlines can exact a high price from potential candidates with little likelihood of their efforts realising any return. Even a letter acknowledging receipt of an application is rare. Recruitment takes little account of the 'price' the applicant is expected to pay.

Another hidden cost is the time and effort an applicant is expected to spend working out what the employing organisation is looking for. Additional information from the organisation may be very attractive, well produced and packaged, but unless the needs of the potential applicant are considered, it may not contain the information required to facilitate an application. Some packages are so dense, are written in idiosyncratic jargon, give huge quantities of information about the organisation, its location and internal structures, but add nothing to help the applicant. Many such packs simply require applicants to spend a lot of time working out what they do need to know and what it irrelevant *at this stage*. Sometimes it takes so long for this material to arrive that applicants do not have adequate time to submit a considered application before the imposed closing date.

Obtaining additional information can also cost in different ways. How many of us have rung to speak to the named person, only to find that they are not available? How many times has it not been possible to make contact because the phone line has been continually engaged? This, of course, assumes that the applicant is able to make private phone calls during the working day.

The number of advertisements asking applicants to send self-addressed envelopes for application forms and additional information has declined — but the practice has not disappeared, again expecting the potential applicant to invest time, materials and energy. (Employers place great reliance on the speed of the post and take little account of this when deciding closing dates.) One technique that has been used to good effect is the reply coupon. Placed at the bottom of a large newspaper advertisement for several vacancies, the potential applicant simply fills in their name and address and job reference number and then addresses the envelope. The use of Freepost also helps to make the process cheaper for the applicant.

The value of applying

It is worth spending some time thinking about why people apply for jobs. Many different assumptions are held about the precise reasons why people do and do not work. Some of these are influenced by political persuasion as much as empirical evidence. Rather than getting into a detailed debate here about the issues, it is sufficient to say that there are probably as many motives as there are people in and out of work. Nevertheless, some general drivers can be recognised.

For those out of work, the need for a job is an obvious motivator. Jobs bring companionship, social esteem and useful ways of passing the time — and they bring money. Maslow's hierarchy of needs (discussed in Chapter 2) also helps us to understand what drives people. Nicholson and West (1988) conducted research into the career moves of over 2,000 managers. They found that managers respond to three broad types of motivation force: circumstantial; avoidance; and future-orientations. Most gave the latter reason — but they would say that wouldn't they? Further analysis showed mixed motives concerning avoidance (reasons for escaping current circumstances) and the wish to improve career prospects or standards of living. (Interestingly nearly twice as many men than women wished to improve their living standards.) Generally, people who are happy in their jobs do not scan the situations vacant columns as a matter of course, yet the best applicants for the vacancy may be in this group. These people will not be prepared to put a lot of energy into applying for another job if there is no particular reason for them to do so. Other ways of attracting these people and trying to ensure they apply need to be considered.

If employers want to attract a strong field of applicants they must make it as easy as possible for potential applicants to make contact, obtain information and submit their first application. One way of simplifying the process for applicants is for employers to ask for just enough information to enable a first screening, and then to ask those who reach the second stage for extra material to support their application. Extra information about the organisation can also be given to applicants to help them. Application forms, if used, should be designed to be easy to complete. Tests and trials can be carried out to make sure the forms are simple for the applicant, while supplying the information needed for the purposes of selection. Applicants should be told what needs to be included with their CV or application. The advertisement is the first place where potential applicants are told what the organisation is looking for and what skills, abilities or experience they need to have.

Promoting the vacancy

If a communication is to be effective, the audience at whom it is aimed should be defined. According to Torrington and Hall (1991), for the purposes of recruitment this is 'suitably qualified, experienced individuals who are able and willing to perform the job to the agreed standard for the organisation in question'. Similarly, the content of the message should portray the image the sender desires to communicate (which should be an accurate representation), and there should be some mechanisms for checking whether the message has been received as intended. The vehicle used for the transmission of the message is also an important factor to be considered. The means of promotion should aim to reach the majority of the target audience, and how best to do this depends on a number of factors:

- How rare are the people with the skills?
- How difficult will it be to attract them?
- Where are they located in the labour market?
- Which media will reach them?
- How long will it take for them to receive the message?
- How much will the chosen medium cost (money, time, imagination, effort)?
- Will the chosen medium comply with equal opportunities legislation?
- Will the chosen medium help to promote the organisation as well as the job?

The marketing concept provides some ideas that are not usually considered when preparing to advertise a vacancy. The application of the four Ps (place, product, presentation and price) can offer some suggestions on ways to improve targeting and the success rate of recruitment activity. An effective recruitment campaign is one that attracts suitably qualified and experienced candidates, and the size of the response should be large enough to provide choice and comparison. Too many applicants defeats the purpose because decision making can be paralysed by having too large a choice.

A marketing approach can contribute to effectiveness — focusing the message concentrates resources. It forces the recruiter to consider what the contents of the message should be and at whom it should be aimed. The assessment of what the target audience knows already and what the organisation wants the market to know enables the advertisement to make a contribution to the wider communications function.

Once the broad parameters of the message have been decided, it is possible to draft the contents in detail. The text for the advertisement comes primarily from the job description and person specification. It is the first, and in some cases the only chance to persuade the 'best' applicants to express their interest. The image created and language used could say to potential employees, 'This is the job for you in an organisation you will want to work for'. Alternatively it may say, 'They want a repeat of last year's model — the job will be uninteresting' or even, 'The organisation doesn't know what it wants.' Once the message is drafted in broad shape and detail, it is possible to decide how best to transmit it. The medium is part of the message. It too says something about the job and the organisation and can influence the success or failure of the campaign.

When the huge range of media available for the advertisement of a vacancy is considered, the use of the market concept as a framework can produce some radical solutions to the problem of how best to get the message to the right people. Some ideas are discussed in the following sections. Obviously, the most appropriate method for the purpose should be chosen and some care needs to be exercised, especially in relation to the equal opportunities legislation. Frequently, the only thought given to the problem is which newspaper or agency to use, but the other possibilities are numerous and some will be described briefly below, while Fyock (1993) provides some interesting American ideas.

RECRUITMENT METHODS

The second part of this chapter will put to use the concepts outlined in the first part. Most of the personnel textbooks give brief indications of how to place advertisements in newspapers and outline the services offered by recruitment agencies and search consultants. These descriptions will be taken further and the practicalities of these and other methods will be discussed. Some ideas of alternative approaches will also be offered, a few of which may seem bizarre. The labour market is changing rapidly and sometimes, therefore, it is appropriate to try out different ways of attracting the attention of people who may not be looking for another job. The role of recruitment in promoting the organisation must not be neglected. Combining both the need to fill a particular post and the wish to contribute to the organisation's overall image can produce some innovate and effective approaches.

Advertisements

Press advertisements

Advertisements are placed in both newspapers and trade journals, and three factors influence the choice of these media — cost, profile of the readership and circulation. The first is variable, depending on the size of advertisement, type and location. A national daily or Sunday paper can cost thousands of pounds; a local paper a few hundred pounds. Against this must be balanced the nature and number of the paper's readership and the profile of its market share. (This information can be obtained from *British Rate And Data* (BRAD), a monthly publication serving the advertising industry.)

Readership profile is an important factor when choosing trade journals. These include journals aimed at occupational groupings (such as members of a professional body — eg *The Architects' Journal*) or those engaged in a particular area of work (eg *Construction News*). Cost can vary considerably, as does publication frequency, which can delay the filling of a vacancy. Most journals appear monthly, but when the lead time and the time needed to ensure that the majority of likely applicants have had long enough to obtain the journal, read it, seek additional information and prepare and submit their applications are taken into account, the closing date may need to be as much as six weeks after publication. Newspaper advertisements usually have less than a week's lead and are read within one or two days.

Table 3.2 lists some design factors that need to be taken into account when preparing advertisements. Decisions about these will determine the size, style, wording and use of graphics and colour. As with other aspects of life, press recruitment advertising has fashions and its own agenda. Agencies operate on behalf of their clients (the employing organisations) as well as attempting to satisfy their own needs. Competition between agencies is fierce, and satisfactory filling of vacancies is only one of several measures of success. Profitability is another obvious measure, as are the annual advertising awards which have a significant influence on style and the use of graphics and colour. The employing organisation when commissioning an advertisement is very much in the hands of its agent and, unless it provides a tight brief, is prey to fashions and the agency's priorities.

Table 3.2   Factors affecting the design of advertisements

Factor	Comments
The image of the organisation	Recruitment advertisements should match and enhance the public image of the employing organisation. For example, a traditional bureaucracy would not best sell itself using avant-garde, full-page colour spreads, nor would it recruit staff who would fit easily into its culture.
The nature of the job	The advertisement for a chief executive demands very different treatment to that for a working charge hand.
The chosen media	Different media have distinctive styles that affect the 'fit' of an individual advertisement. It is well worth looking at a few back issues of the selected newspaper or journal to see what works on its pages and what does not. A frivolous advertisement placed in a serious paper is not likely to work as well as it might if it were placed in a more suitable medium.
The predilection of the target market	An advertisement for a chartered accountant working in a large, long-established, traditional organisation would hardly attract the 'right' sort of candidate if it were headed 'Do you have a creative way with figures?' While sometimes it is worth flouting the normal, it needs to be done with a certain amount of circumspection.

An advertisement has to compete for the reader's eye on the page. Most readers are unlikely to be engaged in a systematic search for a particular vacancy. They are more likely to be scanning the pages to see if there is anything of interest. They will be looking for a word or image that attracts their attention and then they will read on to see if the advertisement contains anything that is of interest. The design and layout of the advertisement influences initial eye appeal more than the text. Equally, the overall 'picture' on the page is important. Attractiveness, balance and readability all have an effect, and getting these right is the skilled work of a graphic designer. Some argue that what works and does not is largely a matter of personal taste, but this is not totally true. Some variables have a predictable effect on eye appeal and readability, such as size of type, the length of lines and clarity. Above all, the black-to-white ratio can make the difference between an attractive and an unattractive advertisement. Consider the following two layouts advertising the same post, both of which take up the same amount of space on the page.

SYSTEMS DEVELOPMENT MANAGER

ABC, an advanced integrated graphic reproduction & design group specialising in magazine production on paper & multi-media, seek a Systems Development Manager. He/she will be responsible for staff training & development using a variety of Mac, PC and Scitex equipment. The successful candidate will also be capable of producing full-colour design and multi-media work on system and be able to show a strong track record in both staff development & client contact. Send CV to Mickie Smith, ABC, 3rd Floor, Luker House, 3/5 Baker Street, Luton

---

The black-to-white ratio — version one

Systems Development Manager

WANTED to work with Mac, PC and Scitex equipment and be responsible for:
- **training and development**
- **client contact**
- **full-colour design**
- **multi-media work**

You should have a strong track record in these areas. We are a design group specialising in advanced integrated graphic reproduction on paper and multi-media for magazine production. Please send your CV to
ABC, 3rd Floor, Luker House, 3/5 Baker Street, Luton

The black-to-white ratio — version two

Newspaper advertising is something that most employers have to do at some time in their history. Consequently, advertising professionals face a similar problem to that familiar to catering professionals — because everyone eats, everyone is a food expert. The difference between a good press advert and one which passes without notice is not always cost. Yes, being able to engage a graphic artist and copywriter can help, but thought, careful wording and careful use of space can make a big difference as these two examples demonstrate.

Radio and television advertising

Radio and television occasionally broadcast job advertisements. Most local stations have a community service and a commitment to their area, especially if it earns them income and audience share. But radio and TV advertising is expensive when air time costs are added to the time, expertise and expense involved in preparation. Most viewers and listeners are experienced and sophisticated and so expect to receive professionally produced messages. Yet, despite the drawbacks caused by the expense and planning needed to ensure a professional end-product, this media is worth considering, particularly for the recruitment of large numbers or when the employer wants to get to a 'hard to reach' group.

TV and radio have extremely good market research data and know who is tuned in and when. This knowledge can help advertisers to decide when best to broadcast their message.

Ross Services is a supplier of office equipment and stationery. Recently it has diversified to provide secretarial and clerical services in response to a need expressed by its customers. The modest pilot project proved to be an overwhelming success and so Ross has decided to expand and extend this part of the business. Part of the expansion plan is to offer its services at the 'edges' of the normal business day. Some valued customers have said how much they would welcome early morning and early evening support to help prepare for rush meetings and to tidy up after hectic days.

The town in which Ross is based, however, has suffered from a long recession and most experienced office staff are in well-paid jobs. Those registered unemployed tend to be lacking in experience but it is known that there is a large number of potentially suitably qualified people (mainly women) who are not registered as seeking work. Ross realises that using the Job Centre and advertising in the local newspaper would not necessarily reach people wanting to work only a few hours at unsocial times of day. Daytime radio advertising would reach those people at home whose domestic commitments may well be covered by other family members in the morning and early evening.

Fliers

The use of fliers (ie leaflets or small posters) is mainly found in targeted recruitment campaigns. The target audience is defined by the requirements of the person specification, market research identifies potential candidates, and ways of reaching that group are devised. Take, for example, a job that requires the specialist knowledge normally possessed by people who belong to a certain professional body. Most organisations are now prepared to make available their mailing lists for a fee, and it is worth calculating the cost difference between a press advert and the chance of it being seen by the desired candidates, relative to a mailshot and certain delivery via the postal system. But mailshots must be used with discretion because people may get fed up with unsolicited job details and so the technique will lose its impact. However, used judiciously this technique can produce impressive results.

Some organisations, especially large ones and those operating on a number of sites, send out internal vacancy bulletins. These can be used in similar ways to fliers, as existing employees will pass the bulletin on to family and friends who may be looking for jobs. The Commission for Racial Equality and Equal Opportunities Commission advise against advertising solely within closed groups, and the internal bulletin can thus be used to promote the organisation and its vacant posts to the outside world. Some employing organisations distribute bulletins via community groups so they are seen by under-represented groups. Others send them to similar, nearby employers. It needs to be made clear, however, which jobs are restricted to internal applicants so that false expectations are not raised and unnecessary applications generated.

Fliers and bulletins need to be produced to as high a standard as possible and can take a similar form to that of a press advertisement. They may also need to be supported by an appropriately worded letter. However, fliers need not be expensive to produce. The principles about giving emphasis to job title, employer's name, salary and location that apply to press advertisements also apply to fliers. The design should allow them to be used as posters or leaflets to be passed on to interested parties. Word-processing technology now makes the production of an eye-catching flier very easy.

Fliers produced in conjunction with a small newspaper advertisement have been used very successfully to encourage members of under-represented groups to apply for posts. Not only did the advertisement attract more than normal enquiries, letters were received from individuals expressing their support for the action and thanking the organisation for contacting them. The general quality of the applicants was higher than the standard previously attracted, so the flier did its job of encouraging suitably qualified applications and also contributed to the public image of the employer.

Fliers can be sent to organisations and locations where potential applicants are to be found. Sometimes, one employer will approach other employers and ask them to circulate job vacancy advertisements, although it seems that this practice has declined as the competition for skilled and experienced staff has increased. Fliers can also represent an effective way of getting to people who do not see normal advertisements. Distributing vacancy notices to venues such as libraries, post offices, doctors' surgeries and community groups need not be restricted to organisations trying to recruit staff from under-represented groups; it can also be a useful way of contacting people not in paid employment, such as the self-employed or those caring for relatives.

OFFICE STAFF
wanted for
Manor Community Forum
To work Monday, Wednesday and Friday
10.00am to 2.00pm

Duties will include	**Skills needed:**
Filing	Word processing
Typing	(using Easiword)
Reception duties	Telephone skills
Bookkeeping	Elementary bookkeeping

If you would like to apply, please call into the Forum Office,
236, Princess Way or telephone Robin on 345987

A sample flier

Mailshots

Fliers can be used for mailshots, or the information can be put into a letter with or without enclosures. Mailshots are best when a large number of people spread over a large geographic area need to be contacted, but they should be used with care. We all know how irritating it is to receive unsolicited 'bumf'. Usually distribution takes place via the postal service or, alternatively, distribution agencies can be employed to leaflet a town or area. If designed well and produced to a high standard, accurately targeted mailshots can be very effective. Their primary purpose is to attract the attention of potential applicants who do not read the situations vacant columns in newspapers or the professional press. These may be people out of employment or those who are content in their present jobs. The audience may also include people who possess skills not normally associated with a particular job and who would discount their suitability before any advertisement could make an impact.

Some professional bodies are prepared to make their membership lists available for a fee, and some are able to produce sectional lists sorted into specified categories. Alternatively, it may be possible for mailshots to be included with the normal material being sent out to members by the professional body. The response level for this sort of campaign, however, is known to be very low — perhaps one out of every 1000 leaflets. Nevertheless, careful mailing can achieve some startling results.

One organisation was trying to attract more female applicants into a traditionally male occupation. The women members of appropriate professional bodies were sent a letter and a copy of the advertisement due to appear in the professional journal. The women were told of the vacancy and the organisation's wish to increase the number of women in a group in which they were currently under-represented. The approach and wording had been checked and, on the advice of the Equal Opportunities Commission, it was stressed that any appointment would only be made on the grounds of merit. The number of well-qualified women applications increased considerably.

The most surprising pay-off, however, was the number of people who wrote in to say they had never considered that particular area of work before, and even though they did not wish to apply for the particular vacancy, they would bear such work in mind for the future. The approach achieved its objective and made a significant contribution to the organisation's image as a progressive employer.

Brochures

Additional information packs or material aimed at a particular category of recruits, such as graduate trainees, are frequently packaged as brochures. These are distributed through outlets like careers offices, 'milk round' events (discussed later in this chapter), Job Centres or training venues. Traditionally they have been glossy and high cost, but modern reproduction methods have brought brochures within the price range of most employing organisations. Again, they can be used to reach groups of people who do not read newspapers or visit the normal venues used by job-seekers.

Most brochures tend to fall into one of two categories. The first covers the high-cost, mass-produced glossies. Most commonly they are used for bulk recruitment in areas of work where there is a skill shortage or competition for staff is high. They are most economical when it is possible to target large numbers of potential applicants quickly. Exhibitions, displays or recruitment fairs are usually supported by such quality publicity material. While the use of brochures can enhance the image of the employer, the glossy should convey an accurate message. Over-egging the publicity eventually leads to disillusioned staff or high turnover rates.

The other main use for brochures is to support the basic material used to attract applicants. It is not uncommon for large organisations to send enquirers additional information describing the organisation and the job in greater detail. Many smaller employers simply ask interested individuals to submit CVs or letters of application without providing any additional information, but this can be a mistaken economy. Research into the factors influencing the success or failure of an appointment suggests that the more information the appointee has in the early stages, the more likely the appointment is to be successful. The provision of early information ensures that applicants are more able to select themselves in or out, thus reducing the time and cost of shortlisting. It also helps them to provide information the selectors need in a form that helps shortlisting and later selection activities. Moreover, it means that applicants are able to build a more complete and accurate image about the job, the organisation and the expectations that will be placed on them.

These brochures need not be too ambitious or high cost. A very attractive folder can be compiled from single sheets describing the organisation, its mission, the terms and conditions of employment, the job and, for organisations wishing to attract out-of-town applicants, information about the locality, its housing, schools and so on.

Recruitment fairs

Recruitment fairs can be general, offering a large range of career opportunities (such as those organised in major cities for school leavers); they can be local (some careers services organise events); or they can be arranged by an employer (eg caterers and other employers who need to take on large numbers of staff for particular functions).

Recently, about 100 temporary office staff were needed to help an organisation over a period of peak workload. A recruitment fair was organised and publicised via the press, local radio and posters. Possible applicants were invited to take some work-related tests (such as typing, completing a clerical aptitude test and drafting a simple letter). They also had the chance to talk to existing staff about the work before deciding whether to submit an application. The tests and the chance to talk to staff cut out shortlisting.

The event also opened the organisation's doors to people who previously had no contact with it. The professional arrangements for the event and the friendly approach taken by the staff did a lot to build the organisation's local reputation. The abilities of the applicants called back had already been assessed systematically, so the final selection interview could concentrate on checking experience, understanding of the role and social fit. The whole project proved to be economic as well as effective, and eventually some of the applicants were engaged as permanent employees.

A variation on this theme is an open day, perhaps most suitable for, say, the establishment of a new store, branch, office or unit. Inviting interested people to visit the location, meet existing staff or representatives and talk about the work may seem time-consuming, but it can be a low-cost way of attracting and meeting potential employees. It enables information to be transmitted, questions answered and initial assessments of potential applicants to be made, which can, if appropriate, be extended into a work trial. Obviously, preparation is needed to ensure that the flow of visitors is controllable and that staff running the event are adequately prepared and briefed. It is also essential to ensure that work samples and tests are planned and well set up, and that enough copies of paperwork, documents and supporting leaflets are available for the anticipated size of response. Some organisations hold such events in hotels or public venues, but the disadvantage of this is that potential employees do not have the chance to see the working environment.

Other people's meetings

The main weakness of placing advertisements in newspapers and trade journals is that their effectiveness depends on suitable people obtaining a copy of the paper or journal in the first place. Then they need to turn to the vacancy pages where the chances of your advertisement being seen are very small. The 'flag is flown' usually on one day only. There are some people who do not buy newspapers and others who do not join professional bodies or read trade journals. If they are not members, they will not be on any mailing list. So, how does an organisation reach people who do not make themselves available?

Head hunting (or search as it properly called) is one way, while another is to go to where these people are likely to be — at meetings, exhibitions and conferences. For example, if there is a need to recruit a specialist to help deliver a critical part of the organisation's business plan, or special skills are in short supply, it may be worth negotiating with organisers to hold a recruitment event and so make a public impact. Any display or exhibition should be staffed so that questions may be answered and an initial assessment of potential made. However, if this is not possible or the event organisers are unwilling to go this far, fliers, brochures or leaflets may be enough to elicit some expression of interest from suitable individuals.

Vehicle displays

Until recently, the idea of mounting vacancy advertisements on the side of motor vehicles seemed like an American fad that would not translate very well. However, a small news item in one of the personnel journals (*Personnel Today* on 28 June 1994) told of a multinational company wanting to recruit a number of staff for a new outlet being opened in Bristol. The way they chose to advertise themselves and the job opportunities was on the side of buses! Broadcasting the need to fill vacancies in such a public way can result in more than attracting potential applicants. It can help an organisation demonstrate its commitment to other policies, such as its wish to be 'environmentally friendly'.

Off-the-wall approaches

Vacancy boards used to be one of the most common methods of recruitment used by large employers in industrial areas. Notice boards or posters in windows were displayed listing the vacancies and inviting applicants into the employment office. The reduction of numbers employed by this type of organisation and the decline in the traditional industrial estates has meant that this approach to recruiting is now less common. Nevertheless, sandwich boards have recently been seen outside employment agencies in city centres, displaying a range of jobs — not just office vacancies. Employers with suitable external display space are also using boards or posters to draw people's attention to vacancies, and posters or cards are seen in the windows of post offices, supermarkets, etc. These tend to be for part-time, temporary or casual jobs and are placed by small employers believing the method to be low cost and effective. However, the Equal Opportunities Commission warns against recruiting by word of mouth or from closed communities: the danger in each of these approaches is that the profile of the current workforce is replicated and opportunities denied to members of other groups.

Milk round

The 'milk round' is the term used for the series of annual events designed to help organisations find graduate employees. Mainly large organisations mount staffed displays at exhibitions organised by universities and colleges. The process is very much like the traditional hiring fairs, except the meeting between prospective employers and employees can lead on to discussions to ensure that the match will produce the 'best fit' for both parties.

Agencies

Careers offices can help to bring potential employees and employers together, as well as providing guidance to school leavers and job-seekers. This role has expanded as the careers service has moved from providing 16 and 18 year olds with information about jobs and careers into a more advisory role encompassing work training, retraining and educational opportunities for people of all ages.

Job Centres have also broadened their role. The huge numbers of people unemployed for long periods of time, the variety of government schemes to help people back into work and the wish to introduce 'business' methods into the public sector have all led to a revamping of the traditional 'Labour Exchange'. Job Centres have long tried to match vacancies and job-seekers, but now they offer a wider range of services to employers. These include shortlisting services, pre-interview screening and search. The Department of Employment also has links with the Rehabilitation Service and is able to work with employers to help those with disabilities find suitable work.

Employment agencies have a popular image as suppliers of temporary office staff, but they too have changed their services in line with changes in the labour market and have increased the range of occupations they cover. They can provide a full service which includes the recruitment of suitably qualified applicants, initial screening, profiling and assessment of skills and shortlisting for temporary, locum and permanent staff. The better agencies also provide support during the induction stage and can help train placed and existing staff. Some are working with employers to take over areas of outsourced work such as telephone switchboards, office services, data processing, etc. The way in which fees are calculated for placed staff varies. In some cases fees are charged in relation to the salary of the post, or sometimes as a fixed consultancy fee. The major contribution played by an agency is their ability to provide a total, professional service and, for organisations with little experience of recruiting staff or when anonymity is needed, the benefits may be worth the price.

Recruitment consultants

Consultants provide very similar services to employment agencies, but there are two major differences. One is that consultancies tend to work on more senior, professional and management posts, whereas agencies concentrate on lower paid jobs such as catering, office, stores, manual and junior management. Secondly, consultancies also engage in search. The advantages of engaging a search consultancy is that they can provide expertise and labour, and it also enables the employing organisation to remain anonymous if it so wishes. The consultancy can carry out checks on candidates that would not be so easy for a potential employer to arrange. Search consultancies have networks that allow them to make discrete enquiries about past records, reputations of individuals and their current activities.

'Head hunting' is the derogatory name given to the process of positive search. This technique has attracted much criticism from equal opportunities activists who see it as a means of ensuring that the status quo is preserved and that clones are appointed. Indeed, the use of established networks and 'old boys clubs' can limit the pool of potential applicants, and this approach may have been favoured in the past. But search consultants now have a professional body and have developed a code of ethics, and the better ones are very conscious of the equal opportunities requirements and are ready to engage in proper positive action. They can ask challenging questions when taking the initial brief, thus broadening the horizons of the employing organisation by exploring assumptions, suggesting alternatives and proposing searches through previously unconsidered sources. They can also add value and difference by presenting applications from people from non-typical backgrounds for consideration. Moreover they can encourage reticent individuals to put themselves forward. Research has indicated that members of minority groups devalue their skills and themselves to such an extent that they will not apply for some posts they are well able to fill. This is due to the potential applicants' belief that their chances of success are so low.

As regards the typical process used by a search consultant, the first step is usually to take a brief and translate it, via the job description and person specification, into a profile of the best person for the job. The likely location of suitably qualified people is considered and a search strategy developed. This could include desk research — ie looking for people in similar areas of work or who, for example, have published or spoken on a relevant topic publicly. A search of recent applicants for similar posts also adds names to the list of possibles. Information about these individuals is then sought, either from them directly or from colleagues, peers, employers or informed others. Sometimes known 'experts' are asked to make nominations or newspaper advertisements (either confidential or publicising the name of the employing organisation) are run. The individual is usually approached directly and asked to submit a letter of interest or a CV. From this initial data, the search consultant checks basic requirements against the job requirements and, if these align, arranges to meet the individual. The individuals and consultants have discussions about the job, their expectations and understanding and their suitability against the job requirements. Checks may also be carried out to back up the longlist which is then submitted to the client organisation. Selected individuals are then invited to meet the prospective employer, and more discussions take place, other checks are made and formal references taken up. This degree of preselection screening makes it possible for the final selection phase to involve only a very few candidates.

The services of search consultants are being used more and more. So far, little research seems to have been carried out to assess the predictive validity of the process, whereas most other common forms of selecting staff have been subjected to scrutiny and rich evidence exists to enable the comparative benefit of each to be assessed. The whole process of search and its reliance on data obtained from others would benefit from examination.

The search process

There are several distinct steps, each of which is prone to error and bias.

Initial briefing

It is easy for a busy manager to believe that, by engaging a consultant, responsibility for finding the best person is handed over. This may seem to be the very reason for using a search consultant but, in effect, it can amount to avoidance. The manager is able to avoid thinking deeply and critically about the job requirements, the content of the person specification and the selection criteria. Unless the consultant is very competent, the abdication on the part of the manager can lead to a superficial image being painted, full of assumptions and stereotypes. And, of course, because similar words are used to convey commonly held values, it is so easy for misunderstandings to occur.

'I want a good communicator who can lead the team through a period of rapid change.'

Intended meaning — 'I want someone who can write really sharp, concise reports and who is able to steer good people gently through a short period of externally imposed turbulence.'

Heard message — 'I want a good public speaker who can sell a convincing story to a group of people who are resisting the need to change their working practices.'

Search strategy

Again, it is easy for the manager to hand over the whole recruitment phase to the consultant but, in practice, it is better if this is planned jointly. The role of the consultant is to give professional advice, front the process and to provide the labour, while the role of the manager is to ensure the organisation's requirements and values are embodied in the process. If search is to be used, the employing organisation and existing staff may be able to suggest appropriate individuals or likely sources of suitable applicants. Confidential advertising is being used increasingly but, if the organisation's name is to be used for recruitment, it should ensure that the opportunity is not lost to contribute to its overall public image.

The search process

How the names of potential applicants are gathered needs to be planned as part of the search strategy. One criteria for the selection of a consultancy is the size of the database — ie how many people do they know about. These names may be gathered from previous recruitment activities, contacts made with individuals in other organisations, from other business transactions, meetings attended and so on. Each economic sector has its own circles and being able to tap into these is one aspect of the consultant's skill. But there is a danger of concentrating on the easy circles — those that are very well known and public, like the conference circuit or professional meetings. There are many competent people who are not active in these circles but who need to be sourced if the employing organisation is to be presented with a balanced selection from which to longlist.

Preliminary meetings

The nature of biases and errors in the way in which we form initial impressions is described in Chapter 4, but the simple point to be made here is that the interview process is flawed. It is well known that initial impressions are formed within 30 seconds on the basis of previously held assumptions, stereotypes and prejudices (prejudgements). Subsequent interactions are used subconsciously to confirm that initial impression, while efforts are made to discount any contradictory information.

The meeting between the consultant acting as an agent of the employer and the prospective candidate is used to 'screen out' and 'select in' people who are perceived to be suitable. The consultant will endeavour to make use of the briefing given by the employer but, inevitably, this will be underpinned by the consultant's existing beliefs and value patterns.

One-to-one interviews are regarded as a poor predictor of subsequent performance. As Smith, Clegg and Andrews (1989) point out: 'Many researchers over the past 30 years have confirmed that interviews are very bad predictors of job performance. In other words they are not a valid selection method.' Yet they continue to be used extensively as a main source of information and point of decision making. As a result, efforts have been made to improve the process — for example, the use of criterion-based and behavioural event interviewing. In most cases the interview is conducted by an existing member of the organisation who is versed in its culture and has an understanding, from the inside, of its values. The use of a consultant means that this critical part of the selection process is being externalised. Consequently, the criteria used for selecting the candidates put forward for the employer to consider will have been chosen on the basis of the consultant's opinion. This is another reason for ensuring the initial briefing is more than a half hour chat about the job. At the very least, the consultant should have an appreciation of the organisation's values and some insight into its culture.

The consultant is also acting as an agent of the organisation and therefore as an ambassador. Prospective candidates will make judgements about the organisation from the behaviour of people who represent it, regardless of whether they are direct employees or agents. There have been reports of consultants acting in less than professional ways with some applicants who have been written off early in the meeting. This sort of response does no good for either search consultants or employing organisations.

References

Checks on applicants and opinions about them are sought in order to inform the compilation of the longlist. Some of the references are those supplied by individual applicants and are approached with their agreement, while some are people who know of 'Person X'. They may have worked with the individual at some point in the past — as a manager, colleague subordinate or co-worker on projects, or perhaps as customer or supplier. The better consultants obtain opinions from a range of sources, looking for common themes and contradictions. From these opinions, a picture of the individual applicant is compiled.

Again there are dangers. One factor is the size of the population from which information is obtained. (Similar opinions of several people formed at different points in Person X's working life in different situations may have some validity, but the views of two or three people formed at one point in time will have been influenced by the situation and the circumstances of the moment.) Another factor is the quality of their judgement. We tend to place great weight on the views of others without knowing the reasons for their opinions, their abilities or expertise, or if there are any 'axes to grind'. The halo effect (a well-developed skill in one area of work or one good comment being taken to reflect total competence) and the Satan effect (a lack of skill or negative comment being taken to reflect low overall competence) are phenomena that influence perception when making judgements about other people. A third danger to be aware of is the validity of the referees' opinions. People change and develop, their performance varies in different surroundings with different people, with different pressures and stress levels, and interpersonal skills are affected by the emotional and physical climate of their working environment.

The House of Lords has ruled concerning the use of references that a previous employer has a duty of care to be honest and informative in order to safeguard Person X's future employment prospects, while providing the future employer with an accurate as possible portrayal of the individual's abilities. Also, the provider of the reference should not slander or defame Person X. These restrictions can deter people from providing written references and there is a tendency to ask for verbal comments. Some people believe these 'off the top' comments to be more revealing, but whether this is so or not is questionable. In addition, because the consultant is obtaining the opinion, confidentiality can be preserved; the consultant need not pass the source of the information on to the prospective employer.

Presentation of the longlist

The longlist, drawn up by the consultant, is often presented in writing but supported by a verbal explanation. This is the occasion for the employing organisation to check on the assumptions being made by the consultant and to ensure consistent application of the selection criteria in the context of the job requirements. The employer should check also the relevancy of the references and opinions of others sought during the checking phase. The breadth of the search and the nature of the rejected candidates also need monitoring. The latter check is not to doubt the consultant, but rather to safeguard against Type II errors. Type I errors, in selection terms, are made when the wrong person is appointed. Type II errors occur when the best person is rejected. There is also the need to monitor the backgrounds of those being put forward in the longlist against the profile of the applicants to ensure that minority groups are adequately represented.

Feedback to unsuccessful applicants

Normally this task is undertaken by the search consultant, but this should not be seen as a chance for the employing organisation to avoid responsibility for an unpleasant duty. The content of the feedback should be considered by both the consultant and the employer, then delivered by the consultant. The latter has had the contact with individual applicants and will have developed some form of relationship. Nevertheless, the employer must remember that applicants will associate their treatment with the employing organisation as much as the consultant. Therefore it is in the interests of the employer to ensure that applicants are given good quality feedback (ie information they are able to learn from and can use to develop their skills) and that they are left with positive feelings about the process.

Selection events

Normally the employer organises selection events in accordance with the organisation's internal procedures, although consultants can help and advise as needed. The appointment decision *must* be that of the employer. Asking an external agent to be involved is not reasonable; the employer must live with the consequences of the decision so cannot share or pass on the responsibility. However, consultants can offer opinions, advise and provide additional information.

Consultants can also help with the negotiations following a decision to offer employment to the successful candidate. At senior levels, the decision making and subsequent discussions seem to be becoming more protracted as contracts become more involved and complex. Getting out of such contracts is also becoming more difficult and costly. The preliminary stages of contract negotiations consequently need to be conducted with care and professional advice. For smaller employers this type of arrangement is not an everyday occurrence and, because employment law is a specialist subject, not every company solicitor is well versed in its intricacies. Some recruitment consultancies are developing an expertise and can therefore offer this service at the closing stages of the recruitment and selection process.

Feedback should be given to unsuccessful candidates as indicated above.

They should also be debriefed about the process. With the arrogance of the powerful, it is considered acceptable to provide feedback to candidates on their performance and inadequacies relative to the person specification, but how often are candidates asked to provide feedback to employers about the recruitment and selection process? Obviously, consideration must be given to their feelings at a time of 'rejection', but their views can help an employing organisation and consultant to improve practice. How else do we learn, if we do not obtain feedback from the recipients of our services?

Selecting consultants

In common with the selection of most suppliers of services, recommendations from those with experience of particular companies tend to be the most widely used method of finding and commissioning search consultants. Directories, such as that produced by the consultants' professional body or *The Personnel Managers' Handbook*, list the largest and provide information that helps with the choice. Other companies invite a small number of consultancies to make presentations outlining their services and facilities and make their choice on that basis. The following checklist may guide the selection:

- How long has the consultancy been in business?
- Which individual consultant will be handling the assignment?
- What degree of experience has that person had of recruitment and selection in general, and in your specific sector?
- What support will be available to the individual consultant?
- Is the consultancy able and willing to provide names of previous clients?
- Can references be obtained from previous clients?
- Can the consultant produce examples of previous assignments, such as advertisements placed, literature produced or an anonymous report on a candidate?
- How large is the database?
- How extensive is the consultant's knowledge of employment law and equal opportunities issues (perhaps a recently reported case can be used as a check)?
- What are the terms of business? Consultancies have their own idiosyncratic methods of charging that can make direct comparison difficult. If it is not clear, get the consultant to work through an example.

Managing consultants

As indicated above, once the consultancy is selected the employing organisation cannot simply hand over the whole process and wait for a few plum candidates to appear for interview. The managers of the organisation have two responsibilities. First to foster the partnership that is needed with the consultant throughout the assignment (and described earlier) and, secondly, to manage the consultant. The following notes have been developed in the light of working with several consultancies:

- Brief thoroughly and check to make sure the brief has been understood by asking questions later. Take early remedial action if there is any doubt about the clarity of understanding. It will save time later, avoid wasted effort and misleading applicants.
- Check any advertising copy to ensure that it gives the messages the employing organisation wants to convey.
- What of extra charges? Unquoted costs that can be loaded on top of agreed fees include 'extras' for advertising (such as premium space payments), production costs, redrafting costs and consultant's expenses incurred in visiting applicants.
- Selection and decision-making techniques used to compile longlists: consultancies have their own preferred methods that may differ from those of the employing organisation (eg some use tests, questionnaires and different forms of interviewing). The consultant should be asked about working methods and appropriate registrations should be checked.
- Is the consultant treating the applicants in the way in which the employing organisation wishes? There is anecdotal evidence to suggest that some senior women applicants have been bullied and harangued to see if they are able to withstand pressure. While this reflects on the consultant, it also has a negative impact on the organisation employing that consultant and the use of search consultants in general. It is worth perhaps directly testing the way in which interested individuals are dealt with by the consultancy.
- Ask the consultant to make explicit the criteria on which the longlist was compiled. Reiteration of the person specification and job requirements is not enough. Ask how they have been applied. This helps to confirm that the consultant has understood the brief and the culture of the organisation and it also helps to ensure that Type II errors (the best candidate being rejected) have been avoided. If the working relationship with the consultant has been developed as a partnership, this discussion should flow as part of the continuing dialogue, but if the consultant has been working with a 'magic box of tricks', assumptions and personal prejudices, it will be more difficult for the decision-making criteria to be made explicit.

- Remember the ultimate objectives are different: the consultant's main measure of success is filling the post, whereas the employing organisation wants a person in the post who will be effective for some time. A common method used for charging fees is for staged payments to be made. For example, the first within two weeks of taking the brief, the second on production of the longlist and the final payment when an offer of appointment is made. The consultant will be looking for an appointment to be made as quickly as possible so that another assignment can be started, but the employer may decide that not to appoint is the best decision. This possibility should be considered when the assignment is agreed.

Search committees

Using a committee (usually of employees) to find suitably qualified candidates is a traditional technique most commonly used in professional organisations such as universities. It relies on networks and relationships. This approach can favour the preservation of the status quo unless a deliberate effort is made to avoid replicating the known, safe and predictable.

The use of a committee, while broadening the network and scope of the search, can introduce group dynamics that may inhibit the search for the best candidate. Power plays and positioning by the members and other people involved with the search committee and selection process have been known to take over, resulting in a compromise appointment that suits no one and a postholder who cannot do the job. Despite the pitfalls, this technique can be operated satisfactorily and has advantages in very small communities of specialists where social fit with existing teams is as important as skills, knowledge and understanding. Search committees can also be used to challenge assumptions, introduce different criteria and provide alternative ways of encouraging diversity within an organisation.

Invitations to nominate

Although occasionally seen in advertisements for senior or specialist posts, this technique is not widely used. It does, however, have potential because peer appraisal is reported to be one of the best predictors of performance. Once a nomination has been received, some mechanism needs to be put in place to contact the individual concerned, obtain information to enable an assessment to be made of their abilities to perform the job to the standard required and to validate that information. Nominations provide a way of getting people, less confident in their abilities, to apply for posts. Reference has already been made to the evidence that suggests that members of minority groups do not apply for higher salaried posts. There is also some suggestion that people do not put themselves forward for posts paying 15–20 per cent more than their current earnings. Perhaps nomination is one way of encouraging people with talent to progress. However, if this approach is to be used, care needs to be taken:

- to avoid the halo effect;
- to push people with talent too far and too fast;
- to ensure that job-related criteria are used to assess suitability rather than personal preference; and
- to justify the final decision to those making the nomination.

Positive action

Under the provisions of the equal opportunities legislation, positive action can only be taken if it can be demonstrated that members of one group are significantly under-represented in relation to other groups. The purpose of this form of action is to enable members of the under-represented groups to arrive at the situation where they are able to compete on the same terms as members of the majority groups. Training schemes, confidence-building activities and practical support are examples. For instance, a group of media companies has worked in concert to provide training and experience to members of ethnic minority groups. There is no job at the end of the period, but the aim of the initiative is to encourage participants to seek permanent employment in the industry and to equip them to compete fairly on the same basis as other applicants who have had preferential treatment because of their membership of the majority group.

The other form of taking positive action is to urge, publicly, members of under-represented groups to submit applications for particular posts.

A SENIOR ENGINEER IS REQUIRED TO TAKE CHARGE OF QUALITY ASSURANCE

Women are under-represented at this level in the company. Applications from them will be particularly welcomed. The appointment will be made on the grounds of merit.

Seeking applicants from an under-represented group

This tactic is most frequently seen in press advertisements inserted by public sector and other organisations committed to equal opportunities policies. It can also be used in fliers, letters informing potential applicants about the existence of the job, mail outs and other proactive methods of publicising a vacancy. Nor need the tactic be confined to attracting applications from individual members of particular population groups; it can also be used to find particular skills or experience needed to balance the staff profile.

ZANIZBAR CAFE WANTS CHEFS

Qualified to C & G 770, with several years experience of fast food outlets, you will be required to work 7 hour shifts between 10.00 and 12.00 over 5 from 7 days and should have a good public manner. We particularly seek applications from those experienced in vegetarian cooking to help us expand in this area. Ring 789345 if you meet the bill.

Balancing a staff profile

Speculative letters and filing applications

Job-seekers are often advised to contact possible employers on a speculative basis, asking for help to find suitable employment or offering themselves for work. The most common response to these letters is nothing, although sometimes a letter of regret is sent or one directing the author to press advertisements. Occasionally the letter will attract a positive response and a meeting. One reason for disregarding such letters was the large number of inexperienced, unqualified, unemployed people desperately seeking work in the early 1980s. Times have changed, however, and the labour market contains a different profile of workers; additionally, mature women returning to work are being more adventurous in their job-seeking strategies. The cost of press advertising also means that organisations genuinely have to find other ways of looking for candidates. Employers ignore these letters at their peril because they are a source of information about possible suitable candidates.

It is good practice for organisations to keep a file of past applications in case anyone complains about their treatment and the fairness of the procedures. If these records are being maintained for one purpose, there is no reason why they should not be re-examined if another similar post falls vacant. Possible candidates may have been overlooked, especially if a large number of applications were received. Even if the application was rejected the first time round, the second job could be sufficiently different to make them close enough to the new person specification to merit reconsideration.

Training schemes and work placements

The measures taken to alleviate unemployment among young people and those out of employment for a long time have included training schemes and work-based opportunities. These intend to provide practical, relevant experience to support any theoretical work-related training given as part of the scheme. Some schemes aim to refresh skills or help individuals change direction. They also bring those out of employment into direct contact with potential employers. Cook (1993) argues that work sampling is one of the best predictors of performance. It follows that getting to know someone and their standard of work through direct experience while they are on a training placement is a good way of assessing whether that individual is capable of doing the job and will fit into the work group. For the applicant, being able to have direct experience of a job before deciding whether to sign a contract is a good way of finding out whether the work meets the individual's needs and whether future colleagues are convivial.

Many employers who recruit graduates find that using work-based learning placements is a very good way of assessing the fit of individuals with the organisation. These placements can vary in length from a few weeks to a full year. Most colleges and universities have liaison staff who are happy to discuss the different types of work-based placements, outline the pros and cons and explain the procedures.

How will you know you have succeeded?

As with any process, the success or otherwise of recruitment should be reviewed and evaluated. The review should be used to provide feedback so that adjustments to the separate parts of the process and its overall operation are made on the basis of evidence and experience. The information needs to be systematically gathered and combined with the impressions gained by all those involved. Normally, some form of review is carried out by managers and other people involved after an appointment is made, but how often are the views of those who were processed sought? Benefit can be obtained by asking the people who took part in the process for their opinions about their experiences and what they thought of the organisation's recruitment material and actions.

The evaluation is an assessment of the effectiveness of the recruitment campaign at each stage and as a whole process:

- What was the full cost of recruitment action in
  — effort (expertise/time)
  — actual expenditure (in comparison to the salary or value of the post)?
- How many enquiries were there?
- Were many enquiries lost and, if so, why?
- How many applications were there?
- How many applications were there from suitably qualified applicants?
- Did potential candidates get the sort of information they needed to help them make decisions?
- Did the information produce an attractive impression of the organisation to applicants?
- Did the information give an adequate picture of the organisation so that newly appointed individuals' expectations are realistic?
- How long did it take to get the new person in post?
- What is the likely long-term effectiveness of the appointee?
- What was the contribution to the overall image of the organisation?

More will be said about the evaluation of each stage of the recruitment and selection process later. It is important to view recruitment in the same way as marketing and so the same sort of rigour should be applied in order to ensure it serves its dual purpose — of attracting suitably qualified (appointable) applicants and contributing to the public image of the organisation.

SUMMARY

The marketing concept has been used in this chapter to demonstrate how recruitment can be (and should be) more than choosing which newspaper should publish the advertisement. The 'four Ps' can help the recruiter to think through and make systematic decisions about how best to bring the existence of the vacancy to the attention of likely and suitable applicants.

Newspapers' situations vacant columns were, traditionally, the most frequently used means of communicating with applicants. However, as the labour market has changed, so have the media and the message. For example, skill shortages and mismatches mean that sometimes potential applicants need to be wooed and the competition between employers can be fierce. The wish to promote equal opportunities policies has led some employers to take positive action to encourage members of under-represented groups to apply. The various training schemes designed to counteract the effects of high and long-term unemployment have provided employers with opportunities to trial individuals without commitment from either side. The greatest area of change has been in the role of recruitment consultants. Because of this, the selection and management of consultants has been discussed at some length. In most organisations, recruitment, especially at senior levels where most consultants concentrate their efforts, occurs infrequently. Therefore, the opportunities to become 'expert' in the use and management of recruitment consultants are few.

Recruitment practices, as with many aspects of the recruitment and selection process, tend to vary between different industrial sectors and types of organisation. These cultural idiosyncrasies contain a tension. People in the know tend to come from similar backgrounds and share assumptions and values. There is a school of thought proposing a convincing argument that, for future survival, organisations need to be able to draw from and develop a wide range of diverse talents. Recruitment is the way in which people from different backgrounds are brought to an employer's attention, and the existence of the vacancy is brought to their's. The perceptions of potential employer and potential employee are formed on the basis of the information provided during the lead up to the submission of an application and on compilation of a shortlist, and the information is used to build the framework within which decisions are made. As with any other human decision-making process, recruitment decisions are known to be flawed and based on bias. How these errors are made and the ways in which information can be used to improve decisions is the subject of the next chapter.

4

The Information Needed to Make Decisions

This chapter explores how the information supplied to applicants by employers and vice versa influences the decisions made by both. These decisions are taken at various points throughout the process — some are free standing, others are determined by previously taken actions and all are based on information. This may have been deliberately supplied by one to the other (for example, details are given in an advertisement or as a part of an application) or may have been given unwittingly (for example, the announcement of poor half-year profits at the same time as advertising for a new marketing director is bound to affect the response rate).

Moreover, impressions and images combine with existing views and beliefs to inform prejudgements that influence decisions taken later. The decision processes used by human beings to make judgements and decisions about other people, particularly when the outcome is uncertain and information is missing, is known to be full of flaws and to result in error. However, these can be minimised by improving the flow and quality of the information on which such decisions are based.

This chapter describes some of the more common mistakes applicants and recruiters can make. Ways of improving the exchange of information are suggested as a means of helping improve the quality of decision making and ensuring that judgements are made on the basis of job-related factors rather than personal inclination.

INFORMATION FLOW

The recruitment and selection process can be described as a flow of information that is systematically exchanged. Both parties supply and obtain increasingly more detail about each other as recruitment leads to application and on to shortlisting. The flow has two facets — the contents of the information and the medium used to transmit it. The contents need to be planned, written and presented in a way that complements the message and suits the audience, while the medium chosen to transmit it must be effective and also complementary.

Traditionally, there have been two ways to provide information about a vacancy — some form of public advertisement or via a third party. These contain a distinct power imbalance in that the employing organisation is offering a job (take it or leave it) and it is for potential employees to demonstrate their fit to the job and the organisation, not the other way round. Roe (1989) has proposed that the following four information functions are the most significant:

1. **Information gathering**: obtaining information about job openings, job content, job requirements etc, and about physical, behavioural and biographical characteristics of applicants.
2. **Prediction**: transforming information on (past or present) applicant characteristics into predictions about their future behaviour and resulting contribution to organisational goals.
3. **Decision making**: transforming predictive information on applicants into a preferred action.
4. **Information supply**: producing information on applicant characteristics, predicting behaviour, plans for action (decisions), etc.

The recent changes in the labour market mean that traditional approaches to the design of recruitment and selection procedures are no longer good enough. People applying for jobs expect and demand more information about the job. They also want to know about the nature of the organisation to help them decide if the job is likely to offer what they are seeking. Especially in areas where skills are in short supply, applicants are increasingly seeing themselves in control — and they are, if the organisation depends on the skills these potential applicants possess for its ultimate success. Some employers responded to this by jacking up salaries and introducing other pay-related perks, but conditions have changed again. More and different skill shortages are being reported. More people have skills on offer in the same way as more organisations have jobs to sell. People are looking for other benefits from their jobs aside from just the take-home pay packet. Consequently, the ways in which information is exchanged and decisions are made demand more systematic and considered approaches.

Improving both decision making and information exchange can have mutual benefits. Providing good quality information via effective media helps individuals make better, more considered decisions. It helps applicants decide if the job is for them and if they are qualified to satisfy the selection criteria. This initial self-selection reduces the number of spurious applications. Good quality information also helps applicants present their applications in ways that are easier for the employing organisation to consider and shortlist.

However, the exchange of information has a cost impact. The production of high quality information takes time and thought and the physical design costs money. Consequently, the proposed methods of supplying information to and obtaining information from applicants must take into account constraints and practicalities facing the employing organisation.

WHAT INFORMATION IS NEEDED TO MAKE DECISIONS?

There has been some interesting research into how the exchange of information during the early days of an employment contract can affect its subsequent success. Herriot (1989a) has examined many aspects of the recruitment and selection process and sees the nature of the psychological contract formed at the beginning of the employment as critical. He also argues that unless organisations recruit and retain the quality of staff they need to conduct their own unique business, they will not stay in existence very long in today's rapidly changing conditions. As a consequence, the efforts in the early days to ensure that expectations and requirements are matched could pay off. Similarly, if misunderstandings are not clarified and discontent is allowed to develop, the ultimate cost could be very high.

Quality staffing does not necessarily mean the highest qualified or the most experienced. It means that staff at all levels are equipped and competent to do their current job, and are able to learn and adapt to meet the needs of the future. Experience is important, but when the problems of tomorrow are totally different to those of yesterday, staff cannot rely on previously used solutions. They need to be creative and forward looking. Moreover, if they are to feel genuinely involved and part of their employer's business, staff need to have some idea about where the job is likely to take them. Thus, when appointing employees or transferring or promoting existing staff, employing organisations must find ways of conveying a realistic assessment of the future and what it means for the business and the people who work in it.

The nature of information

Handy (1985) takes a similar approach and describes the employment contract as:

> ... essentially a set of expectations. Individuals have sets of results that they expect from the organisation, results that will satisfy certain of their (different) needs and in return for which they will expend some of their energies and talents. Similarly, the organisation has its set of expectations of the individuals and its list of payments or outcomes that it will give to them.

Makin (1989), in describing the selection of professional staff, says that current practices need to change to enable employing organisations and individuals to engage in a process of matching. This, he argues, will allow parties to determine whether the other will satisfy their expectations and requirements.   They need information about each others' future expectations, possibilities and opportunities. In particular, potential employees will be asking possible employers questions such as:

- Where is this job going to take me?
- What will I learn?
- How will I be treated during the selection process and as an employee?

Relevant and accurate information given to applicants via the advertisement and additional information packs lays the ground for the negotiation of the employment contract. It can also act as induction and initial training material (as described in Chapter 9). This information creates an image in the future employee's mind about the organisation and the job. If this picture is accurate, the employee will find that matching his or her expectations with reality is no problem. The understandings of both employer and employee about key objectives, performance standards and working methods will be in harmony as they will have been built up through discussion and exchange over a period of time. The new employee's 'fit' into the organisation's culture will be eased as the underpinning assumptions will have been explored and values made explicit.

The information flow in detail

The exchange and flow of information during the recruitment and selection process is shown in Figure 4.1.

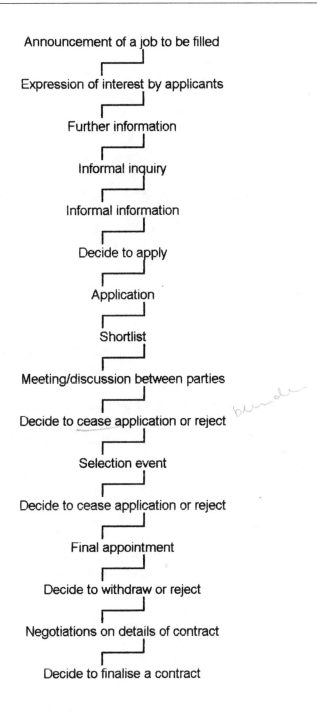

Figure 4.1 Information flows during recruitment and selection

A new sales manager was needed when Peter, after 20 years with the company, was due to retire. In discussing how best to replace him, the MD agreed with the personnel manager and Peter that no one inside the company would be able to do the job. A new set of skills and experience was needed.

Because the company's products were highly specialised and technical expertise would be needed by the new manager, they decided not to advertise the post. (They also felt that such an advert would do little for their customers' confidence in the company's stability.) Instead they decided to put together a list of likely candidates they knew in the industry. The personnel manager contacted other personnel managers, asking them to suggest possible people, the MD contacted the employers' association and Peter made use of his own networks. (In view of this breadth of the search, separate initial lists were drawn up to avoid 'group think'.) When the MD, Peter and the personnel manager were satisfied they had searched far enough, they compared lists and found that eight names were common to all three lists. These individuals were invited to the company to discuss the job, see the firm's location and, most importantly, to meet potential colleagues. After these initial meetings four of the visitors said they were interested in the job and, at this stage, a traditional selection process was instigated. The individuals' CVs were checked against the person specification and suitable activities were designed to explore what each candidate was able to do in practice. Reference checks were made and an appointments panel constituted.

Meanwhile, the candidates were sent information about the company's products, its annual report, and an edited version of its business plan. They were also given the names of the company's major customers and were encouraged to seek as much information about the organisation as they wanted. The final interviewing process was seen by all the parties as a negotiation — the candidates were supplying skills and the organisation was purchasing them. The candidates knew they were competing for the contract and the company knew it would have to give out sensitive information if it wanted the candidates to give a good 'pitch'. After all, the job was for a sales manager and, if the candidates could not sell themselves, would they be able to sell the company's products?

Research and experience have indicated that if clear messages are not transmitted early, the damage done by the mismatch can be costly to both parties. For the employee, being in the wrong job damages:

- job satisfaction;
- self-esteem;
- career progression;
- family life; and
- future prospects.

For the organisation, a poor appointment decision can be as a result of appointing someone unable to do the job, leading to:

- mistakes;
- loss of productivity;
- low quality customer service;
- shoddy goods; and
- the lowering of morale of other staff (worse than a high turnover).

Appointing someone too well qualified for a job can lead to:

- boredom;
- frustration;
- rebellion; and
- disgruntlement.

The information given builds an image of the job in the mind of an individual and, when applying, we all consider what we want from a job and an employer relative to the image being presented. We decide whether to submit an application or self-select out on the basis of the evidence given and obtained. If the picture does not match our requirements we do not submit an application or we withdraw.

Another type of recruitment mistake is made when the right person for the job, from the point of view of the employer, decides not to proceed. This is particularly serious if the decision is made on the basis of inaccurate information, but it is difficult to prove that this type of error (Type II) has happened. If an enquiry about the vacancy has been received but no application results, it is possible to investigate what deterred the enquirer.

And if applications are withdrawn, it is possible to ask the applicants why. But if the interest generated by the advertisement does not result in even an enquiry it is very difficult to discover what has happened.

THE DIFFICULTIES IN MAKING DECISIONS

Human decisions are never perfect. Judgements are inevitably made on the basis of limited information under uncertain conditions. We make errors of judgement and are biased but, by exploring some of the more common flaws, it is possible to improve decision making. Some simple steps can be taken, such as enhancing the quality and flow of information and making explicit the decision-making criteria. But some insight into the more common flaws is also important and the ones most likely to occur in recruitment and selection are described in the following sections. For those wishing to explore these issues at greater length, Bazerman (1994) is a useful guide to individual and group management decision making.

Escalation

Research into decision making suggests that the more one has invested in a decision the more one becomes committed to that particular course of action. Escalating one's commitment results from a typical chain of events:

1. The original decision is made on a limited amount of information, but making the decision will have been costly in terms of time, effort and expenditure. (Running even a modest recruitment campaign can cost several thousand pounds. Submitting an application can take days and considerable thought.)
2. Early indicators suggest that the decision is not achieving the desired results. (For example, the advertisement does not attract the size of response expected.)
3. The size of the initial commitment is seen as being too great to waste. ('We can't go back now.')
4. More is invested to try to remedy the situation and save the face of the decision maker. ('We had better re-run the advertisement.')
5. The situation gets progressively worse. ('We had better interview the people who have applied.')

Can you think of selection decisions that have resulted in the 'wrong' person being appointed?

The response to the big advertisement has been disappointing. It had been very well planned and designed, and so had been extremely costly. The employer had expected in the region of 100+ applicants, but only 30 applications had been received and they were not inspiring. Nevertheless, a shortlist was drawn up and the candidates were interviewed. After the final interview the employer was relieved because two candidates were appointable. One was definite, the other marginal, but the interviewers thought he might 'do at a pinch'. An offer was made to the best candidate who, the next day said, 'Thank you, but a better offer had been made by another organisation.' Rather than go back to the drawing board, the employer decided to offer the job to the second choice who accepted.

Nine months later the employer was trying to work out what to do with the new appointment who was clearly not up to the job, and the individual was wondering how to get out of the situation.

Rather than face the real problem directly, the parties involved are likely to try to make the best of the decision. Actions such as providing additional training, adding extra resources to fill the gaps and making excuses about the time needed to settle in are commonplace, and represent an escalation of the commitment to the original decision.

Over confidence

Another common error found in decision making concerns the confidence levels of those involved. Individuals have unwarranted confidence in their judgements and abilities to predict uncertain outcomes. 'Good' interviewers who over-assess their abilities to select the right person are more likely to make a decision on the basis of scant evidence than those who have less faith in themselves and prefer to make informed decisions. How many interviewers ask for feedback about:

- their questioning abilities;
- how they develop a rapport with candidates;
- their skills at encouraging candidates to open up and discuss their aspirations and concerns about the job?

Similarly, applicants with limited opportunities to compare their skill levels with others in their peer group and who are unable to obtain good quality feedback will find it difficult to accurately assess their abilities and suitability for a particular type or level of job:

- How many of us show our CV or application to a colleague for critical appraisal?
- How many of us actively seek feedback after an unsuccessful application for a job we really wanted?
- How many organisations are prepared to spend time with unsuccessful applicants, especially those who were rejected at the long and shortlisting stages?

Availability of information

The rational model of decision making suggests that a search phase takes place during which information about *all* available options is systematically gathered. Once a sufficient quantity and quality of information has been obtained, the alternatives are weighted and the 'best' decision made. The 'best' decision is the one that satisfies the predetermined requirements and obtains the maximum results. This model is recommended for strategic and large investment decisions. Surely the decision to appoint a member of staff constitutes both a strategic and a substantial investment? Yet the normal approach to recruitment and selection is to limit the amount of information supplied and obtained:

- The advertisement publicising the vacancy is often the only information given out.
- Applicants are frequently asked to submit brief letters of application and short CVs.
- Applicants are kept at arm's length. If they ask questions, the information given is superficial and the people supplying it are guarded.
- Reference checks are made at the end of the process and tend to be obtained from previous employers rather than colleagues or customers of the individuals concerned. (As discussed in Chapter 6, employers may have their own reasons for giving good or bad references.)

Research into the biases in decision making indicate that if sufficient information is not available we tend to fill the vacuum. We do not exactly make up information to fill the gaps; rather, we use our experience to explain, interpret and predict. We all possess these idiosyncratic rules of thumb, and use them to help us make decisions about the future and judgements about people.

First, if information is easily accessed (ie it is readily available and can be recalled from memory) it will be given more value than if the information has to be sought out. Thus, in an application form, if the sought-for information is given in a way that stands out, or the applicant says or does something that is very noticeable, then a stronger impression will be formed.

We also tend to make connections between previous events and experiences. If we have good feelings or memories of an event or a place, we will transfer these on to other things or people who are linked in some way to that event or place. (For example: 'The best manager I ever had studied at Durham University. Anyone who has a Durham degree is likely to be good.') Likewise, we tend to believe that if one aspect of an individual's performance is good then this standard will be found in all other aspects. Similar judgements are made about employers: for example, it is easy to believe that employers with equal opportunities policies are likely to provide generous sickness payments. These presumed associations, the halo effect, are often the basis for unreasonable expectations.

Confirmation of initial impressions

Another foundation for unreasonable and unrealistic expectations can be seen in the tendency to seek confirmatory evidence for our initial impressions. We are all good judges of character — infallible in fact. We also hate to be proved wrong. We form our initial impressions within a very short timescale (sometimes in less than 30 seconds), and this is not just confined to when we meet people. The phenomenon also occurs when we open the envelope containing additional information about a job vacancy or look at an application. The factors used to form these initial impressions are the products of each individual decision maker's biases, prejudices and stereotypes. Unless the decision maker is very self-aware, these biases influence judgement without being checked or balanced.

The best example of dubious evidence used to form an initial impression is handwriting. British selectors deny using graphology as an aid to the recruitment and selection process, but it is well known that people who produce small, neat script with uniform letters are quiet, almost introverted, and with precise habits. On the other hand, someone with large, untidy handwriting is bound to be an extrovert and disorganised. Backwards facing letters indicate a pessimist, while someone who writes with a forward slant is adventurous. Rounded ascenders and descenders indicate a mature personality but spiky, stubby ones are produced by a short-tempered individual. Whether these assumptions are accurate or not is immaterial; they serve to indicate the sort of prejudgements that create images of the person behind the handwriting.

The error in decision making comes from the effort made by the decision maker to confirm that these initial impressions are correct. At the same time, any evidence that disproves these impressions is discounted. For example, if the vacancy appears to offer the very opportunity a job-seeker is hunting for, even on the small amount of information contained in a simple newspaper advertisement, the individual will invest considerable time and energy in submitting an application. This could be followed by visits, information gathering and meetings. Unless the evidence to the contrary is very strong and undeniable, the applicant is likely to avoid recognising indicators that suggest the job or the organisation might be less than ideal. Unfortunately, more often than not, the time when the individual can no longer deny errors of judgement comes when the offer of a job has been accepted and the individual has started work.

Predictions of success

For both parties, selection of the right person and the right job is an assessment of risk. The employer assesses the comparative features of each applicant, perhaps against the person specification and job requirements, to predict the chance of long-term successful performance. Each applicant will assess the chance of the job providing the desired outcomes sought for in a job and a career. Research into the predictive validity of recruitment and selection has explored the final stages of the selection process. Yet each stage of the whole process concerns gathering information, assessing the goodness of fit for both parties and predicting the chance of obtaining the desired solution. Decision making in uncertain conditions can be improved by the gathering of relevant and accurate information. This will help to reduce the degree of uncertainty and convert some of the unknowns into knowns. The quality and quantity of information supplied and obtained during recruitment will inevitably improve the decisions made by both parties.

The recruitment and selection process can be represented as a series of decisions made on the basis of limited information obtained from, and provided to, a small sample of the total population of suitably qualified individuals. In summarising the flaws commonly found in decision making, we can identify ways of reducing their negative impact:

- Take action to match expectations — the whole process can be seen as an exchange of information between two parties (job-seeker and job provider) who want to 'do business' with each other, rather than a seller of jobs displaying wares and then choosing which possible buyer to sell to.
- Provide accurate information — the purpose of giving out information about the job and the organisation is to help the decision-making process. Over-egging the job and prospects or over-selling the application will eventually be discovered by the other party and lead to disappointment and dissatisfaction.
- See the process as a negotiation between two parties, each possessing equal amounts of power, and with rights and responsibilities to each other. Honesty and the provision of helpful information can facilitate power balancing and contribute to positive exchanges.
- The social fit is important to both parties and requires different types of information to that traditionally provided. Applicants will want to know more about the job than simply its post title and outline. They will at least expect, in addition to a brief description of the organisation and its location, a summary of the requirements to be found in the ideal postholder. Details such as conditions of service, priorities and key policies are other basic essentials. On the other side, a skeleton CV does not tell a prospective employer whether the potential employer's values and aspirations match those of the organisation.
- Treat the recruitment and selection process as a flow of information. Details are gathered and exchanged at each stage to allow both parties to build up a picture of the other. If the process is seen in this way, it is possible for both parties to check information supplied for consistency of the message, validate it against information obtained from other sources and ensure that initial impressions are correct by actively searching for disproving evidence. It is also possible to assess the usefulness of the information to the individual and to the employing organisation.

- Key decision makers can became more aware of their normal biases and the limiting effect of their rules of thumb: increased awareness will help to reduce their negative impact and check for false assumptions and preconceived stereotypes. (A technique to help check for biases is to explore the decision from the alternative point of view — consider 'why not' rather than 'why'.)
- The amount of information supplied should be adequate. Supplying too much can be as bad as not giving enough. Oversupply can be off-putting; undersupply encourages the reader to fill in the gaps to confirm the initial impression, which may or may not be accurate.
- Be aware of first impressions because the subconscious tendency is to give them more value than the information gathered later, whereas, in reality, both should have equal weight. We also give undue value to final impressions and distinctive features or factors, which may, in fact, be irrelevant. These are the biases of primacy, recency and saliency.
- Avoid making judgements too soon in order to limit the importance of first impressions. Wait until all the evidence has been accumulated so that pros and cons can be weighed against each other.
- No one is a perfect judge of other people, so expect to make mistakes. As we all make mistakes, it is important to gather data from a number of sources and to seek the (independent) opinion of others. The collection of information from a variety of sources helps to balance bias. Checking the quality of a decision with others and comparing logic will help to validate the decision and the process used to make it. However, responsibility for the decision must remain with the person so charged.
- Job-seekers and seekers of people to fill vacancies are all in the selling business. Don't expect the whole truth and nothing but the truth to be given by either party. Approach the decision in the same way as you would a major investment decision — gather information and check it, as described above. If there is no evidence available, accept that this does not confirm or disprove anything at all; it simply means that there is no evidence. Don't make it up if it doesn't exist!
- Take positive steps to check assumptions and interpretations at all stages of the decision. Be sure that impressions are founded on evidence and that the factors that have been discounted are really irrelevant to the decision.

WAYS OF PROVIDING INFORMATION

Many employers supply little if any information to prospective applicants about the organisation or even the job. According to Herriot (1989a):

> Typical personnel practice in the 1980s fails to inform.... There is likely to be little about supervision, career development or training. There will nothing about the boring routine parts of the job, or the organisational culture and lifestyle. And problems will be avoided like the plague. The only exceptions are those organisations appealing specifically to the macho market — people who need to prove themselves really tough.

However, high levels of unemployment have led to large numbers of enquiries being made when jobs are advertised. It is not unknown to receive over 1000 responses, while 200–300 enquiries are quite common. As only about 50 per cent can be expected to be translated into applications, the cost of providing additional information can be seen to be prohibitively high. On the other hand, if the process of recruitment is seen as an exchange of information to aid a complex and high risk investment decision, the initial expenditure can be regarded as a necessary part of the set up costs. It must be remembered that the risk of making the wrong decision is greater than making the right one — even the techniques that have the best predictive validity achieve a co-efficient of 0.6. Moreover, if the decision to employ is seen as a substantial capital investment instead of a revenue cost, the need to invest in the initial decision will be seen from a different perspective.

If, for example, average earnings stand at about £15,000 and a typical appointment is likely to last 5 years, when the employment costs (National Insurance contributions, etc) are added, the total estimated investment could be in the region of £90,000. When the cost of producing extra information is estimated (for example 1000 booklets at £1 each) we can see each aspect in perspective.

Most of the research into the effectiveness of recruitment and selection has concentrated on selection techniques used in the final stages of the process. According to De Witte (1989):

When searching through the literature on personnel policy there are almost no publications on personnel advertising. Notwithstanding the enormous total budget spent on personnel advertisements, no systematic research has been done. A lot of research about interviewing and psychological testing is available. Theories about how persons choose an organisation have been developed. These theories assume the existence of the applicant. The question remains how the organisation can influence the potential employee. In many cases the first contact is through a personnel advertisement. The effectiveness of this, therefore, is very important.

The same is true of all other forms of attracting applications, and means that some of the important earlier stages have not been investigated or recorded thoroughly. However, this gap can quite adequately be filled by empirical and anecdotal evidence. Generally the lack of information is quite evident and, where it is provided, the quality is usually low. This need not be the case: it is possible for the decision to apply and shortlist to be informed by good quality information supplied for and to both parties. The information need not be costly because 'good quality' implies only that the information is accurate, concise and relevant. Some ways of achieving this are described in the following sections.

Packs

Some organisations (mainly those in the public sector or those engaged in mass recruitment — for example of graduates) produce packs giving additional information about the job. These packs can range in size from one or two pages to a large booklet. They also range in quality. Some seem almost to be a random collection of documents produced for other purposes; some are as carefully constructed as any product sales leaflet. Regardless of style, the pack reflects the culture of the employing organisation and adds to the prospective candidates' impressions.

A poorly constructed pack contains long, waffly documents that do not have any obvious connection with the job in question. Some include detailed and general explanations of the organisation's environment, descriptions of its management structure, detailed explanations of every department (but not their relationship to the post in question) and masses of facts and figures without any effort to put them into context.

Another example of a poor pack is the glossy brochure. These are generally produced when the size of the recruitment exercise is large enough to justify the cost of employing copy writers and graphic artists. These sorts of information packs (which can be very imaginative and attractive) are often used when the competition for employees is fierce. They are promotional literature painting an image of an organisation with a bright future, offering potential employees careers with prospects. The real purpose of this sort of pack is to sell the organisation, and providing candidates with the information they need to decide their future is a secondary consideration.

A good pack is one in which information relevant to the job in question is provided concisely and attractively. The latter does not necessarily mean that huge sums of money need to be spent on design and layout. Most word-processors allow simple, clear layout that makes the information easily accessible and readable.

The contents of an information pack might include brief descriptions of the following topics:

- The organisation, outlining its mission, priorities and the context in which it is operating.
- Key statistics relevant to the job in question.
- An outline of the management structure, showing the location of the job.
- A summary of major employment policies and the area of work on which the future postholder will be engaged.
- A description of the department in which the job is based, outlining its key targets and priorities.
- The job description and person specification.
- A summary of the main terms and conditions.
- A description of what it is like to work for the organisation, indicating major facilities, non-pay benefits and values.
- Information on how to apply and a description of the selection process.

The cost of such a pack will vary considerably depending, for example, on length, fanciness of the graphic design and quality and thickness of the paper. At 1994 prices, a pack of average size has been estimated to cost in the region of £1.00 per copy, including the cost of postage, and even for jobs attracting 1000 enquiries this would add up to the cost of perhaps 2 display advertisements. Providing good quality information can help to encourage those with little chance of being appointed to select themselves out in the early stages. It also helps those who are suitably qualified and interested in applying to provide information aimed directly at the organisation and the job. This will aid the selectors' decisions because the information submitted will be relevant and more likely to be presented in a form that enables comparison to the person specification. Moreover, candidates will be gaining an impression of what the organisation is expecting from the successful candidate. Initial job training and induction starts here.

Meetings

Some organisations encourage preselection meetings, while in others this is seen as being tantamount to canvassing! There are ways of arranging for applicants to meet existing staff and visit the organisation without influencing the decision makers. (They should be concentrating on assessing candidates against the person specification, not just the social fit.) Preselection meetings can be organised in several ways to ensure that all candidates are treated fairly and have equal opportunities to make an impact on selectors.

Some organisations hold the recruitment equivalent of open days. These events have a dual purpose: first, they aim to provide information and, secondly, they enable potential applicants to perform some sort of screening or initial selection exercises.

A holiday tour operator launched a new series of holidays with an innovative promotions campaign. This immediately captured the public's imagination and the number of enquiries and bookings exceeded expectations. Consequently, a large number of temporary data processing staff were needed to cope with the processing of enquiries and bookings.

Time was short and the tour operator knew there would be difficulty finding the staff. Computer-literate and office-skilled staff were in short supply in the town. The computer program used to process bookings was simple to use, yet the staff to be appointed needed to be accurate and able to work at speed. The tour operator decided to repeat the innovative approach that had already proved successful, and a radio advertisement was broadcast for three days, inviting interested individuals to meet the tour operator at the local college one afternoon and evening the following week.

With the college's help, the tour operator's data processing suite had been replicated in one of the computer studies classrooms. The 'guests' were offered refreshments and a chance to try their hand at data processing. Even if they had not used computers before they were encouraged to assess their own potential and preference for this type of work. A photographic display had also been mounted showing the tour operator's offices. The operator's existing staff who hosted the open day described the company's holiday tours and the reasons for the unusual recruitment drive. The nature of the work was explained and the system demonstrated. Those seriously interested in working for the company were given written information about the pay, hours and conditions and were able to discuss the job with the staff.

The operator managed to appoint adequate numbers of staff — and sold some more holidays.

Other types of meeting can be organised in response to speculative letters or can simply be chance meetings. Meetings are also commonly used by smaller organisations that tend to see recruitment and selection more as a negotiation process. Regardless of the stimulus for the initial contact, the prospective employer and potential employee arrange to meet to explore if they could work together. This sort of meeting is much more about information giving and gathering than the traditional interview and the power is more equally balanced. The prospective employer has a need — a job to be done — while the potential employee has skills and knowledge to offer. In addition, there are social considerations. The employer has existing staff and a new employee will need to fit with the team, complement and enhance the skill profile, perhaps be different, but not too disruptive. The new employee will expect, for example, job satisfaction, colleagues who are sociable, the opportunity to use skills, knowledge and expertise and to be treated as a unique individual. The meeting, conducted without prejudice, can be an effective way of exploring the degree of fit before either party makes a formal commitment. In these circumstances, it is possible to arrive at a mutually satisfactory contract. Even when it is not possible to agree terms, both parties are able to withdraw without the loss of face that occurs with the more normal recruitment process. As no advertisement of the vacancy has been published, there has been no failure to fill the job.

No formal application has been made, so none has failed. The parties have simply been unable to find enough common ground to justify formalising their relationship.

Informal discussions

Informal discussions normally take place before a formal application is submitted. Giving the potential applicant the opportunity to talk to someone knowledgeable about the job enables information about both the vacancy and the organisation to be exchanged. This helps the interested enquirer decide whether to become an applicant because it is possible to probe potentially sensitive areas without jeopardising an application.

These discussions may be conducted face to face, but more often they take place over the telephone. The information disclosed during the discussion provides additional insight to augment that contained in the advertisement or other form of announcement. This can also constitute another level of screening. It helps enquirers decide for themselves if the job is what they are looking for and if they meet the specification. Similarly, the discussion provides information to the employer. If a brief record of the conversation is made, these notes can be used to assist shortlisting. However, if this is to be the case the enquirer should be told.

Finding a new director was proving more difficult than had been anticipated. The job itself was challenging — the company's customer liaison division was not without its problems — and the pay was not outstanding. Nevertheless, the chief executive had not expected it to be this hard to replace Simon. Advertising twice in the leading newspapers had been expensive and had produced a lot of applications from people who had no real understanding of the meaning of quality customer service. The search consultants had produced names with track records, but none of them had had the imagination to take the service forward while tackling the deep-seated problems that had grown up in the 20 years of Simon's 'reign'.

Then a conversation took place by chance. Lucy was talking to an old friend one weekend about the difficulties the company was facing in several areas, including appointing a new customer liaison director. The friend said he knew just the person and promised to fix a meeting the following week. The 'person' indeed seemed ideal, having most of the qualities outlined on the person specification. Saleem had been abroad for several years and had only just returned home to Britain. In fact, he was not really looking for a job just yet. Nevertheless, he said the post seemed to be an interesting challenge and he agreed to submit a formal application and meet other members of the board later that week.

Following several exploratory discussions with board members and staff in the division, Saleem became enthusiastic about the job. Lucy satisfied herself that he matched the specification and made the necessary checks. A recommendation was made to the chair of the board and Saleem was appointed within a month of the weekend conversation.

Visits, open days and social events

Letting potential applicants into the organisation before they have made a formal expression of interest is not the normal way of encouraging applications and exchanging information. But it is not uncommon for applicants to be invited for a pre-interview discussion. Search consultants hold screening interviews and senior academic and medical appointments are often finalised after candidates have made several visits to the employing organisation. This is not canvassing; it is more a way of ensuring that people who will have to work very closely with each other believe they will be able to form working relationships. However, this technique does contain dangers.

Makin (1989) describes some of the problems of selecting professional staff, especially when a number of individuals are involved in the decision. He argues that the process is prone to a number of errors and supports Herriot who suggests that selection should be a 'matching' process between the individual's occupational self-concept and the organisation's purpose. Putting these two views together, the following appears to be the way in which professional selection and perhaps selection strategies in general should be developed:

1. Techniques need to be developed that are acceptable to candidates and that accurately assess a candidate's track record.
2. These techniques need to be acceptable to the decision makers.
3. The crucial criterion for selection is an adequate match between the individual's self-concept and the role required by the organisation.

These techniques are designed to take account of normal biases. For, when new members of a group (or tribe) are being sought it is normal behaviour for existing members to seek others who are like them in some ways and to reject people who are dissimilar. This tendency is the basis for cloning and discrimination. The techniques used for job recruitment and selection should be designed to avoid this. The key is to separate the job-related selection criteria and those relating to social fit. Another key to avoiding indirect discrimination is to ensure that the methods used to attract applicants are open and accessible to *all* suitably qualified individuals. Many of these methods were described in Chapter 3.

Sometimes, during the course of normal business, working relationships develop between an individual working for one organisation and another employing organisation — for example, as supplier and customer. This frequently occurs between individuals and organisations working in competition with the former's employers. Poaching employees is not uncommon, and some employers have tried to impose clauses in employment contracts to prevent an employee taking employment with a competitor, but these are difficult to enforce. The situation is most common among senior executives and highly skilled specialists, and the reasons, obviously, concern confidentiality, the disclosure of sensitive information and competitive advantage. In this context the individual employee is a business asset.

A typical pattern follows a predictable path:

- A manager in Organisation A witnesses the performance of an employee of Organisation B.
- Organisation A has a need — a skills shortage or lack of specialist knowledge — or can see the individual's developmental potential for the business.
- The employee of Organisation B is approached to see if he or she would be interested in moving or strengthening the working relationship.
- A meeting is set up to explore the possibility of the individual changing employers.
- Several other meetings and visits to the new employer may occur before any final decision is made by either party.

Initial visits and open days are more commonly used when a large number of new employees are being appointed, such as trainees, graduates, staff for a new venture or temporary staff to cover short-term peak workloads. Interested individuals are invited to visit the employing organisation via a newspaper advertisement, flier, radio announcement, a billboard or similar media. The purpose of the visit will be to enable potential applicants to become familiar with the job and the nature of the employment, compare their abilities and fit against the employer's requirements and perhaps undergo some initial selection assessments. In this way a lot of information can be exchanged without the high cost of paper, postage and the labour needed to send out material. It also gives both parties first-hand experience of each other and judgements can therefore be made about social match. The visit can also enable expectations to be matched because they will be based on actual information rather than interpretations of written material.

The Bouquet House was planning to open a new store. The new manager had been appointed to finalise the plans and appoint the staff needed to run the outlet. In total, 60 people would need to be ready to start work for the opening, 2 months hence. The town in which the new store was located was known to have a ready supply of clerical, retail-experienced and stores staff because a large supermarket had recently closed in the face of fierce competition. Even though the nature of Bouquet House's business (predominately in the leisure market) and merchandise were different, the personnel director believed that if staff of the right calibre were appointed, they could be quickly retrained.

Consequently the director arranged for a suite of offices to be ready four weeks before the store's opening date. A radio announcement and an advertisement in the town's weekly newspaper informed the local population that the offices would be open the following weekend and staff would be available to meet anyone interested in working for Bouquet House. Publicity material was prepared and distributed to libraries, surgeries, hairdressers and community centres.

The local population responded enthusiastically. Everyone was curious about the new store because it was promising a 'new experience in leisure shopping' and, not surprisingly, those now without jobs were anxious to find new employment. Hundreds of people arrived to see a video showing the company's other stores and explaining the nature of the business. Examples of the company's stock were available for inspection and various items of equipment were demonstrated.

Individuals who expressed genuine interest in working for the company were asked to complete, with the help of a member of staff, a simple form that requested biographical data. They were also asked to take some aptitude tests. These examined, among other essential abilities, trainability, customer orientation, numeracy and computer literacy. Those matching the person specifications were asked to return for a final discussion with the store manager the following week.

The result of the exercise was 55 appointments within 10 days and a huge amount of pre-opening publicity and public goodwill. The cost in comparison to traditional recruitment practices was minimal.

Reputation

Most people involved in marketing know that the best publicity is what other people say about you. This is as true for recruitment as it is for any other sort of publicity or promotion. The public perception of the organisation is formed over a long period; a single advertising campaign (unless the scale is enormous) will make only a small impact. Building an image as a good employer takes time, thought and a strategic approach, and using marketing techniques, as described in Chapter 3, is one way of creating the image of being an organisation worth working for. However, unless that image is based on reality, it will be built on sand and will fall quickly as people find out that the recruitment activity is merely gloss.

Word-of-mouth recruitment goes against the spirit of equality of opportunity and is strongly discouraged by both the Commission for Racial Equality and the Equal Opportunities Commission. However, the public's image of an organisation is largely built around the tales told by one person to another. Similarly, the reputation of an individual, especially in the close-knit professions, can precede consideration of their application, and using information based on the opinions of others can lead to some very successful appointments. The appointment of judges is known to rely on 'soundings'. As Cook (1988) points out: 'Research dating back to the 1920s finds that people are surprisingly good at predicting who among their peers will succeed, and surprisingly honest too. Even when they know their opinions will help determine who gets selected or promoted, people say (fairly) willingly what they think of each other and are (relatively) uninfluenced by who they like and dislike.' Reference checks (discussed at length later) are partly based on this research.

However, basing recruitment and selection decisions on the opinions of others can lead to some very bad appointments or, at the best, some near misses. Moreover, using reputation as the main source of information can often lead to accusations of unfairness and favouritism. Action can be taken to reduce the dangers, for, as Cook (op cit) suggests, reputation can be an effective predictor. One way of reducing bias is to obtain actual evidence of achievement and the types of achievement. These can be gained from others who were actually involved with the individual, rather than relying entirely on what individuals say about themselves. This is not intended to imply that all individuals are dishonest (although it must be said that some are!). An individual's memory naturally distorts the past and alters the perception they have of their involvement and responsibility. It is known from the theories of human perception that self-perception is inaccurate. Consequently, obtaining confirmatory evidence can help to ascertain a fuller picture of past achievement. It must also be remembered, however, that the individuals who are providing additional information about an applicant are inclined to distort their memories and overemphasise their own contribution!

Many recruitment consultants use reputation as a base for their initial searching for candidates. Anecdotal evidence suggests that this is, at best, leading some organisations to fail to appoint. There are also some reports of very bad appointments being made as a result of an individual's achievements in one industrial sector not translating into another. Some search consultants take an initial brief and look for people who have applied to them for similar jobs in the past, who are known to occupy similar or subordinate roles in other organisations or who have contacted the consultant because they wish to change jobs. The individuals are matched against the brief and likely candidates are interviewed. From this information a longlist of very likely candidates is drawn up and presented to the employing organisation. A possible shortlist is compiled and further checks are made about the individuals by contacting people who are likely to know, or know of them. Using this supplementary information, a final shortlist is presented to the employer. This approach does work: search consultants would not be increasing in number and their use would be declining rather than expanding if it did not!

Nevertheless, problems can emerge when the values and cultural norms of an organisation are distinctive. Matching skills and knowledge is a comparatively straightforward process and canvassing factual evidence about an individual's attainment and expertise should be uncontroversial. However, matching *how* a job has been done as well as *what* has been done is more tricky. Sometimes the differences are intangible and the employing organisation is not explicitly aware of the distinctiveness of its ways of doing things. It is mismatches in these respects that lead to appointment failures — for both parties. The public sector has many experiences of this.

As a result of the growth of 'managerialism', the belief developed that 'a manager is a manager is a manager'. The public sector in the late 1970s and 1980s recognised the need to introduce other methods of working in order to improve productivity and the effectiveness of service delivery. The easy answer was to import managers and other staff straight from the business world and expect them to change working practices, thinking and organisational culture. Very little preparatory work was done to help these individuals understand the nature of public service and its implicit value systems. And even if such attempts had been made, the chances of their rejection would have been high. Induction and introduction to organisational culture would have been seen as indoctrination aimed at contaminating the newcomers and reducing their scope to change the organisation radically. On the other hand, it can be argued that to change an organisation effectively some insight into the status quo is needed. An organisation's ability to preserve itself through the forces of dynamic conservatism is very strong!

The chief executive designate of Ravenscliffe Public Utilities Company (RPUC) saw the coming of independence as a major opportunity to do things differently. Releasing the bureaucratic shackles of direct government control would allow decisions to be made locally and remove the dead hand of central control. Richard Bramskill was excited by the prospect and was determined to do things right. He realised that, as finance was the one area in which he and his staff had no experience, a 'whiz' from industry was essential.

Time was of the essence, so Bramskill engaged the services of a recruitment consultancy specialising in the financial sector. The brief was to find an executive who had experience of introducing change and restructuring systems — quickly. The consultancy's search soon found a financial manager currently working for a confectionery company: the firm was facing a hostile takeover bid that would probably be successful. The financial manager, Rosemary Howerd, was looking for other openings because she believed that the new owner would replace her once the takeover bid had been finalised. Rosemary had a history of initiating new financial systems and procedures, and then leaving each organisation as her work changed from innovation to maintenance. Reports of her talents were glowing.

Bramskill had no doubt, this was the person for RPUC. He told the consultant to look no further and arranged to meet Howerd the following week. Richard liked what he saw. Rosemary was a no-nonsense type, quickly picked up the issues facing the company and had some good, far-seeing ideas about how to tackle them. Her confidence about her ability to negotiate an early release from her present employer made her an even more attractive proposition.

Within a month Rosemary was working for RPUC. Two months later she had drawn up proposals to restructure the internal accounting methods, had ordered new computer software to support the systems and had developed the financial framework. It was this last point that caused the real problem. The framework laid down the limits of individual managers' responsibilities and established a system for internal trading. The managers had never had any real budgetary responsibility before, did not understand how to use financial management information and were more used to fighting between themselves than being part of an internal customer/supplier relationship. Rosemary failed to appreciate that the organisation had been driven by internal competition, and that it had no history of the sort of collaboration she had previously experienced. This lack of understanding was exacerbated by the managers' reluctance to accept instructions. They were used to being involved in lengthy consultations, discussions and protracted decision making.

Nevertheless, Rosemary's proposals were approved by the management board and implementation began. The line managers gave taciturn acceptance to the framework but implemented it with no enthusiasm. The managers were enthusiastic, however, about finding ways of defeating the new system.

After a year Rosemary moved on. RPUC was left with a financial system in tatters and a vacancy to fill. This situation had been caused by a lack of understanding of the organisation's culture and the failure to adapt working methods and practices to suit. The chief executive had not been aware of the need to take account of these factors. The recruitment consultant's brief had been to find certain skills, knowledge and experience, and Rosemary's previous successes had left her blind to the sensitivities of others and the need to take people along with change. Her approach had been to impose the 'right answer'. The lesson that emerged for Bramskill was that the best person for one organisation is not necessarily the best for another.

A way to avoid the sort of problem described in the case study about RPUC is to ensure that the values and cultural features of the organisation are reflected in the recruitment brief and person specification. If these factors are made explicit it is possible to take them into account when gathering information about an individual's reputation. It is appropriate to compare the context in which the individual's previous achievements were attained against that of the employing organisation. The ability to transfer skills and experience should also become a key feature of initial assessment. Additionally, when seeking opinions from others about the reputation and history of applicants, questions should be asked about the sort of organisations the individuals have worked for and the style and norms of those organisations.

It would be wrong to make assumptions about people's ability to change organisational types. Many people leaving the military services, for example, have experienced discrimination because civilian employers have not recognised their skills and did not believe that ex-service personnel would be able to adapt. As with any other part of the recruitment and selection process, it is better to check directly with the people concerned rather than rely on assumptions and the possibly uninformed opinions of others.

WAYS OF GETTING INFORMATION

The exchange of information during recruitment and selection is a two-way affair. Just as applicants are cautious about the information they supply to prospective employers, so employers are cautious about what they say to potential employees. Both wish to portray themselves in the best light, but this need not be the true light. Organisations are also careful about what they allow applicants for jobs to see and who they allow them to meet. In the same way applicants are wary about giving access to referees.

The advice to applicants is 'Go see for yourself'. Also, applicants are well advised to obtain information about the prospective employer through supplementary channels. One way to appear enthusiastic and keen about the job is to be seen to be doing your homework. It goes down well at interview because it shows that you are serious about the job and are interested in working for the organisation. In addition, it prepares the applicant to ask the prospective employer searching questions about what it is really like to work for the organisation. In the same way as organisations seek references and seek the opinion of others about applicants, there is no reason why potential employees should not ask the opinion of others about the organisation.

Applicants had been invited to attend informal meetings before participating in the final selection process. During the morning they were given the opportunity to discuss the job and the organisation with key individuals during a series of one-to-one meetings. These were all very amicable and low key. The applicants were told that a buffet lunch had been provided in the restaurant, or they could avail themselves of the staff facilities before the final interviews which would be held in the afternoon.

Only one applicant declined the formal lunch. Instead he went 'walkabout', ended up in the staff room, where he found two members of staff discussing the managing director's behaviour during a recent staff meeting. The applicant had the wisdom to recognise staff room gossip for what it was, but had some concerns about the tone of the conversation.

During the final interview the applicant asked the panel about the frequency and conduct of staff meetings. The panel's answer indicated a well-ordered, information-giving type of meeting at which debate, albeit limited, was encouraged. Sadly, this confirmed the impression given by the staff room conversation. The overheard discussion had given a graphic portrayal of the other face of a dictatorial style which took questions as indications of disagreement and discussion as open rebellion.

Even though the applicant was offered the job, it was declined.

SUMMARY

This chapter has explored how recruitment and selection decision making occurs in conditions of high uncertainty and risk, and how the exchange of information can facilitate the decision-making processes. To be effective, however, the provision of information needs to be equal and a two-way flow. Information flow mechanisms need to take account of the biases and errors that naturally occur in human perception, and should be designed to make explicit the factors used to form prejudgements. If these mechanisms are of good quality (ie fit for their purpose), the risks of making the wrong appointment or losing the right applicant can be reduced.

If an individual is to convert from an enquirer into an applicant, he or she needs to know from the organisation:

- What is the job to be done?
- What is to be achieved?
- What standards are expected?
- What skills, knowledge and expertise is the postholder expected to possess?

- What challenges and problems are to be faced?
- What rewards are to be obtained?
- What job satisfaction will the job offer?
- What opportunities for growth, development and enhancement will there be?
- Will I be able to do the job?
- Will it give me what I want?
- What is it like to work for that organisation?
- What are the other people who work there like?

If an applicant is to convert into a candidate, the organisation needs to know:

- Does the applicant have the skills, expertise and knowledge required to do the job?
- Has the applicant worked for employers previously who will have provided the right sort of training and experience?
- Has the applicant had the right sort of education and training?
- Are the referees the right sort of people with the right addresses?
- Do the applicant's interests complement the values of the organisation?
- Does the applicant say the right sort of things in the application letter and in the other information supporting the application?
- Is the application presented in an acceptable form to a standard that complies with that expected by the organisation?

As can be seen from these lists, there are many opportunities for bias, assumptions and discriminatory prejudice to influence decision making. This chapter has concentrated on ways of supplying information to applicants to help them make their decisions and submit their applications. Chapter 5 will explore the format for collecting information from applicants in ways that can aid the assessment of risk, help predict successful performance in the job and organisation, reduce uncertainty and facilitate negotiation between the two parties. Redressing the balance of power between the employer and the potential employee can contribute to the development of a positive working relationship based on matched expectations and shared understanding. Early concentration on the provision and gathering of good quality information can only enhance the major capital investment that is the reality of recruitment and selection.

5

Applications: Their Format and Uses

Once potential applicants have been attracted, information exchanged and firm expressions of interest made by both the prospective employee and the employer, the employing organisation needs some systematic method to enable it to assess applications against the job requirements and person specification. The assessment of applications is a process shrouded in mystery. Little research has been carried out to investigate how decisions to include an application in a long or shortlist are made. Similarly, the text books on personnel practice, while describing other parts of the recruitment and selection process at length, only make passing reference (if that) to sifting, screening and shortlisting.

This chapter considers the nature of initial sifting and what happens in practice. It goes on to explore the mechanisms that need to be available to ensure that the best candidate for the job makes it through the recruitment and selection phases. These mechanisms should also ensure that the candidates rejected are those who do not meet the job requirements and person specification.

The question of discrimination will be explored at some length. The word 'discrimination' tends to be used pejoratively and is given to mean the differentiation between individuals, often unjustly. However, it can also mean to make or see a distinction. Initial screening is the occasion when the person seeking a job and the potential employer 'meet' and make comparisons about each other. The employer has a job to be done and a specification to be met, while the individual has wants and needs to be satisfied. Consequently, the whole process of recruitment and selection is about discrimination.

Initial screening is the first occasion in the recruitment and selection process when decisions are made by people about people, deciding if one will satisfy the requirements of the other. The deliberate intent of the employer is to reject applications from those people who do not meet the person specification. The process, theoretically, should be one of rational decision making, but this is rarely the case. While the equal opportunities legislation attempts to eliminate unfair practices, the very fact that there is little reported evidence about how the shortlisting process works in practice indicates that the way in which these early decisions are made is not fully understood.

Bearing this lack of knowledge in mind, the chapter suggests ways to make more explicit the decision-making processes that can be used to exclude some people's applications and carry forward those of others. There is little point in pretending that human beings are not biased and, consequently, in making these suggestions the existence of prejudgements and assumptions will be taken fully into account. These will help the person faced with a selection decision understand how such factors influence judgement. A brief description of how an individual develops and applies a personal decision frame will be given, and action that can be taken to minimise the negative impact of these normal processes of human perception will be described in the examples. As Torrington and Hall (1991) point out: 'Care with shortlisting increases the chances of being fair to all applicants and lessens the likelihood of calling inappropriate people for interview'. Moreover, care and systems designed to minimise inappropriate discrimination increase the chances of making the right decisions and getting the best person for the job.

HOW TO SHORTLIST — IN THEORY

Shortlisting is the transition phase between recruitment and selection. It is the stage where the total number of applicants is reduced to the select group the employer wishes to carry on to the selection phase. Shortlisting has not been subjected to the same degree of research as some of the other stages of recruitment and selection. Cook (1988) cites some work showing that 'people who wrote a lot were considered further, as were people who wrote neatly and people who use certain keywords' — unspecified. People from certain parts of Britain — also unspecified — were more likely to be rejected. He also quotes American research that 'finds women widely discriminated against at shortlisting stage. Women are also stereotyped as more suitable for some jobs, or for working with other women. Both men and women shortlisters were equally biased against women.' There is a need, therefore, to understand better how shortlisting occurs, and ways in which biases and prejudgements distort the fairness and quality of the decision. Once an insight has been gained from this examination, methods can be designed that improve the decision making and reduce the chances of rejecting the best applicant.

Shortlisting may comprise several stages depending on the number of applications received, the complexity of the job requirements and the sophistication of the selection processes used by the organisation. For example:

- initial screening using biodata or reference checks;
- longlisting against criteria, then drawing up a final shortlist;
- pre-interview testing against particular abilities; and
- pre-meetings with key individuals.

Other techniques, such as psychometric tests, are more often used after a shortlist has been compiled, and so will be described in Chapter 6 about techniques for selection.

The most common way to reduce the number of applications is to examine them and apply some decision criteria in order to construct a shortlist. The nature of decision criteria and the way they are used will be discussed below, but shortlisting is rarely the simple, rational process described in textbooks and seldom are *all* the criteria made explicit. The use of a decision aid, such as the checklist in Table 5.1, can help to reduce bias by making the steps and decision criteria used open and obvious.

Table 5.1   Shortlisting — a decision aid

Steps	*Comments*
Decide who is going to shortlist.	This could be the line manager, a member of the personnel staff, a recruitment consultant or a team of selectors.
Design the process to be used and consider the difficulties presented by each and ways of dealing with them:	
Shortlisting by an individual — a system is needed to ensure that application of the criteria is consistent and personal bias reduced.	For example the matrix or decision checklist shown in Table 5.2 can help a line manager to examine a lot of applications and be reasonably confident that the same sort of judgements about the criteria have been made against predetermined factors.

Steps	*Comments*
Group shortlisting — some processes and systems are needed to reduce the negative effects of group dynamics and the introduction of side issues to ensure the individuals involved use the same explicit and implicit criteria.	Techniques such as nominal group technique can help to reduce the effects of peer group pressure while enabling each individual to make an equal contribution. A matrix or checklist will help to retain consistency.
Shortlisting by several individuals separately — again some mechanism is needed to ensure consistency but the effects of group pressure are removed.	Integrating the opinions of shortlisters can be done in a group setting or by one individual from the completed matrices, using, for example, the principles of the Delphi technique.
Person specification requirements form a matrix or decision checklist.	Only those criteria that can be evidenced from the application or other specified sources of information should be used.
Decide which requirements are essential and which are desirable.	The essential criteria (ie basic requirements) are those used in the matrix or checklist for the first sift (for example, qualifications or certain types of experience).
Weight the criteria into priority order	eg basic knowledge, skills, training or experience deemed essential for adequate performance.
Sort against the overriding priority. The reasons for the rejection of each applicant should be noted against the relevant criteria.	
The applications remaining form the longlist If a further reduction in numbers is needed, examine the remaining applications for the best 'fit' against the desirable requirements.	The desirable criteria are those which are supplementary to the adequate performance of the job, provide an added extra or an area which would normlly be acquired through development or additional training.

Steps	Comments
The remaining applications can then be sorted into possible and probable candidates.	The possibles are kept on hold in case anything prevents the probable applicants participating in the selection activities. The probables are those applicants about whom all (or the majority of) shortlisters agree should be seen.
These applicants form the shortlist	

This model, like all technical models, seems to be a rational and perfectly logical process. However, its application inevitably will be flawed, because judgements made by one person or a group of people about others are distorted, biased and based on errors. Even when standard criteria are used, the way these different judgements are applied is inconsistent. Because all human beings make their decisions from a unique and individual framework of experiences, assumptions, beliefs and values, the same piece of evidence is interpreted differently by each shortlister.

DECISION FRAMES

Decision frames are the mental constructions that help an individual choose whether or not to act, or to ignore a situation. To be able to function effectively in society we all need to make judgements about ourselves, other people and the situations in which we find ourselves. Without these judgements we (and everyone else) would act in a totally random fashion and be unable to make sense of the world. Because we are not very good at coping with high levels of uncertainty, our lives would be extremely stressful.

Kelly (1955) suggested that we are all natural scientists, struggling to make sense of our world and the people in it. We build a template that is overlaid on our current situation for use as a means of interpreting, simplifying and predicting. This template is constructed from previous learning — ie experiences, messages and images conveyed to us by influential others (such as parents and teachers) and from the conditioning of the society around us. We do not seek to have our constructs disproved, but rather we seek to validate them, even in the face of contradictory evidence. If, for example, there is no evidence to support a particular belief, the evidence is constructed so that events, our behaviour and that of others fit.

This phenomenon sways our judgements and reduces the possibility of dispassionate decisions. When this is considered in conjunction with the heuristics, biases and errors described in Chapter 4, the idea of making objective and impartial decisions about other people is shot down in flames. The reality is that we all make judgements on the basis of our own internal constructs, prejudices and assumptions about others. In other words, we all decide subjectively.

Research has demonstrated that training interviewers to improve their decision making did little to change their behaviour. The actual result was that they became more aware of their prejudices. But even though this outcome was not the one intended, some improvements to interviewing practice must have resulted. Four levels of awareness are used to help learning and lead to changes in behaviour:

1. **Unconscious incompetence**. ('This is the way I have always conducted an interview. I am good at asking probing questions.')
2. **Conscious incompetence**. ('I should not have asked that question like that.')
3. **Conscious competence**. ('I had better prepare and think carefully about the questions I will ask every candidate.')
4. **Unconscious competence**. ('This is the normal way I conduct interviews now. How did I used to do it?')

Thus, training to increase awareness of the flaws in decision making can lead to some measures being taken to accommodate the sources of errors, biases and prejudices and, ultimately, can influence performance. One of the most practical ways found to accommodate the flaws in decision making has been the use of behavioural criteria. Also, the construction of mechanisms to force decision makers to make explicit the grounds on which they make their decisions can lead to improvements.

Changes to the law and court judgments are also influencing the need to use systematic methods to aid decision making and are resulting in the creation of records that demonstrate that decisions were made on criteria relevant to the job. Moreover, if the organisation's need is to ensure that the right person for the job is appointed, it too must be satisfied that the criteria used to make the decision to select or deselect are the right ones. There is little consolation in knowing, after the event, that the best candidate is working for a major competitor because, for example, the manager responsible for the decision did not approve of the candidate's hobbies.

Decision matrices or checklists can demonstrate the reasons why applicants were carried through the selection procedure or rejected. They can also help comparisons to be made between applicants, even if their qualifications, experiences and attributes are dissimilar. Evidence can be collected or areas in need of further checking identified. The use of aids enables decisions to be validated, and the main measures of validity are the following:

- **Face and content validity** — the method appears plausible to those being assessed and to 'experts' in the area.
- **Criterion validity** — the method predicts who will be the best applicants as determined by relevant modes of assessment.
- **Construct validity** — the method measures meaningful, relevant criteria.
- **Reliability** — a manager can check if the same decision would be made about the same applicant at a later time.
- **Consistency** — other managers can be involved to check if they too would make the same decision.

The decision matrix set out in Table 5.2 shows how the person specification criteria can be used for the compilation of a shortlist. It provides a process of elimination using the information supplied by the applicants as evidence.

Table 5.2   Decision matrix based on person specification criteria for a branch manager

	Criteria	E/D +W*	Mode of assessment	Candidate 1	2	3
Attainment	GCSEs (or equivalent) in English and Maths	E2	Application			
	Evidence of post-16 training	E4	Application			
	Management or supervision training	D	Application			
Experience	Customer service (including dealing with complaints)	E3	Application and interview			

	Criteria	E/D +W*	Mode of assessment	Candidate 1	2	3
	Staff supervision	D	Application and interview			
	Keeping financial and other records	E5	Application and interview			
	Use of computer-based systems	D	Application and interview			
Abilities	Leadership	E6	Application (?), selection activities and interview			
	Independent decision making	E7	Application (?), selection activities and interview			
	Planning and organisation	E8	Application (content and presentation), selection activities and interview			
	Promotion techniques	D	Application and interview			
Aptitudes	Social skills	E1	Selection activities and interview			
	Financial acumen	E5	Selection activities and interview			
	Coaching	D	Interview			
	Concern for quality	E9	Application (content and presentation), selection activities and interview			
	Assertive	D	Interview			

	Criteria	E/D +W*	Mode of assessment	Candidate 1 2 3
Interests	People	E1	Application (interests given) and interview	
	Improvement	D	Interview	

*E = essential
D = desirable
W = weighting
(importance 1–9)

Each application can be assessed against the matrix and judgements made about which applicant best fits the criteria being sought. Anyone should be able to take a batch of applications and check for the factual evidence being sought. Missing pieces of information can be checked at other stages. Failure to meet the essential criteria would mean that the application would not be carried on to the later stages. The matrix can enable comparisons to be made between candidates and ensure that the priority requirements are satisfied. A checklist can also pose a series of questions to be asked about each applicant (see Table 5.3).

Table 5.3 An applicant checklist

Criteria	Source of evidence	Indicators
Does the applicant demonstrate social skills?		
Does the applicant demonstrate an interest in other people?		
Does the applicant coach others and help them develop their skills?		
Does the applicant possess GCSEs (or equivalent) in English and Maths?		
Has the applicant ever had experience of providing direct customer service, including dealing with complaints?		
Is the applicant assertive?		

Criteria	Source of evidence	Indicators
Does the applicant make use of promotional techniques?		
Has the applicant participated in any post-16 training?		
Has the applicant experience of keeping financial and other records?		
Does the applicant demonstrate financial acumen?		
Has the applicant experience of using computers?		
Does the applicant possess leadership skills?		
Has the applicant received any management or supervisory training?		
Has the applicant ever supervised the work of other staff?		
Is the applicant capable of making independent decisions?		
Does the applicant demonstrate planning and organisational skills?		
Is the applicant concerned for quality?		
Is the applicant interested in making improvements?		

The use of some form of structure can simplify and improve the process of compiling a shortlist. The matrix, checklist or a similar form of decision aid ensures that all relevant factors are examined and irrelevant factors are excluded from consideration, and facilitates the co-ordination of views if more than one person is involved in drawing up the shortlist. They also provide a lasting record that enables the decision to be checked, and this can be particularly useful if the selection process fails to appoint to the vacancy and it is decided to reconsider applicants. It enables the employer to answer challenges about the fairness and equity of the process, and also helps to short circuit the process if another similar post needs to be filled.

Decision matrices and checklists speed up shortlisting, simplify it and help to maintain consistency. They enable a first sift to be made for the absolutely essential criteria, thus eliminating the need to read every application in full. By requiring the shortlister to search for specific information, the chance of distraction is reduced, and this means that the process is more straightforward.

The choice of decision aid depends on the culture of the employing organisation and the application method (both discussed in later sections). Some forms of application can eliminate shortlisting aids because the application itself will provide a mechanism (such as Biodata). Other forms of application require more sophisticated decision aids. Application forms and letters of application encourage applicants to use their own words and structures when presenting their submission. Some way of analysing and comparing the varied and various styles of individual applicants has to be constructed.

FORMS OF APPLICATION

The advertisement or the additional information should tell applicants how to express their interest in the post. The most common methods involve the application form or the curriculum vitae (CV). The latter should be a *brief* summary of the applicant's education, qualifications and previous occupations. Alternatively, sometimes applicants are asked to write a letter of application.

Some employers (mainly organisations trying to encourage applications from under-represented groups) provide guidance to potential applicants, advising them about the preferred form of application and indicating the desired contents. Some organisations ask interested individuals to make an initial telephone call or to attend an initial selection event in person (as discussed in Chapter 4). Each of these methods of making applications, with the exception of meetings, will be explained below, and examples given of their use.

Application forms

Application forms ensure that the information sought by the employer is presented in a uniform fashion. Shortlisters and selectors have biographical data arranged for them in a standard way, which enables them to compare the details in separate applications. The use of a form is also beneficial for applicants. Once the skill of completing a form has been learnt, submitting another is relatively straightforward.

Torrington and Hall (1991) point out that application forms were initially intended as the basis of the personal personnel record, rather than as an aid for selection. When they were first used, most appointments were the result of an interview of sorts which relied on the premise that the interviewer was a good judge of characters. Since then, workers' mobility has increased, the labour market has changed from being local to national and employment legislation has become more prescriptive. Reliance on face-to-face interviews as a fair means of making such contractual decisions has been recognised as no longer sufficient, and more systematic methods have been introduced to sort applicants into candidates. Consequently, the application form has been developed to convey the information needed to aid and record decision making. Standardisation of presentation has also been found to be more useful than idiosyncratic letters of application.

A typical application form asks for the following information:

* Personal details
  — name, address and phone numbers;
  — interests;
  — the names of people able to supply a reference.
* Information needed for monitoring the effects of equal opportunities action
  — gender, ethnic origins, age and the existence of any disability;
  — some employers require information about marital status, age, children, medical conditions affecting the applicant's abilities to carry out the job and unspent convictions.
* Education and training
  — schools, colleges and universities attended with dates and qualifications attained;
  — training received;
  — other development activities that have led to skills or knowledge acquisition.
* Employment history

- — employers and their business;
- — dates of periods of employment;
- — main duties of each job;
- — salary;
- — reasons for leaving.
- Additional information to support the application
  - — It is this section that can cause the most problems for applicants. In effect, it offers the same scope as a letter of application for the individual applicant to 'write their own thing'.

Application forms are mainly used in large organisations that can afford to supply the forms to applicants and need the standardisation to satisfy their internal bureaucracy. Like any method, application forms have their pros and cons. Some people cannot imagine running a proper recruitment and selection process without them, while others see them as an unnecessary encumbrance that prevents applicants from expressing themselves, thus showing 'what they are really like'. Some of the negative aspects and benefits are outlined below. As regards drawbacks:

- The style and format of the form can be constraining.
- The applicant may omit vital information that does not fit into the standardised form.
- Having to fill in the application form may be off-putting to some applicants. It can take a considerable amount of time and effort to complete some of the more complex forms.
- The additional information section can lead to lengthy discourses that are difficult to analyse and compare. Even when applicants are advised what to say, the open nature of this section (after the tightness of the previous ones) can encourage some applicants to include everything they have ever done in an attempt to prove their suitability for the post. Alternatively applicants can be so brief that they provide no information worth speaking of. To make the best use of the open section, applicants need to be told what is expected of them. If they are then too verbose or wide ranging, the shortlister is able to draw conclusions about applicants' comprehension and communication skills. Similarly, if the conciseness is uninformative, this may also convey a message about their suitability for the post in question.
- Should an application be completed in an applicant's own hand or should it be machined? Some shortlisters want to see applicants' handwriting, hence the belief that graphology is used more extensively than is acknowledged. There are, however, questions about legibility and space.

Some people write in a small script, while others do not — how much space can be reasonably provided on a standard form? When typewriters were commonly used, it was possible to complete the form in print and to include a hand-written covering letter; thus applicants were able to supply an example of their handwriting and present a neat, legible form. However, as word-processors have replaced typewriters, it is becoming increasingly common to see returned application forms filled with the phrase, 'please see attached sheets'. How much longer can pre-printed application forms last?

- Shortlisters expect to see a customised application for each job. The common assumption is that if applicants are really motivated and committed to the particular job, they will make the effort to fill in the form. In other words, shortlisters believe that 'my vacancy is more important than any other'. But how realistic is it to expect applicants, at times of high unemployment, to spend the considerable amounts of time needed to complete an application form for every job?

- Application forms are part of the public relations effort of an organisation. They transmit a message to the outside world about the organisation's style and so contribute to its image. Even if that image is simple, printing costs and the cost of postage can be considerable. There are also design costs and decisions to be made about the quality of reproduction, and these of course add to the unit cost.

The main benefits of application forms are as follows:

- Asking applicants to present factual information in a standardised form makes it easier for shortlisters to search for the desired aspects of an individual's history and makes it simpler to compare applicants.

- The form helps to focus applicants' attention on the information required by shortlisters. One of the weaknesses of less structured methods is that applicants have to guess what is wanted. A form can also discourage applicants concealing gaps or weaknesses in their history. For example, having to give dates of attendance at college makes it difficult for an applicant to hide the fact that a fourth year was spent completing a three-year course.

- The information provided on the application form suggests openings for interview questions. This is the occasion when gaps (such as reasons for leaving previous employers), over-egged achievements or ambitious statements can be checked. Analysing the information given on the forms requires the ability to read between the lines — a level of skill not commonly found among managers who recruit only occasionally.

- The application form can be used to obtain information other than that needed to support shortlisting and selection. Details needed to form personnel records, monitor the effectiveness of recruitment activity and the effect of equal opportunities can be requested.

To summarise, application forms can facilitate systematic shortlisting by requiring applicants to structure the information they are providing about themselves — but at a cost. They reduce the opportunities for applicants to demonstrate their individuality. On the other hand, if a particular applicant wishes to demonstrate their idiosyncrasies, they will do so. The use of forms is most cost-effective for organisations that recruit regularly enough to justify the printing and production costs, and also when the employer receives enough applications for each vacancy to require a mechanism to facilitate comparison between them.

The CV

The submission of a curriculum vitae is possibly now the most common way to apply for a job. They are cheap for the employer and, because they are used almost universally, their form is almost standardised. Typically a CV comprises:

- Name, address and telephone number(s).
- Date of birth, marital status and (perhaps) number and ages of children (but not other dependants!).
- Education and achievements.
- Employment history with a brief description of main areas of responsibilities and duties. (Salary and reasons for leaving are frequently omitted.)
- Professional activities such as membership of professional bodies, training etc. (Personal interests are often excluded.)
- References may or may not be given.

The main omission from a CV is 'the additional information supplied in support of your application' section. This is when the applicant can 'sell' their skills and have an opportunity to tell shortlisters what they would bring to the job if appointed. As with the application form, there are arguments for and against using a CV as a basis for shortlisting and selection. As regards drawbacks:

- there is no additional information;
- the mode of presentation will vary, and it is difficult for shortlisters to

make comparisons between applications;

- the length of each CV submitted may vary from brief (one side of A4) to lengthy (a full narrative); and
- all the information needed for shortlisting may not be provided.

The arguments in favour of CVs are:

- there is no cost to the employer;
- there is no delay while the application form is sent out and returned;
- it is possible to draw inferences about applicants' skills of communication and presentation; and
- CVs tend to be shorter and can be easier to use for shortlisting. The reduced amount of information makes it easier to isolate sought-for details.

For organisations that recruit infrequently it is more economic to ask applicants to submit their CVs. It is possible to reduce some of the drawbacks by providing potential applicants with guidance about the desired form of the application. The boxed example shows how this can be done tactfully while helping applicants decide whether they match the person specification.

How to apply: You are asked to consider your attainments, experience, skills and abilities against those given in the attached person specification. Your CV should demonstrate how you match the profile of the ideal job holder.

Letters of application

Applicants can be invited to submit a letter of application, or letters may arrive unsolicited at the organisation. Invited letters tend to be the opposite of CVs. While CVs focus on factual aspects of an individual's history, demonstrating the match between the individual and the job requirements, a letter tends to be a narrative 'selling' the individual's abilities and fit. Of course, letters may include a brief summary of qualifications and experience, but they tend to contain what the individual wants to tell the employer rather than what the employer may need to know in order to make a decision. It is not uncommon to see advertisements asking for interested parties to write, explaining how they meet the requirements of the job. The major disadvantage is that each letter will be unique and therefore straight comparison will be difficult. However, the letter does allow individuals the opportunity to demonstrate their own approach. Indeed, some shortlisters believe that they provide invaluable insights on which to base decisions about suitability. Asking for letters is, once again, a low-cost option and advice on content and presentation can be given in the same way as with CVs.

Individuals seeking employment are often advised to send speculative letters to potential employers. At one time it was regarded as courteous to acknowledge these letters and then keep them on file for examination when a vacancy arose, but the massive unemployment in the early 1980s meant that the number of letters outstripped the possible vacancies and the practice of using letters as a pool of potential applicants fell into disuse. Moreover, the belief that commitment to equal opportunities required all jobs to be open to competition discredited the idea of using a file of previously received letters. There was something secretive about them — possibly a 'fix'. Nevertheless, some employers do act on unsolicited letters; if they were totally ineffective, specialists and consultants would not advise job-seekers to send them to possible employers!

The main disadvantage for the employer is that such letters contain only what job-seekers wants to say about themselves, not what the employer may need to know about applicants. Another drawback is that they are sent when job-seekers are looking, not when the vacancy exists, and this means taking the chance of the right letter arriving at the right time. Alternatively, the employer needs to set up a system for maintaining letter files. Even if this is done, however, when the vacancy arises it is always possible that the best applicant will have already been successful in their hunt for a suitable job. Even so, as an initial introduction, letters can be useful. The obvious advantage of these letters is that they cost the employer nothing, although maintaining files and checking them does take time and resources. However, compared with other recruitment methods, this cost is low.

Telephone calls

Some advertisements ask interested individuals to telephone the prospective employer. This approach is used by search consultants and agencies as well as employing organisations, and the main advantage is speed. It can restrict the field to those individuals who are able to gain access a telephone, although it is possible to widen the opportunity to those who are not able to make private phone calls during working hours by offering the chance to call during an evening or weekend. Regardless of when the call is made, its cost is carried by the applicant.

The telephone call can act as an initial screen. It can also preserve confidentiality by allowing factual information to be exchanged in confidence about both the job and the applicant. It is possible to envisage a situation when an employer does not want to give away too much information about a vacancy for competitive reasons yet needs to attract applications. The telephone conversation thus enables the organisation to check who is calling before giving out any more information. If needs be, the employer can return the telephone call to check the identity and validity of the enquiry (in the same way that some banks do this before agreeing to give personal details to telephone callers.)

It is better if the organisation makes use of structured interviewing techniques during the conversation. The enquirer can then be asked for information about qualifications and experience and to discuss some of their perceptions of the job in an organised fashion. This will enable comparison to be made against the person specification and between applicants. It will also enable a record to be maintained that both assures and demonstrates fairness and consistency of treatment. Likewise, the employer can give out details about salary, location, purpose of the job and expectations. If a match is achieved, the enquirer can be asked to submit a written application, further information can be sent out to help the applicant, or a meeting can be arranged.

This sort of approach can be used as an initial screen to cut down the number of applications received. The enquirer is in a better position to decide whether to submit an application as a result of their personal contact. Similarly, the employing organisation can decide and tell enquirers that they do not fit the person specification without them having invested too much of their time and energy in submitting an application. Also, shortlisting is simplified: the number of applications submitted will have been reduced to only those who have attained a certain degree of fit. The manager or someone else responsible may need to devote time to answering the telephone calls, but this should be quantified against that saved dealing with unwanted applications at later stages of the process. The benefit obtained from the early personal contact between potential employee and employer also needs to be included in the equation.

SCREENING METHODS

Once applications have been received, some way of analysing their contents and comparing their degree of fit with the person specification has to be devised. Some shortlisters read each and every application and then try to decide which to reject and which to carry forward. This can be a totally unsystematic approach that does not facilitate consistent and fair judgements. Too much information is in circulation to enable simple yes, no, or not sure decisions to be made. The tendency is to compare applicants against each other rather than against the job requirements, and the biases and heuristics of the shortlister provide the underlying rationale. The prejudgements and errors described earlier then come into their own and dominate the decision-making process. If several people are involved there is also potential for conflict. Each individual will, rightly, be using their own personal decision frame that will be different from those of the other shortlisters. There are methods (some of which are described below) that can reduce the potential for this unhelpful conflict and the flaws of human decision making. This is achieved by focusing shortlisters' attention on to the person specification and job requirements rather than their own internal criteria.

Biodata

Biodata draws from the biographic profiles of previously successful postholders and uses certain discernible features as an aid for the selection of future postholders. A database is built from personal details and typical career paths. The type of personal data used may include family background (such as whether the typical postholder was the first or youngest child), schooling (such as type of school, subjects studied, roles played in school activities) and social life and preferences (eg involvement in clubs or social groups, theatre visits and sporting activities). Also included are attitudinal issues and judgements (such as what factors do you think influenced your personal success). Smith, Gregg and Andrews (1989) claim that biodata is one of the best predictors of job performance.

To collect the information needed to develop a database, several steps have to be undertaken:

1. Analyse the job and/or the performance of previous postholders to identify the skills and characteristics needed. These establish the dimensions to be used.

2. A pool of items relevant to these dimensions is created and an instrument devised that enables the characteristics of applicants to be compared to the dimensions. Multiple questions are used that have built-in checks and an appropriate scoring system is devised.

3. Validate the questions and system by testing them against a sample of postholders whose standard of job performance is known — for example, from the results of appraisal. Smith, Gregg and Andrews (1989) recommend that this sample consists of at least 300 people.

4. Analyse the findings statistically to see which combination of questions best predicts job performance. Checks must be made to ensure that no gender or ethnic bias exists in the system and that it is consistent and reliable.

Obviously only large employers can develop such a system effectively. Moreover, repeated analysis is needed to ensure that the dimensions remain up to date. Despite the researchers' endorsement, Biodata as a shortlisting device from which to predict future performance has several weaknesses:

- It is expensive to construct and maintain a proper system.
- It assumes that certain factors outside the control of an individual (such as family size) have a direct effect on job performance.
- Biases, albeit unconscious, are built into the system, and using existing and previous employees as the sample population is limiting. Some of the features identified as leading to successful performance may be cultural, if not ethnically or gender-bound. For example, it may be difficult for a young person to develop an interest in going to the theatre if they grew up in rural Northumberland. Team sports have been considered by some local education authorities as being unhelpful to the development of socially responsible, collaborative adults and therefore have not been encouraged in schools. Similarly, team sports tend to be encouraged as a male rather than as a female pursuit.
- History does not always predict the future. If it did, very little growth, development and innovation would happen. We would simply go round in a never ending circle of sameness.

The main use for Biodata is in sifting a large number of applicants for a large number of vacancies. It enables factual comparisons to be made between applicants and the requirements and desired features of the successful job holders. This acceleration and systematising of the shortlisting process allows it to be completed by comparatively junior staff.

This plus the predictive validity of Biodata, can compensate for some of the high set-up costs.

Graphology

The use of graphology, as a means of predicting success or failure in a job has been the subject of some heated debate among personnel professionals and occupational psychologists. One reason for the recent revival of interest is its widespread use in Europe. Some recruitment agencies are developing graphology services and have run workshops to explain the benefits and practicalities of the method to employers. Very few British companies admit to using handwriting as a method of screening, and reviews suggest that the lack of interest is well founded because the method has low predictive validity. According to Smith, Gregg and Andrews (1989):

> ... many systems have tried to use handwriting to predict personality. The simplest and most scientific methods have used physical characteristics such as pressure on the page or speed of writing. The second approach focuses upon single features such as slant, regularity and connections between letters. The third, holistic approach is the method adopted by most graphologists and uses complex analyses that are based on combinations of features.

Unfortunately, many of the studies of graphology have been flawed. People, tests have shown, are able to change their handwriting at will and handwriting has been shown to have no correlation with personality and subsequent actions. However, despite statements from employers, it can be argued that handwriting is used extensively as a method of screening and shortlisting applicants, albeit subconsciously and unsystematically. If it were not so, why are applicants still generally expected to include at least a hand-written letter supporting their application? One reason for this is our tendency to make assumptions about people based on evidence gleaned from personal factors such as their handwriting. However, it must be remembered that handwriting style is influenced by additional factors. School teachers have had fashions and have taught different generations of children differently. We have passed from copper plate through forward sloping script via italics to big semi printed letters. Moreover, we make unsubstantiated assumptions. For example, tidy, small handwriting is generally seen as being produced by a neat, introverted individual; large, scrawly script comes from an extrovert. None of this, of course, is true, but it illustrates how easy it is to form false assumptions.

Shortlisters, as we have seen before, each have their own personal preferences and prejudices which, unless a great deal of care is taken, serve to inform their decisions. If one of these concerns handwriting and prejudices are allowed to lead to assumptions being made about the individual, subsequent decisions will be influenced accordingly. A way of dealing with these biases is to be aware of them and to use more valid techniques to aid decision making.

Tests

Testing is a very well-known method of exploring applicants' knowledge and abilities. Tests are given a coefficient of predictive validity of about 0.5 by Smith, Gregg and Andrews (1989). Whereas interviews range from 0.15 to just over 0.3 depending on their degree of structure. (These figures are explained in greater depth in Chapter 6.) Tests take two major forms — work-related ability tests and cognitive ability tests.

Work-related ability tests

These generally require the applicant to complete some sort of task, such as typing a piece of work. In some cases applicants are asked to submit evidence of their previous work in the form of a portfolio or examples of products, while in others tests are sometimes specially constructed by individual organisations.

The opening of a new restaurant provided Bruce's Burger Bars with the opportunity to develop a systematic method for screening new staff. Previously the company had just taken people on and relied on its ability to sack them if they did not come up to scratch within the first few weeks. It was realised that this was in fact costly, and did nothing to add to the company's reputation as an employer.

The personnel staff and line managers carried out an analysis of the most common jobs, identified the skills needed to perform those tasks adequately and established benchmarks for sub-standard and competent performance. They then designed a battery of simple tasks that realistically represented the jobs to be filled. These included a test of money handling, an exercise designed to examine manual dexterity, a verbal question and answer exercise to explore attitude to customer care and a test to discern levels of understanding about safe and hygienic working.

People interested in applying for the vacancies were asked to submit letters of application giving education, previous employment, preferred hours of work and personal details. After the initial sift, potential candidates were asked to participate in the tests, and applicants who passed were then invited for a formal interview.

Care must be taken when devising such exercises to ensure that they do not contain any gender or ethnic bias. They need to be a fair representation of the real job, rather than a series of difficult exercises designed to 'get applicants to show what they are made of'. Similarly, the administration of the tests needs to ensure that each applicant is treated in exactly the same way as every other applicant. Some organisations have abandoned their own tests because of the pitfalls of bias or unfair discrimination and instead rely on those that are available commercially. Most of these have been carefully researched and checked to remove any unnecessary source of bias. However, they inevitably test only the features they have been designed to test, and these may not be the ones required by the organisation. There is a great danger of looking at a catalogue and thinking that one particular test looks good rather than deciding which behaviours and knowledge need to be explored. Fortunately most test suppliers are very cautious and helpful, and they also supply instructions on how to use the tests.

Cognitive ability tests

These tests explore mental rather than physical skills (and sometimes they are referred to as intelligence tests). They can test specific abilities such as numeracy, understanding and cognitive skills, or they can explore general intelligence at different levels. The latter tend to be batteries of the former, drawn together to look at a range of abilities in a way that enables overall conclusions to be drawn. These tests can also be devised internally but this is not to be recommended. Nor should they be used casually.

Numeracy, reading and aptitude tests are often used for the initial screening when a large number of staff are being recruited — for example, graduates to a trainee scheme. The aptitude tests can include tests of trainability as well as preferences for particular types of work. (For example, clerical aptitude tests explore speed and accuracy as well as literacy and numerical abilities. Mechanical and spatial reasoning ability tests are also available.)

Mental ability tests go beyond mental tasks to explore more sophisticated skills such as reasoning. We need to be sure that when using tests at this level we are not building in assumptions, bias and halo effects. For example, it would be wrong to believe that a graduate engineer had well-developed report writing skills. Sternberg (1988) claims that there are seven different forms of intelligence:

1. **Verbal abilities** — the ability to use and understand speech.
2. **Quantitative abilities** — computation such as adding, incrementing and interacting between numbers.
3. **Problem solving** — the ability to represent problems and to identify solutions.
4. **Learning abilities** — to remember through repetition and rehearsal.
5. **Inductive reasoning** — the ability to perceive relationships between related terms and concepts.
6. **Deductive reasoning** — the ability to draw conclusions from information provided about a problem.
7. **Spatial abilities** — forming and identifying visual representations.

Therefore, when selecting a test an employer needs to be sure that the one chosen is actually testing the abilities needed for the job in question.

Generally, tests are administered and interpreted by occupational psychologists or those licensed by the test suppliers as being suitably qualified and experienced. These safeguards are necessary because cognitive ability tests are powerful instruments and, in the hands of inexperienced or careless testers, can inflict psychological damage on the individuals taking the test. They are usually interpreted with the aid of data that enable an individual to be compared with normative tables. These tables are drawn up from population samples (eg Army entrants, sixth formers, students in their second year at university, senior executives, etc). The validity of these tables depends on the size of the sample used to compile them. Using a small sample or one that is biased in some way leads to in-built discrimination. Most test suppliers are now very careful to ensure that their samples are as large and as representative as feasibly possible, and that they are statistically valid. More will be said about the use of tests as selection instruments in Chapter 6.

The opinion of others

When an organisation employs a search consultant to find suitably qualified applicants, part of the service supplied by the consultant is an initial screening. This aims to reduce the number of applicants the potential employer needs to consider. Applications or telephone interviews supply preliminary information from which the consultant draws up a longlist of individuals who seem to match the person specification and appear as likely candidates. The quality of screening depends on the quality of the consultant's skills and understanding of the employing organisation's requirements. It must also be remembered that the one-to-one interview is regarded as among the worst predictors of final performance. The main benefits of employing a consultant are:

- The preservation of confidentiality and anonymity for both parties. Some organisations do not want the knowledge of their search for a new appointee to be public, while some applicants do not wish to divulge their interest in another job.
- Paying an agent to conduct the screening can save time for the employing organisation.
- The consultant can bring much needed expertise to bear, particularly if the employing organisation does not recruit new employees very often.
- The consultant can ask questions that a potential employer cannot. Similarly, an applicant is likely to give information to a third (independent) party that they would not be prepared to give to a potential employer. (For example, not many applicants would admit to a prospective employer that they did not get on well with their current boss.)

The main disadvantages are:

- Interviewing is a poor predictor of job performance.
- The consultant will be seen by applicants as a representative of the employing organisation, and therefore the way in which they are treated will be taken as indicative of the organisation's treatment of staff. (There are anecdotal reports of search consultants grilling applicants and being aggressive in their questioning. This has not reflected well on the organisations as well as the search consultants.)
- The interviews, being one to one, are prone to all sorts of poor and unfair practice, with little redress available for the applicant.
- The briefing given to the consultant needs to be thorough and action

should be taken to check understanding. There is a danger that the consultant, naturally, will use personal interpretations and prejudices that may be contrary to those implicit in the organisation's culture.

Competence-based applications

The competence/competency approach is becoming more popular. The main use so far has been for development, but it is now spreading into other areas of human resource management. Application forms, supplementary questionnaires or guidance notes for applicants can be designed to elicit experience, attainment, skills and knowledge against predetermined competence/competency statements. In a way this can be seen as an updating of weighted application blanks.

In their original form, weighted application blanks were very similar to Biodata (as described above). They were designed to elicit information about applicants that could be compared to the idealised profile of a successful postholder. Cook (1988) describes how this approach was used to recruit department store staff, and shows how the idealised profile was developed from empirical data. The 'perfect' individual was between 35 and 54 years old, had 13–16 years of formal education, had over 5 years sales experience, weighed over 11.5 stones, lived in a boarding house, etc. The application blank was designed to explore these and other desirable features of applicants' background. The criticisms of this approach are very similar to those levelled at Biodata. Unless the sample of previous postholders is very large and broad, it is very easy for distortions to occur. It is also possible for bizarre factors to become included. Similarly, it is easy for discriminatory factors to be introduced, justified because previous postholders possessed them. In short, without some check, this approach can merely replicate history.

The modern use of competency or competence-based applications is much more systematic, depersonalised and forward looking. 'Competencies', briefly, are the skills and knowledge needed to perform a job satisfactorily (ie more than adequately), while 'competences' are the outputs of satisfactory performance. Both or either can be used to develop a structured application form that will facilitate shortlisting. The example in the panel draws on the Training and Development Lead Body Standards.

APPLICATION FOR THE POST OF TRAINING OFFICER

Please complete the following questionnaire (see in Table 5.4). You should give actual examples of work activities that demonstrate your achievement in each of the areas. You should also indicate your level of skills, using the ratings given below, remembering you will be asked about your answers if you are called for an interview:

- *poor — (ie you have very little experience or skill in this area);*
- *satisfactory — (ie you can make some significant improvements to the level of your skills or experience);*
- *competent — (ie you are able to perform this area of work at a level regarded as above average most of the time).*

Table 5.4   Competence-based questionnaire

Area of work	*Evidence*

1. Identification of training and development need
Is able to analyse complex situations and distinguish between training and other problems.

Rating
- ☐   poor
- ☐   satisfactory
- ☐   competent

2. Design training and development strategies and plans
Is able to organise resources for the achievement of objectives and implementation of plans and to prepare contingencies.

Rating
- ☐   poor
- ☐   satisfactory
- ☐   competent

Area of work	*Evidence*

3. Provides learning opportunities, resources and support

Is able to implement and monitor the plans designed to achieve objectives and accommodate the needs of individual learners.

Rating

☐ poor
☐ satisfactory
☐ competent

4. Evaluate the effectiveness of training and development

Is able to review actions on the basis of information gathered from a range of sources.

Rating

☐ poor
☐ satisfactory
☐ competent

5. Support training and development advances and practice

Engages in action to ensure own professional learning and development.

Rating

☐ poor
☐ satisfactory
☐ competent

From the information given, the shortlister can make judgements about which of the applicants best match the requirements for the job. Obviously there are risks of applicants overestimating their own abilities, but the warning in the introduction should be sufficient to safeguard against all but the most determined boast. The evidence column should provide examples of previous life or work experience that can be used as being indicative of abilities. For example, in response to question 4, a typical answer might be:

I conducted a staff survey to assess their views of training and development. I designed a questionnaire that covered how needs were identified, what action had been taken to satisfy the needs and how the staff were able to implement the results of the training received. The answers to the questions were analysed by staff group and section. The section results were discussed with the respective managers and the overall findings of the survey reported to the management group.

The value of using competencies and competences is that the application, using the words of the applicant, can be directly related to the requirements of the job. It is accepted that, at the initial stage, the word of the applicant only is available but, depending on the way questions are phrased, two checks are possible. One is to ask the applicant to provide factual evidence of achievement. This, of course, can be checked via references. The second way is to tell applicants that their application will be used as a basis for other selection activities, such as criterion-based or behavioural event interviewing (discussed in Chapter 6).

Moreover, the use of criteria that can be directly related to the job requirements offers shortlisters a practical way of comparing applicants in a systematic and fair fashion. To enhance this process further, a matrix can be built using the competencies and competences from the job description and person specification.

Shortlisting matrix

The matrix provides a means of comparing applications to the criteria and the applicants to each other, so that the strongest field — on paper — is shortlisted. It also creates a record that is able to demonstrate the grounds on which each applicant was shortlisted or rejected. This latter consideration is important because individuals have the right to ask an employer to justify its decisions to an Industrial Tribunal if the applicant believes he or she has been subjected to unlawful discrimination.

The matrix takes the criteria as one of the dimensions and lists the applicants along the other. The shape of the matrix makes it possible to give applicants a number, thus creating a system that preserves some anonymity. This may be necessary in order to remove bias or to assess potential — for example, if some or all of the applicants are existing employees of the organisation. The matrix provides a mechanism for pooling the opinions of several shortlisters.

Some organisations hold shortlisting meetings at which several shortlisters exchange their opinions of each applicant and collectively decide a shortlist. This method is prone to all the dynamics of group working and can result in decisions being made on criteria that are very different than those required for the successful performance of the job. Even if the meeting is a necessary part of the organisation's way of working, the use of a matrix can facilitate the decision making and reduce some of the negative effects. For example, the process could follow these steps:

1. Each shortlister is asked to complete the matrix before the meeting.
2. When the shortlisters come together in person they are asked to compare their assessment of each applicant against the criteria.
3. The applicants who fail to achieve the minimum essential criteria are eliminated immediately (in a way that can be evidenced factually).
4. The applicants who best fit the criteria, as agreed by all shortlisters, are carried on to the next stages of selection.
5. The remaining applicants will be those about whom there is some disagreement between the shortlisters. The shortlisters can then compare on the matrix where their differing views occur and the reasons for them. If there is a need, further discussions about the fate of the application can take place and informed decisions made.

Table 5.5   Office manager shortlisting matrix

Criteria for office manager	Candidate			
	1	*2*	*3*	*4*
Attainment				
Successful completion of a post-16 further education course	Yes	Yes	Yes	Yes
Some job-related, management training	Yes	No evidence	No evidence	Yes
Experience				
IT office applications	No evidence	Yes	No evidence	Yes
Customer service	Yes	Yes	Yes	Yes
Staff training and supervision	Yes	No evidence	No evidence	Yes
BS 5750 and record maintenance	No evidence	Yes	Yes	Yes

Criteria for office manager	Candidate			
	1	*2*	*3*	*4*
Abilities				
Communication skills	Untidy application	Yes	Application badly produced	Yes
Leadership skills	Trainer with no supervisory responsibilities	No evidence	No evidence	Yes
Planning and organisation	Poor organisation of information on the form	No evidence	Application badly produced	?
Training and instructional skills	Yes	No evidence	No evidence	Yes
Aptitudes				
Customer focused	No evidence	Yes	No evidence	Yes
Accuracy	No evidence	?	Application badly produced	Yes
Concern for quality	Untidy application	Yes	Application badly produced	Yes
Interests				
Involved with people	Yes	Solitary interests	No evidence	Yes
Learning and self-development	No evidence	Yes	No evidence	Yes

On the evidence shown in the Table 5.5 matrix, applicant number 4 would be shortlisted and number 2 held as a reserve. Numbers 1 and 3 would be rejected. The grounds for holding number 2 as a reserve would be the lack of supervisory experience. The criteria that were not evidenced are gaps. Applicant number 3 has similar gaps. But the poorly presented application could be taken as a reflection of the standard of communication skills or a lack of concern for quality and accuracy. Applicant number 1 has not had leadership experience and has many other gaps.

Used in this way, the matrix can aid decision making:

- It makes the criteria explicit and gives the shortlisters a tool that simplifies the process.
- It facilitates the pooling of several shortlisters' opinions.
- It enables comparisons to be made between shortlisters and between applicants and the job-related criteria.
- It provides a record of the decisions and the grounds on which they were made.
- It gives a mechanism for checking the validity of decisions. If needed, the applications can be re-examined and the decisions checked to see if other shortlisters reach the same decisions on the basis of the evidence supplied by applicants.

SUMMARY

This chapter has considered how applicants express their interest in a vacancy. In doing so, it has attempted to indicate how steps can be taken to reduce the negative effects of the biases and errors found in normal human decision making. Shortlisting is the main point in the recruitment and selection process when decisions are made about people and their abilities to match the requirements of the job. This is the stage when the best candidates can be lost and inadequate individuals carried forward. Therefore it is essential that judgements are made on the basis of explicit criteria and evidence obtained from the applicants. Not only do employers need to be fair, they also need to be able to demonstrate the quality of their processes. Aggrieved individuals do have the right to claim against unfair treatment if they feel that they have been subjected to illegal discrimination. It is up to employers to maintain adequate systems and records to demonstrate that this has not happened. Examples of simple ways of doing this were given in the form of checklists and matrices.

Managers are obliged to make decisions throughout recruitment; it is a process of discerning between applicants and predicting which will best meet the criteria and fit the organisation. Consequently it is worth gaining an insight into some of the mental processes and constraints that inhibit effective decision making. A brief introduction to decision frames, constructs, heuristics and the use of decision aids was given to help managers learn how to improve. Even if decision making were to be faultless, the processes used contain some inherent flaws. There are several measures of validity that can help to ensure the design of techniques and methods act as effective predictors of subsequent performance.

The strengths and weaknesses of the common methods of submitting an application were discussed. Each has its own advantages and difficulties that need to be taken into account when deciding how to sift and shortlist. The need to make transparent the criteria for decision making and decision processes has been stressed.

Some examples demonstrating the uses of matrices have been given. This approach is used in a number of organisations and has been found to be easy to use to administer by personnel staff and line managers alike. It can act as a decision aid and provide a vehicle for combining the views of several shortlisters who may or may not meet. Regardless, however, of the method used, what is important is that all those involved know how the decision is to be made, their part in the process and the decision criteria to be adopted.

Similarly, applicants need to know what is happening to their application and when they are likely to get a response. It is also useful for them to know the criteria by which they will be judged. Indeed, this allows them to decide whether or not to submit an application in the first place. The most effective recruitment campaign, after all, is one that results in a manageable number of suitably qualified and experienced applicants. If self-selection is exercised by the applicants, shortlisting is almost unnecessary and the process can move straight to selection.

The next chapter considers the selection process. This is the time when applicants become candidates and meet representatives of the employing organisation in person. There is therefore more discussion about the effects of biases and prejudgements, because inter-person perception has a major influence on decision making during selection and needs to be taken fully into account when choosing selection methods. The usefulness and uses of the different techniques are discussed in the context of their predictive validity and feasibility. Techniques, however, do not make decisions — they facilitate them. It is the human decision makers that must exercise their flawed judgements. The advice given keeps this fact firmly in mind.

6

Selection Methods

This chapter describes some methods and techniques that can aid decision making during what is perhaps the most critical phase of the recruitment and selection process. Already we have accepted that getting the right person in the right job at the right time is a vital part of any manager's job. Unless the decision to appoint an individual to a job is 'good', the chances of the appointment being successful are severely limited. A good selection decision is one that results in the person appointed attaining a satisfactory level of performance in an acceptable amount of time at an acceptable cost.

The common pitfalls and danger spots that litter every stage of the run up to selection have been described earlier. Most mistakes are caused by the fact that managers generally give little thought to the critical nature of the decisions. Employers are surprised and disappointed when an appointment fails, and often the person appointed is blamed rather than recognising weaknesses in the process and methodology. If the steps outlined above are followed, the chances of some of the most common errors occurring will be reduced, and a sound basis will be laid for selection. Nevertheless, the techniques available are not 'fail safe'. Most of the research carried out into recruitment and selection methods, practices and procedures has investigated the validity and impact of selection techniques. This research is valuable in that it highlights areas of concern and indicates how improvements can be made that will have an effect on the quality of the process and its outcome. They also have an impact on the well-being of all the individuals concerned. (The stresses on candidates are recognised, but are those of the managers involved given due acknowledgement?)

Brief summaries of some of the main research findings will be used to draw attention to the fact that even the soundest of techniques and best practice contain scope for error. Some of this is due to the methods themselves, but the main source is the frailty of the human decision makers. Some of the concepts already introduced will be expanded further in order to provide guidance to managers responsible for decision making and help them choose which technique will best improve their practice.

The different selection methods most commonly used will be described and the pros and cons of each will be explained and guidance given on how to choose and use them.* In choosing a selection method, the manager responsible should take account of a number of factors:

- the job in question;
- the impact the method will have on candidates;
- the impact the method will have on the manager and key others;
- the feasibility of running the method in terms of
  - — resources required (space, materials, equipment) and cost;
  - — skills needed to design and operate the method; and
  - — the time required from managers, candidates, experts etc;
- the effect on the organisation; and
- the likelihood of the method achieving the desired outcome.

Some hints will be given in this chapter to improve ways of making the final decision which, as far as the employing organisation is concerned, is the offer of employment to the best candidate and the rejection of the others. However, it must be remembered that the offer is a binding contract and must therefore be made with care, and also that, in reality, this is not the final decision. The final decision is made by the candidate — whether to accept the offer or reject it. Employers would do better if they took account of the ultimate power of the chosen candidates throughout the process and gave due weight to their ability to turn down an offer of employment.

The consequences of the best candidate rejecting an offer can cause widespread ripples in an organisation. These include demoralisation, blaming and fault finding, public embarrassment, uncertainty and delay to projects, and the introduction of changes and confusion for other staff. If the advice of Herriot (1989a) is followed and the process is seen more as a negotiation, much can be done to reduce the chances of the best candidate rejecting the employer. The approaches adopted for the design of the methods to be described have been chosen to take account of their likely impact on candidates. The structured decision-making aids outlined are also intended to help the manager focus on the likely outcomes of choosing each of the available options, including the loss of the best candidate.

Even after doing the best one can, the research suggests the chances of being able to predict a perfect match between the candidate and their performance in the job are lower than one would wish (or believe to be the case.) The findings of the most significant research is summarised by Smith,

---

* Assessment centres have not been included here as they are adequately discussed in Dale and Iles (1992) and can be seen as sophisticated composites of other methods described.

Gregg and Andrews (1989), and suggests that the most common selection methods are a little better than chance at predicting a perfect match. The way in which methods are compared is by using a statistic called a coefficient of predictive validity. This indicates the probability of a particular selection method predicting subsequent performance in the job. Performance is judged by a number of different factors and techniques relevant to the job and organisation (such as supervisor appraisal, trainability, production, turnover, etc). The research on which the coefficients are based has been carried out world-wide in a range of organisations on a large number of jobs; the results have been pooled and the findings subjected to a meta analysis (a complex statistical technique based on the use of average correlations to take account of the effects of sampling error). This method, mainly developed by Schmidt and Hunter (1977) and Hunter and Hunter (1984), shows that some selection methods are better predictors than had been believed and that it is possible to generalise validity across jobs and situations.

The statistic these studies produced is a correlation coefficient. A perfect selection method is one that predicts perfectly every time it is used which candidate will best perform the job, and this has a coefficient of 1. A method with a coefficient of 0 may or may not predict the best candidate — employers may as well appoint the first person they meet on the high street. Generally a coefficient of over 0.5 is regarded as excellent, 0.4–0.49 good, 0.3–0.39 acceptable and less than 0.3 as poor. The coefficients in Table 6.1, taken from Smith, Clegg and Andrews (1989), are widely accepted because they are based on a meta analysis.

Table 6.1   Selection method coefficients

Method	Coefficient
Assessment centres (for promotion)	0.63
Work sample tests	0.55
Ability tests	0.53
Assessment centres (performance)	0.43
Personality tests (combination)	0.41
Biodata	0.38
Structured interviews	0.31
Typical interviews	0.15
References	0.13
Graphology	0
Astrology	0

The methods most commonly used for shortlisting and appointment (unstructured panel interviews, references and judgements made about an individual based on their handwriting) have the lowest predictive validity. The methods with better coefficients tend to be used less frequently. The reasons often given for their lesser popularity concern the time needed, the degree of expertise and the cost. Yet any selection decision represents an investment of at least several thousand pounds, and potentially it can take many hours of unproductive work to correct a bad decision.

Another reason why managers are reluctant to use more reliable methods is because they tend to believe that they are good interviewers and good judges of character.

ERRORS AND BIASES

In Chapter 4, the ways in which we form our initial impressions of people were explained. In brief, these are formed on the basis of a personal system of beliefs constructed throughout our lifetime which underpin the judgements we make about situations and people and enable us to make sense of what otherwise would be a confusing world. They help us reduce the anxiety engendered by uncertainty and fit what could be seen as random events into a picture that makes sense. Our constructs are used to explain the past, interpret the present and predict what is likely to happen in the future. We use them to prepare for situations and rehearse the part we are to play, and we also use them to prejudge the people we meet and predict how they are likely to behave. Some of our constructs are conscious and we are well aware that we hold them and why. Others are so deeply entrenched in our subconscious that we are not aware that we hold them, and even less why we hold them or where they came from. That is, until something happens (usually something out of the ordinary) that challenges them or brings them into question.

Subsequent decisions are informed by these impressions and made using heuristics — rules of thumb that are known to work because they have been used before. They are generalisations and truths that save mental energy by reducing the need to gather and process data. They can be wrong and unreliable but are rarely called into question. Subsequent interactions are used to confirm these impressions and opinions; we actively seek information which will do this and discount anything that serves to disprove our opinions. Thus, we gather evidence and make decisions that develop our first impression and build up a firm opinion about the person. We make sure our rules of thumb remain intact and preserve our personal image as a good judge of character. This is known as self-serving bias.

We tend to focus on the person as the centre of attention and ignore other factors that might influence their behaviour, and we tend to assume that individuals are responsible for what happens around them. For example, if an individual has worked on a successful project it is easy to believe that the person has contributed to that success and so is a competent worker. We attribute failure in the same way. If a person is unable to answer a question during an interview it is seen as a reflection on their ability and knowledge, even though their failure may have been due to the fact that the question was confusing. We see people in isolation — giving a soliloquy, centre stage — rather than being part of the play that takes place in the greater scheme of things.

If a person is seen in a good light because of success in one area of work, this is taken as a sample of their total ability. This 'halo effect' also comes from other people, organisations or situations with whom they have been associated. Similarly, if you have a poor opinion of the employer of an individual's referees, you are likely to transfer that opinion onto that individual without necessarily being aware that this transfer is happening. This is the 'Satan' effect.

First impressions are formed from what is witnessed. Judgements are based on what is seen and heard of the other person and assessments are made about personality traits. Conclusions are drawn and then used to predict how the person is likely to behave in other, non-related situations with different people. These tend to be gross generalisations and over-simplifications. Nevertheless, unless this process is challenged in some way, the information gathered is regarded as reliable. In similar fashion, stereotypes are used to classify individuals into groups. These broad 'truisms' are used to describe members of the group in general and are assumed to apply to all individuals who are classed as members of that particular group. The use of these generalities denies the uniqueness and potential of individuals. Even when we are aware of these dangers, we are susceptible to some of the other traps and errors. Impressions, opinions and conclusions are formed on the basis of:

- **Appearance** — hair, facial appearance, dress, demeanour, use of cosmetics and so on. For example, hunched shoulders can be taken as indicating timidity, although it could be that the individual is simply cold. The use of perfume (or aftershave) can be seen as an indicator of extroversion and a quiet voice as demonstrating a lack of confidence.
- **Behaviour** — conformity to social mores, conventions, patterns, body

posture and language. For example, everyone knows that you wait to be asked before sitting down at the start of an interview; leaning implies sloppiness which means careless work; and a hand tremor is a sign of nerves rather than another indicator of coldness.

- **Role** — roles held or thought to be held are used to predict behaviour and state of mind. For instance, a teenager in jeans and a studded leather jacket is likely to be disobedient and disruptive, while a senior manager will not move easily into a lower paid position.

It is also known that, in addition to these errors and biases, our memories of other people are prone to distortion. We tend to remember the first (primacy) and last people (recency) we meet better than those who were encountered in the middle of a sequence. We also recollect the person who had some outstanding feature (salience), like a big nose or a spot, or someone who did something out of the ordinary (such as suffered a coughing fit) better than those who were 'normal'. The outstanding feature may not have any relevance to the interaction but it still fixes the person in our memory. These distortions can influence decisions simply because the decision maker is able to remember those individuals better. This does not necessarily mean that the decision is likely to favour the individual best remembered. On the contrary, the 'best candidate' may be rejected because the selectors were repelled by the after-effects of a common cold.

We prefer to be surrounded by people who share the same values as ourselves. At our first meeting we exchange information to seek common ground and if our initial impressions are favourable, we tend to ignore differences and assume agreement. We seek harmony and consensus and avoid conflict and disagreement, and we like to be with people we like and who like us. Thus we tend to play down or ignore potential areas of conflict. Moreover, we tend to shy away from people if we think they are likely to be different. This can be based on the slimmest of evidence, but the risks contained in the potential for disagreement and, later, conflict are too great.

No selection technique can eliminate these errors, biases and distortions. The reasons for the existence of these subconscious processes is to safeguard us by protecting our physical and mental health. Therefore they should be seen for what they are — part of the normal human perception and decision-making processes. They can play a useful role in ensuring co-operation and effective working by helping us to find like-minded people who share our values. But as they contain prejudice and unfounded assumptions they should not be allowed to govern modern recruitment and selection practices. Effective selection methods should take account of the existence of these processes and enable decisions to be made according to the organisation's needs, rather than the selector's prejudices and assumptions. No method can (or should) take over from human judgement, but it can help to structure the process and make explicit the criteria on which the decision is to be made. In this way, the risk inherent in predicting the behaviour of another person can be reduced.

SELECTION METHODS

Selection methods do not make a subjective process objective. They do not remove bias, nor do they prevent errors. The use of a method does not make the decision or remove the responsibility for that decision and its consequences from the individual manager. Selection methods provide a systematic means by which information can be gathered about candidates and help to predict their performance in that particular job. Some methods are better than others but a good method badly applied will not do its job effectively. Likewise, a method will only explore the aspects of human skills and abilities that it has been designed to explore.

We have seen that the starting point of the selection process is creating the job description and person specification. If these are based on a thorough analysis of the job and are well written, selection decisions can be made against predetermined criteria and the method chosen appropriately. If the job description is unclear and the person specification written in general, unspecific terms then, no matter how sophisticated the selection method, the information gathered will reflect the vagueness of the initial thinking — 'If you don't know what you are looking for, how will you know when you find it?'

Validity

The choice of selection methods should reflect the level, context and content of a job — ie it should be valid.

Face validity

Candidates should believe that they are being asked to carry out an activity that is relevant to the job for which they are being assessed. They should feel that it has some meaning. They should not be made to think that they are being asked to jump through hoops for the amusement of the selectors, nor should they see the selection activities as games.

Content validity

Experts should agree that the contents of the selection method are relevant to the job in question and that they reflect accurately the type of work normally or likely to be encountered by postholders. This is achieved by using real-life aspects of the job during the design or choice of the method.

Construct validity

The selection method, activities and instruments should test aspects of behaviour that are meaningful in the context of the job. These should be those aspects identified in the person specification as being essential for effective performance.

Criterion validity

The selection method should explore what it sets out to explore. If a selection instrument purports to explore a candidate's skills in social settings it should do that on each occasion it is used. Similarly, the results of the activity should not be assumed to demonstrate the candidate's ability in other areas.

Reliable validity

The selection method is consistent. It explores and predicts performance against the criteria it is designed to examine because it has done so in the past and can be relied upon to do so again in the future.

Impact validity

The impact or effect the selection method is likely to have on candidates should be considered. The acceptability of the method and its results need to be questioned and selectors themselves should have experienced similar sorts of activity under similar conditions. The impact of the process will be discussed at greater length later. However at the outset, consideration needs to be given to the likely effect resulting from:

- **The behaviour and role of the assessors**. Will they interact with candidates; in which capacity; will they be intimidating; are they at an appropriate level in the organisation to give the 'right' messages about the level of the job?
- **The number of assessors**. Will the number of internal people involved overwhelm the process; will there be sufficient involved to give a

balanced, all-round perspective on the candidates?

- **Obtrusiveness**. The assessors' behaviour needs to be suitable so that it does not intrude and disturb the candidates' performance.
- **The degree of involvement**. Only have assessors when they are needed. For example, there is usually no need to invigilate — it is not likely that candidates will cheat.

Each selection method has its own particular strengths and weaknesses. Even those shown to have low predictive validity have a legitimate role to play in the selection process. In the following sections, the comparative strengths and weakness of the most commonly used methods are outlined. Certain assumptions have been made about the ways in which each of the methods are applied. It is not possible to describe all the variations as some are prone to the idiosyncrasies of the selector(s) and it must be stressed that any method is only as good as the way in which it is applied.

Interviews

One-to-one interviews

In this method one selector interviews a candidate alone. The method contains many potential pitfalls for the selector, but a way of avoiding them is to ensure that the questions are pre-set and that each candidate is asked them in exactly the same way. It is not easy for a sole interviewer to ensure consistency of treatment between the candidates. It is also difficult for the interviewer to probe in depth and remember fully what was said — note-taking and observing and questioning simultaneously is not easy. The process is open to all the biases and errors of perception described above, and the sole interviewer does not have the benefit of a co-interviewer to counterbalance or check perceptions. The interviewer has to make judgements based on his or her memory of information gathered in what is, in effect, a formal social exchange.

The 'safety' of the process has also to be considered. The interviewer is very open to accusations of malpractice. Disappointed candidates have been known to level accusations of unfair treatment and discrimination. Without another party present, it can be difficult to put up a defence. Similarly, the candidate can in fact be exposed to illegal discrimination and malpractice.

Informal interviews

These are discussions between the candidate and two or more interviewers who feed their perceptions to the members of the final interview panel or appointment board. Mostly unstructured, such interviews allow candidates to be questioned on a broad range of topics, superficially or in some depth. There is the opportunity for the discussion and questioning to be on an equal footing and to flow between interviewers and candidates, but this can be confusing. It is also possible for a false impression of the organisation to be painted in the mind of the candidate. If the discussion concentrates on one aspect of the job, it is possible for this aspect to be overemphasised and for undue weight to be given to it.

The label 'informal' can also be a misnomer. The exact contribution of the interview to the final decision is not always clear to the candidate. Similarly, informal interviewers are not always certain of their role in the final decision. The process, being a social interchange, is also prone to errors and biases of perception. However, this social interaction aspect is important. It helps candidates decide whether they are likely to fit the organisation and its existing staff just as much as it allows the interviewers to assess their potential colleagues. It is possible for the effects of group dynamics and internal politics within the organisation to take the process over. If this happens the assessment of candidates and the decision about who is the best can be subordinated to other (unrelated) considerations.

Panel interviews

Panel interviews are probably the most commonly used and trusted method of selecting candidates. Sadly, this method is not very good at predicting which candidate is likely to be the most successful in the job. The reasons for this are mainly found in the errors outlined earlier.

Panel interviews have additional drawbacks that may contaminate the selection decision. Different interviewers use different criteria, different standards and have different weightings. Without proper planning and preparation, it is difficult to obtain a consistent use of person specification criteria. Every interviewer wants the chance to ask her or his own questions, and this can deny the opportunity for an interviewer to probe the candidate in depth. Moreover, candidates can be easily confused by the rapid changes in the direction from which questions are fired. This may be seen as a reflection of their abilities rather than a flaw of the process. To make matters worse, the dynamics of the interviewing panel may take over. Interviewers can try to score points off each other at the candidates' expense or strive to influence the decision by tripping up less favoured candidates.

Even though they are extremely problematical, panel interviews do have a valid place in the selection process. They are not, however, a reliable predictor of performance. The research carried out by Herriot (1989a) concludes that the interview is best seen as a social event and the main formal occasion when employers and candidates meet face to face. It is also the place where negotiations regarding the nature of the role and the employment contract begin and, as such, it carries out a useful purpose. Rather than argue for the abolition of the panel interview therefore, ways of improving its contribution and separating it from the other parts of the selection process should be introduced. Some methods for doing this follow.

Structured interviews

The interview's underlying format is planned in advance. Each phase and each question is designed to flow from the previous into the next, and to make a valid contribution to the whole. This requires the members of the interview panel to do some preparatory work together. They need to be clear about who is going to ask which questions and when. Thought also needs to be given to the ways in which each candidate may be probed and challenged in ways that are appropriate to the situation.

While asking each candidate exactly the same question in exactly the same way ensures that the required information is obtained, it is a waste of the opportunity for social interaction. Face-to-face interviews allow for particular issues to be explored in depth with individual candidates. If more precise or detailed information is desired, it may be more economically obtained via questionnaires. Interview blanks may be used in conjunction with application forms. Some organisations ask candidates to submit essays, papers and other forms of ancillary data to complement and inform the interview. Other ways of probing in depth can be built into the interview without distorting the structure — providing they are planned and the panel members understand what is happening and what they are expected to do in the process.

This structured approach means that each question has a purpose and is designed to elicit information required to aid the selection decision. The questions should aim to explore the requirements contained in the person specification, explore issues raised in the individual's application and amplify any points that remain unclear. It is also the opportunity for the candidates to ask questions. The type of questions asked by each candidate also provides information about them that will contribute to the picture of the individual.

Needless to say, notes and a record of the interview should be maintained. These are required as reminders for use in the final decision, to reduce the distortions of saliency, primacy and recency and to demonstrate that the correct procedures, designed to ensure that each candidate was treated fairly, have been followed.

Criterion-based interviews

Structured interviews are based on pre-planned standard questions ranging over all aspects of the job. Criterion-based interviews focus directly on elements of the person specification. The interviewers, the structure of the interview and the questions are selected to explore, in some depth, particular aspects of the requirements needed for effective performance of the job. The range of questions is more limited than those posed in the structured interview. This is deliberate because the aim of the criterion-based interview is to probe only specific skills or competencies.

Focused interviews

Focused interviews are similar. The difference lies in the emphasis of the questions, which are designed to cover aspects of the job. Criterion-based interview questions will aim to explore, for example, communication skills, while focused interview questions will concern areas such as the candidates' approach to managing difficult members of staff. If the job contains several distinct elements, it is possible to hold several focused interviews, each designed to explore a particular area. This is known as serial or sequential interviewing.

Behavioural event interviews

Behavioural event interviewing is found mainly in America where it was developed to help the identification of competencies. Its purpose is to explore the skills used by a candidate during a particular event or set of circumstances. Typically, questioning would follow this sequence:

- Tell me about a successful project you have worked on?
- What part did you play in its success?
- What was your most useful contribution?
- How did that help the project's success?
- What in particular makes you think so?

And so on. The aim is to help interviewers assess what the candidate has done and is able to do as opposed to what he or she says they can do. By probing, it is possible to help the individual identify skills they may not know they possess. The questions can be based on aspects of the job that are critical for success and candidates are asked to choose similar tasks from their own experience. Alternatively, projects cited by candidates on their application forms can be used.

Situational interviews

Situational interviews are used to project candidates into the future by asking 'What if' questions. The questions can be chosen to reflect aspects of the job which are known to present difficulties or those that are critical for future successful performance. These should stem from the job analysis used to draw up the job description and person specification. Ideally, they should be challenging but realistic.

There is a temptation with this sort of interviewing to play games with candidates by asking them impossible questions. Asking questions candidates cannot answer does not provide the information needed to predict their future performance. It may test their abilities to respond to direct pressure and challenge. But, unless this is a real feature of the job, games play of this nature should be avoided. Instead, the questions should be designed to enable candidates to think themselves into the situation and explore with the interviewers how they would deploy their skills and experience.

Final interviews

If other selection techniques have been used, the purpose of the final interview is to ensure that all required information has been obtained from the candidates and that they have the information they require. The final interview is the last chance for selectors and candidates to talk to each other. It may be that other selection methods have enabled some candidates to be eliminated (either by their own choice or by their demonstrable failure to meet the requirements). The final interview is the place where decisions are being formulated and negotiations started.

The interview panel will make the ultimate decision after all remaining candidates have been seen. The way in which this decision is made can take several forms (and guidance is given later on techniques to help with this). Whichever method is used, candidates need to be assessed against the person specification, the job description and other explicit requirements. It is also appropriate now to compare candidates against each other in order to judge who is likely to be the best appointment. While this is happening candidates, too, will be making their decisions about whether they will accept the job if it is offered. All too often, selectors forget that in reality it is the candidate who makes the final decision.

It is possible to combine the above forms of interview. If this is done, care is needed to ensure consistency and to maintain a clear separation between different modes of interviewing. Candidates should know what is expected from them at each stage and interviewers must be clear about their role.

Structured activities

The reason for using structured activities as part of the selection process is to explore areas of knowledge and skills in ways not possible in interviews. Various techniques (described in the following sections) are all known to be valid and reliable predictors of performance — but only if they are designed and administered properly. This means that they should conform to the criteria for validity listed above and in Chapter 5, and that they should be aimed directly at eliciting the job-related factors contained in the job description and person specification. They should also be fair and uniquely unfamiliar to all candidates, which means:

- They should not require candidates to possess information not generally available.
- No candidate should need specialist knowledge about the internal workings of the organisation.
- The activities should not have been seen previously by candidates. (It has been found that prior knowledge can actually disadvantage some candidates as well as advantage others.)

Work samples

It is argued by Herriot (1989a) that work samples are the most accurate predictor of performance because the candidate is assessed directly on job-specific activities. However, the research found that when the output of the work sample is rated rather than measured, the potential for bias and hence inaccuracy remains. In the context of most administrative, clerical, technical and professional jobs, rating would have to be chosen to assess achievement; measurement of output can only be carried out for jobs in which volume is produced. Moreover, constructing a sample of a job that does not require specific training or long periods of time to complete is often impractical. Nevertheless, if these constraints are acknowledged, asking candidates to carry out a relevant task or part of the job for which they are being considered is a valid, reliable and appropriate means of assessing abilities.

The choice of task or aspect of the job needs careful consideration. The sample should be discrete and allow candidates to complete it in a reasonable time, and it should also be meaningful so candidates can see the relevancy of what they are being asked to do. They should not need inside information or specialist knowledge. A means of assessing the results of the activity should be devised to ensure consistency between candidates. Above all, each candidate should be asked to perform the work sample under the same conditions as the others. When choosing the sample, consideration should also be given to the stress of the circumstances. It is appropriate for the sample to be performed under similar conditions to those normally encountered as part of the job, but these should not be unduly distracting. In addition, account should be taken of the effects of stress. For example, it would not be reasonable to compare a candidate's work carried out in a simulated situation under stressful conditions to that of an experienced employee who was working under everyday pressure. Therefore, the sample should be chosen to reflect the content, level and context of the job in question, but it should not represent the hardest part.

Tests

Tests aim to explore a particular skill or area of knowledge, rather than an ability to carry out a particular aspect of the job. For example, a typing test would contain a variety of actions designed to examine a typist's capabilities across a range of activities. A work sample would consist of examples of typing tasks normally encountered as part of the job. The latter would not necessarily explore all the skills a competent typist could normally be expected to possess.

Tests should be piloted to ensure they actually test the knowledge and skills they purport to examine. They should produce the same results each time they are used, and be reliable. Mechanisms are needed to ensure that marking is fair and consistent. Ideally, it should be carried out by someone who is not involved in the final decision. The administration of the test should be consistent and care should be taken to ensure that nothing happens to distract the candidate unduly.

Presentations

Presentations explore candidates' abilities to expand their ideas and arguments in a public forum. They provide candidates with the opportunity to demonstrate their abilities in three ways:

- **Making presentations**. Demonstrating communications skills, like clarity and comprehensibility of speech, style of delivery, use of aids, use of time, etc.
- **Convincing an audience**. Making a case and presenting arguments, comprising aspects such as structure of content, logic of arguments, credibility with the audience, engaging the audience, building rapport, the use of influencing skills, etc.
- **Demonstrating knowledge**. This includes soundness of arguments, use of evidence, correctness of facts, choosing the right level for the right audience, and so on.

When using this method, the choice of presentation topic and the wording of the brief given to candidates needs careful consideration. Candidates will need to know the size of the audience and its composition, what aids are available and how long their presentation should last. They should also be clear about the expected way of taking and responding to questions from the audience. The size of the audience and the roles its members are to play also need to be decided upon. If all the members are to contribute to the assessment of candidates, some mechanism and structure is needed to collect feedback and ensure that the assessment is consistent. If only a few members of the audience are to carry out the assessment, the remainder need to have this explained so they are clear about their role and contribution to the process. Assessors will need to be briefed and provided with pro formas to ensure that assessment is made against the criteria contained in the person specification. These will also help to collate the assessments of individual assessors, create records and facilitate feedback.

In trays

In tray activities should comprise a collection of letters, memos, messages, fliers and so on that the postholder could normally expect to receive in their daily mail. Some of the items should be inter-linked in some way, to enable candidates to demonstrate their abilities to make connections, discern issues, make inferences and give appropriate responses. Usually there is a time limit imposed on the activity to add an element of pressure. It is also possible to introduce additional items while the candidates are working through the in tray as an added source of realism. Interruptions are a fact of life for most people at work.

Typically, other skills that may be explored by this method include decision making, planning and organising, problem identification and solution, communication skills and delegation. The in tray can be rated on the basis of the written replies and notes. Alternatively or additionally, a follow-up interview can be held, providing for the assessment of other additional aspects of performance such as assertiveness and influencing skills. It also allows the assessor to explore the reasoning behind a candidate's decisions.

The in tray should be designed to reflect the content, context and level of the job, but should not require specialist or internal knowledge. The size of the in tray should also reflect reality. It would be unfair to give candidates vast quantities of items to deal with if, in fact, the job holder receives very little post. Similarly, it would be misleading to give only a few items if the job really is buried under paper.

Case studies

Case studies are designed in similar ways. As well as asking candidates to work on the case during the selection event, it is possible to ask them to prepare work beforehand. However, if this is done, it must be accepted that candidates will devote different amounts of time and energy to them and may draw on others for help.

Usually, a case study presents candidates with a scenario containing a 'problem'. The task is to identify the problem and to distinguish between symptoms and real issues. Depending on the level of the post, the case study can be straightforward with all the necessary information contained in it, or, for more responsible jobs, the case can contain gaps and misleading or contradictory information so that candidates have to use deduction and their intuition to get to the 'right' answer. In the latter instance, the case study is used to explore candidates' abilities in decision-making processes — ie their abilities to investigate and resolve problems. In the former, cases are designed to explore the ways candidates use and analyse information.

The results of work on a case study can be presented as a written report, the format of which will be determined by the culture of the organisation. It may be, for example, a paper, an argued case making proposals or a brief executive summary. The report can also be used as a basis for a presentation to an audience. Alternatively the findings can be reported verbally in a meeting with the line manager. The process used to communicate reports creates an opportunity for assessing additional skills. Thus, the report can be assessed as one free-standing instrument and its presentation as another.

Problems

A problem differs from a case study mainly as a result of the way in which the situation is outlined. In a problem, the situation to be resolved is not 'hidden' in a scenario. It is presented directly as the question, 'How would you deal with this problem'. Problems tend to be shorter than case studies and more specific. Possibly, they are more suitable for junior to middle level posts because they are best used to explore skills such as problem identification, decision making, and contingency planning, whereas case studies enable more 'senior' skills (such as strategic analysis and complex problem diagnosis) to be explored.

Group discussions

Asking candidates to discuss a topic or problem as a group is quite a common selection activity. It can provide a valuable means of observing the ways in which candidates behave in a peer group and during a meeting. Most other selection activities focus on candidates in isolation or during interactions with assessors and existing employees. Both of these generate different dynamics and contain different types of power distribution. A group discussion can enable selectors to witness candidates interacting with each other as equals.

However, unless the selectors and candidates are adequately briefed and the situation carefully designed and set up, conditions can be created that enable candidates to play games with each other and demonstrate their skills at dominating meetings. Fine, if these are the skills being sought but, if not, the following steps are required:

- Consideration must be given to which skills are to be explored.
- The meeting should be organised so that each of the candidates has an equally fair chance to display their own abilities without detracting from those of the others.
- Observers should be briefed and given specific behavioural criteria to observe.
- The observers should be provided with appropriate paperwork to enable them to record and report their observations.
- Some means of collating the observations and assessing each candidate's performance should be planned and prepared for in advance.

There is also the chance that the candidates will 'play the game' and be nice to each other. If the task is approached superficially by the candidates or if they collude to avoid disharmony, competition or stress, it is possible that the skills to be assessed will not be exhibited. The design of the task should take account of this chance and present candidates with choices. For example, they can compete or collaborate, challenge each other and the task or accept each other and what is given, probe and explore the boundaries or complete the task as it seems to be. The task can be written in a way that gives the candidates indications regarding the direction they should be following without giving them a route map.

Interactions

As Herriot (1989a) points out, the social fit between candidates and future colleagues (as well as the 'boss') is an important aspect of the selection process. This provides a valid reason for building less formal activities and interactions into the selection process. However, it must be clear to all involved exactly what part each activity plays in the formal process; those involved in the social events should know and understand what contribution they are able to make to the final decision. It is not unknown for internal power games, point scoring and feuds to be conducted around selection activities, and less formal activities create opportunities for these internal dynamics to be acted out. But because they contribute nothing to the process and tend to be apparent to candidates, they should be avoided at all costs. Despite this, social events have an important part to play providing their purpose is clear, they are well planned and the roles of the various participants are understood by everyone involved.

Visits

Visits to the place where the post is to be based allow candidates to meet future colleagues in their own setting and to see where they are to work. As well as seeing the physical conditions, candidates are able to 'pick up' a feel for the culture of the organisation and the work group. This advance information means candidates are better able to decide whether they are likely to fit. It will help the new appointee to settle in more quickly because the visit during the selection process will have helped the individual prepare and think themselves into their new job. The impressions gained help to build a picture of what it will be like to do the job.

It is a mistake to pretend that the working environment is different to what it really is like. Sometimes there is a temptation to hide what may seem to be unattractive features, but the successful candidate will soon find this out. In any case, what seems unattractive to insiders may not appear so to others. Neither should certain individuals be kept away from candidates. Dissidents and atmospheres can be detected and 'difficult' employees will meet. It is far better to make sure that everyone in the work group has a proper and active role to play.

Being clear and open about the purpose of the visit helps to decide the role of existing members of staff. The nature of the work site and the job also influence what can be shown during a visit. For example, a trip round an ordinary office can achieve little more than showing candidates the location of their future work space and letting them say hello to their potential colleagues. Conversations about 'What is it like to work here?' are likely to be superficial. One way of giving such visits more purpose would be to give staff a part to play in work sample activities and asking candidates to perform them in the office. This would give existing staff real interaction with candidates and allow them to contribute to the assessment on more than a social level.

Visits to laboratories, workshops and other specialist sites could involve demonstrations, detailed explanations of machinery, equipment processes and so on. This would engage existing staff in a more purposeful dialogue which could allow them to assess, for example, interest, understanding and technical knowledge.

Group discussions

Focused discussions with existing staff can be devised to allow a more systematic assessment. The topics chosen for discussion can include burning issues (eg internal communications), contentious areas (like cover for lunch breaks), aspects of importance (such as quality) or other matters that affect everybody. Topics to avoid, however, are those that would stimulate fierce debate between the staff rather than involve the candidates.

As each candidate will be met separately, a discussion leader (preferably someone independent from the group) should be appointed. This role is necessary to ensure that each candidate is treated consistently and that the process, which will inevitably be different each time, contains enough common features to ensure that treatment and assessment are fair. The final assessment also benefits from there being a discussion leader: the views of group members need to be collated against the criteria and combined to create a feedback report on each candidate for the selectors.

Social events

The Civil Service Selection Board was famed for its assessment of dinner table behaviour. While in some jobs, skills of this type can be important, they are not required as a matter of course in most. Nevertheless, some organisations believe that assessment by dinner knife and wine glass is a legitimate way to predict future behaviour. In these days of restrictive diet and health regimes, vegetarianism and allergies, this sort of social event can cause candidates more stress than the rest of the selection process. Formal dinners also restrict interaction because it is only really possible to talk to one's immediate neighbours and other guests are watched at a distance. Also extra actors interfere with the process (for example waiters) and the success of the event can depend on the skills and organisational abilities of others (such as the chef).

If there is a wish to expose candidates to a social event and give them the opportunity to interact with other people in the organisation, some less formal type of activity, such as a reception or buffet may be preferable. More interaction is possible, less can go wrong and stress levels for everyone are lower.

Regardless of the nature of the event, the selectors need to be clear what role it and the participants are to play in the final decision. These should be determined and planned in advance; the skills candidates are expected to elicit should be decided; and the assessors should be briefed so they are aware of the pitfalls that can easily befall candidates during such activities and are prepared to assess against the criteria.

Psychometric tests

The use of psychometric tests has increased markedly in recent years. One reason for this, in addition to their predictive validity, is that they are relatively simple to administer. A number of tests, which only take about one hour each to run, are available commercially and can be generally applied. Although apparently easy to interpret, they are measures of individuals' psychological make-up and personality and, as such, are extremely powerful instruments. They should only be administered with the candidates' permission (not easily withheld during selection events). Guarantees regarding the use of the information generated and its confidentiality should be given, and candidates should be offered feedback and be assured about the competence of the administrator. Attention should also be given to the ethics of testing.

Ethical issues in this area have caused some concern. Most reputable suppliers claim that their tests have been designed to be free of gender and ethnic bias, and they also say that the norm tables provided should be used for guidance only. However, they can only advise; they cannot control how the tests are administered and how the results are interpreted. It is simple to see the norm tables as containing the ideal profile against which candidates should be compared, but the tables indicate what could normally be expected in that particular population. The way some people use these tables reduces the complex process of assessing individuals to a simplistic level that merely catalogues them into types. The Institute of Personnel and Development is sufficiently concerned about the use of psychometric instruments to have issued a Code of Practice, while most reputable test producers require evidence of competence before supplying their materials.* However, this does not prevent tests from being obtained by untrained or non-registered individuals.

Tests can only measure what they have been designed to measure. Admittedly the predictive validity of such instruments is higher than most commonly used selection techniques but, as with any method, this validity can only be obtained when the technique is administered in the way intended. As has been pointed out above, there are many ways in which they can be abused.

There are several different types of psychometric test in common usage. The most widely used for selection fall into two categories — cognitive ability tests and personality questionnaires.

Cognitive ability tests

These tests have already been discussed in Chapter 5. In some ways they are similar to the intelligence tests that were used at one time to assess and categorise children. Single tests, designed to explore one or a number of similar dimensions, are available. However, the use of a battery combining several measures or dimensions is generally regarded as preferable because a more rounded picture of a candidate's abilities is obtained. The results can be used as individual indicators or (treated with care) can be compared to normative tables. The test or tests should reflect the needs of the job. There is little point in checking candidates' numeracy and mechanical aptitude if the job in question is entirely clerical. Similarly, testing individuals for their creative abilities would be irrelevant if the job demands strict adherence to instructions.

If the tests are selected with care and the results compared to norms with caution, they can provide useful insights into individuals' cognitive abilities. Their administration is straightforward providing that the instructions are followed; there is little that can be done to contaminate the scoring. Feedback does not require judgements to be made about individuals'

* The British Psychological Society has introduced certificates of competence as a means of providing additional safeguards.

personality and the results can be made available to and checked by candidates. The information generated is understandable and accessible and so the influence of subjective interpretation by the assessor can be limited and, if needs be, questioned.

Personality questionnaires

The increasing use of personality questionnaires in selection has been the subject of extensive debate over recent years. They are now freely available in computer form, which makes it easier for non-specialists to administer and score them. Thus, it is possible to carry out a measurement of personality and assess the fit of an individual's personality to the job and organisation. 'We know what sort of person we want' is a common opener when starting the recruitment process, but the problems and disagreements start when we try to define what is meant by personality, never mind how to measure it.

Cook (1988) identifies six different type of personality questionnaire:

- observational;
- situational;
- questionnaire/inventory;
- ratings and checklists;
- projective; and
- miscellaneous.

They usually comprise a series of questions with 'Either or' and 'Don't know' type responses. Candidates are asked to indicate the option which best fits their preferences. The scoring mechanisms usually contain safeguards to check the candidates' consistency of response and to indicate if the candidate has been guessing at the 'right' answer. Specialist skills and training are needed to interpret the scoring. Understanding how an individual's profile compares to norm tables requires a knowledge of both statistical methods and the psychological theories underpinning the particular instrument. The report for the selectors should indicate how the dimensions of the test relate to the person specification, and decisions about the provision of feedback are needed. If candidates are to be given the results, this process needs to be handled skilfully, carefully and sensitively. Real psychological damage has been caused by the bad provision of feedback to unsuccessful candidates.

Some questionnaires have been widely used, piloted and validated over a number of years and are generally regarded as being sound, comparatively free from bias and reliable. For example the 16PF is well known and, being founded on a reputable theory of personality, is generally regarded as being valid, providing it is used ethically and with care. The Myers-Briggs questionnaire has also been subjected to thorough scrutiny. However, there are others which have been developed with less rigour and their theoretical basis is possibly less sound.

One of the main issues concerning the use of personality questionnaires lies in the ways in which the results are interpreted and feedback given to candidates. The results tend to be in the form of tables, numbers, graphs and other seemingly scientific outputs, but the appearance of scientific measurement can seduce selectors into the creation of a preferred idealistic profile. Failure to fit this profile by a candidate may make it seem as though the candidate's personality has failed and that, as a person, they are not good enough. In reality, there is no right or wrong personality. We are all uniquely different, but the use of profiles and norms can mislead us into believing that there is an 'ideal' model that will match the job requirements perfectly.

References

Although the use of references alone has low predictive validity in the selection process, they do have a value, and this value is maximised if account is taken of their weaknesses:

- the referee's abilities to write references;
- the referee's abilities to assess candidates against the job requirements;
- the referee's relationship with the candidate;
- what is not said; and
- the assessor's abilities or tendency to read between the lines.

The strengths of references are:

- the opportunity to check the accuracy of some of the statements made on the application form; and
- the double check on the assessors' reading of the individual candidate.

A 1994 High Court judgment places a duty of care on past employers to provide the potential employer of an individual with an accurate, evidenced reference. If a candidate does not cite their current employer as a referee, this should sound a warning bell, and the reasons for the omission should be explored during the face-to-face interview. No offer of employment (even a verbal offer is a legally binding contract) should be made before references have been taken up in order to, at the very least, confirm some of the candidate's claims.

FACTORS INFLUENCING THE CHOICE OF SELECTION METHOD

The purpose of any selection method is to provide enough and adequate information in support of decision making to ensure that the right candidate is appointed. Therefore, the method must make a positive contribution to the utility of the recruitment and selection process. To do this the method should:

- increase the predictive validity of the whole process;
- be cost-effective;
- be practical;
- make sense to the selectors and candidates;
- be acceptable to the selectors, the manager and candidates;
- be acceptable and transparent to existing staff and key others;
- enable good quality feedback to be given to candidates;
- begin the induction;
- inform the development plan;
- contribute to the organisation's image as a reputable employer; and
- contribute to the personal development of the managers and others involved.

There is a very great danger of deciding to use a selection method because it is fashionable or because it will force candidates 'to show what they are made of'. Bad choice or application of a selection method can do untold damage. Not only can it increase the risk of appointing the wrong candidate, it can also reduce the chance of the right candidate applying for the right job in the future. An organisation's reputation as a good employer is fragile. In a fluctuating job market, damaging it by treating candidates poorly on one occasion, can cause lasting harm. However, careful consideration, choice and design of a selection method can do a great deal of good. It will improve the chance of a successful appointment and, at the same time, it will contribute to the image of the employer, internally and externally.

THE SELECTION DECISION MATRIX

The final selection decision, as with any decision, can only be made by the humans involved. Methods inform the decision-making process but they cannot apply judgement and they should not be allowed to make the decision.

The selection process, in its entirety, consists of a number of phases — each generating information. This information needs to be brought together in some way. Normally this happens in the cognitive processors of the selectors (ie their conscious and subconscious minds). Impressions are formed about candidates on the basis of:

- the factual information provided by the candidates both in their application and as a result of their behaviour;
- the evidence experienced by the selectors — what they have seen, heard or felt about the candidates; and
- the information given to assessors by others — eg other assessors, referees and observers.

The accumulation of these different pieces of information can be formalised via a matrix, and this focuses selectors' attention on the criteria to be matched and away from personal preferences and biases.

The matrix consists of two axes — the criteria from the person specification and the separate activities in the selection process. Cells can be marked to indicate that a particular selection activity is expected to explore a particular skill. A simple matrix is shown in Table 6.2. A hierarchy of desirability can be imposed on the criteria, or a weighting can be built into a rating scale.

Table 6.2　A selection process matrix

Criteria	Application form	Focused discussion	References	Case study	Final interview
Attainment					
Degree	X				X
Experience					
Supervisory	X		X		X
Research	X	X	X		X
Skills					
Communications	X	X		X	X
Decision making		X		X	X
Aptitudes					
Team working		X		X	X
Resourceful		X	X	X	X
Circumstances	X		X?		X

If needed, the rating system can build up the profile of a candidate's degree of fit against the criteria. This would accommodate any weighting and would result in each candidate being given an overall score. The danger of using numbers in this way is that there is a tendency for them to take over from judgement.

A more scientific decision-making technique is called utility or decision theory. Subjective expected utility allows the desirability of possible outcomes to be specified and weighted, while multi-attributed utility allows a number of factors to be combined to enable the 'best' decision to be computed. Both reduce the decision to mathematical calculations. These approaches are intended to aid the process and deal with uncertainty, but they have a limited value, especially when it is not clear what outcomes are likely to result from the different attributes of each possible; they also contain some dangers. They can become ends in themselves and there is a tendency to allow the technique to make the decision. This absolves humans from responsibility by removing human judgement and denies the importance of social fit.

Decision trees can also help to steer a course through a complex, lengthy process and to separate out aspects of performance that are more important than others. Such trees (see Figure 6.1) can provide a means of sifting candidates.

SUMMARY

When choosing a selection method, it is important to remember its underlying purpose. It is not an end in itself, but is intended to contribute to the entire recruitment and selection process. It should thus be designed to get the right person into the right job as quickly and efficiently as possible, and in a cost-effective manner. It should add value and contribute to the quality of the process. It should gather adequate information of the right quality about the candidates, while providing them with the information they need about the organisation, their potential colleagues and the job. Too much detail can mislead and side-track selectors. On the other hand, too little detail tempts selectors to fill gaps by guessing or attributing reasoning and motivation (usually wrongly). Quality information tells selectors what they need to know. There is little point in analysing the job and drawing up a person specification if candidates are assessed against different criteria. The favoured candidate may be highly skilled, but their appointment is only justifiable if those skills are the ones needed for effective performance in the job.

The selection method should not be over fancy, nor should it overshadow the real purpose — ie to aid the judgement of the selectors about the best candidate for the job and to help candidates decide if the job in question and the organisation match their requirements. Nor does the process end once it is decided to make an offer of employment; unsuccessful candidates should be provided with good quality feedback in return for their efforts. The next chapter explores the impact each phase of the recruitment and selection process can have on candidates.

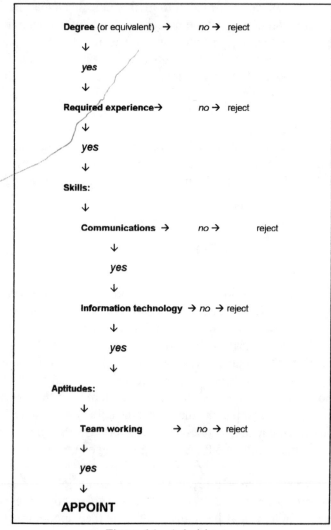

Figure 6.1   A decision tree

7

The Impact on the Candidates

Repeated reference has been made to the two-way nature of the recruitment and selection process. Both parties have needs and both have the means of satisfying the needs of the other. The employing organisation has a job to be done and is prepared to offer the best person certain rewards and benefits, while the employee has experience, skills and potential to offer in return for a wage, other appropriate rewards and a future. These concepts are well accepted, yet when the practices and methods of matching one to the other are discussed, rarely is consideration given to the impact they may have on the individuals involved.

Sometimes, design factors will include ways of reducing the load on the employing manager and provide mechanisms to ensure that legal responsibilities are covered. Managers are trained, prepared and briefed, and are supported by systems, forms and previous practice. But what about the applicant? Changes in work are known to be among the top 20 most stressful life events, but rarely do recruitment and selection procedures place the applicant centre stage. Some organisations deliberately do the opposite by loading on the stress to see if candidates can withstand pressure.

Obviously the needs of the employing organisation must be given high priority. These will centre on the need to offer employment to an individual well able to carry out the duties of the job to the standard required. The processes used to find and employ that person need to be effective, efficient and suitably economic of time and money. As far as the person appointed is concerned, the success of the recruitment and selection process is determined by a range of outcomes, some of which will be unique to the individual. Perhaps the most important for the individual is how much of their self-efficacy — ie their sense of self-worth, self-esteem and ability to achieve is retained after the recruitment and selection process has been completed. Usually the successful candidate is given positive feedback after the selection events and included quickly in the organisation, but it is not that common for consideration to be given to the consequences for the people who are not successful, even though, numerically, the unappointed and rejected individuals are greater than those appointed.

There are times when those rejected by the process need to be given special consideration. Those already in the employ of the organisation may feel that by not being successful they have blighted their chosen career path and future with their employer. The sense of rejection can have a long-term impact on their effectiveness in their current job and on their on-going commitment to the organisation.

This chapter looks at the recruitment and selection process from the point of view of the applicant, and explores the action an employing organisation can reasonably take to reduce any negative consequences. By careful forethought, it is possible that even rejection can provide some benefit for candidates not appointed. Action can also be taken to maximise the opportunity and build on the success of the person appointed.

- **For successful candidates**, following appointment negotiations take place about the explicit terms and conditions of contract. These discussions can be broadened to include implicit terms and development needs. Induction and inclusion phases can be integrated.
- **For unsuccessful candidates**, instead of a 'thank you but no thank you' letter or telephone call, a discussion might be held during which feedback can be offered. This conversation can change a rejection into a learning event that includes positive comments and practical guidance.
- **For the manager**, the process should be seen as the systematic making of an investment decision, during which structured assessments are made of the applicants' levels of ability, their suitability for employment and the potential for their development in the context of the job and employing organisation. The assessment also provides the manager with the opportunity of creating development plans. Recruitment and selection can facilitate the development of the manager's skills which can be translated into other human resource management functions, such as appraisal, performance management and reward allocation.
- **For others involved**, they are offered the chance to work with fellow organisation members in different ways. This can lead to increased understanding of the organisation's business, reduced parochialism and enhanced organisational teamwork. The others are also able to develop their skills of assessment and decision making.
- **For existing employees**, they are able to interact with possible new colleagues in a meaningful way and contribute to decision making. This degree of involvement will help the newly appointed employee to be accepted into the work group and facilitate appropriate participation.

This chapter, in preparation for exploring how to design a recruitment and selection process that has a positive impact on applicants and candidates, considers some of the less pleasant features of the process. Most often, unfortunately, people emerge from the process as losers, while the winners move on, letting the occasion slip into the memory of another everyday event at work. In the worst cases, the scars of being a loser can remain and influence career decisions for a long time. No one deliberately sets out to create a process that does damage, but the sort of examination that recruitment and selection entails makes participants vulnerable. Consequently, exploring the negative feature of the process is a salutary starting point.

NEGATIVE EFFECTS

On the candidates

Submitting an application for a job involves an individual in a series of judgements. The decision to apply for another job is driven by one of two factors, either singly or in combination. People either want a new job or want to get away from their existing one. Thus, the decision to submit an application requires the individual to consider:

- **Their future career and prospects with their current employer**. This means thinking through where their current job is likely to take them and what chance there will be of obtaining desired outcomes.
- **The prospects and opportunities in the new job**. The problem here is that the amount of information (often presented in glowing terms) is limited. Therefore, judgements have to be made based on a very partial and biased picture.
- **The likely impact on life outside work**. Frequently, changing employers will have a knock-on effect on an individual's social life. Many of us find that working relationships spill over. It is possible that such a change will also involve moving house. Thus family members and partners become involved. Dual career partnerships are known to suffer strain as one member's career goes in one direction and the other's in another.
- **The effect of telling colleagues, the boss, family and friends**. Telling people about an application can lead to them asking questions later on about its progress. While these are, no doubt, posed out of genuine

interest, they can add to the stress of waiting to hear about success or failure. If the latter is the outcome, there is the possibility of loss of face and embarrassment. Family members can become unsettled and anxious about the impact on their futures. Alternatively, they can become excited about the prospect of change only to be let down when planned outcomes do not materialise. Some organisations see applying for jobs outside the organisation as expressions of disloyalty, and letting the boss know about applications can have negative effects and blight career prospects. But then if no one knows, where does help with the application and critical feedback on its contents and presentation come from? Where does the support and encouragement come from during the days of doubt and uncertainty? And how can preparations be made for an interview without being able to talk to someone?

It seems, not surprisingly, that most people do not consider the possibility of failure when submitting an application. Yet, if the need for a job change is due to the unsatisfactory nature of the current post, it may be wise to consider other plans to deal with the situation. Pedler and Boydell (1985) give some helpful advice on how to make the most of the current job. For those out of paid employment, rejection letters can seem just that — not just telling the applicant about their unsuitability for the job, but about their general unsuitability for work. The determination needed to continue to submit applications is not easy to maintain, and this is where help and guidance can be invaluable. Some recruitment consultancies offer this moral support alongside practical assistance to job-seekers. The government's Job Clubs are also intended to provide the same service.

Personal disclosure

When individuals decide to apply for a job, they submit themselves to a process of examination and assessment. Applicants are expected to be honest and open with an organisation that may or may not consider employing them. They will be expected to disclose their:

- **Employment history**. Even now, despite high levels of recurrent unemployment, a period spent out of work is regarded as a negative by many employers. Salary details and reasons for leaving previous jobs are also expected.
- **Educational successes and failures**. There is no immediate chance to explain, for example, why a year at college had to be repeated.

Judgements are made on the basis of today's practices rather those current at the time.

- **Personal details**. These may not be relevant to the job and there may be no guarantee of confidentiality. Some organisations still ask for martial status and the numbers and ages of children. It is also common to ask for details of disability, medical history, ethnicity and recent criminal convictions.

Lack of confidentiality

In most cases the confidentiality of applicants is not respected at all. Frequently, application forms are widely circulated to all those with a 'legitimate' interest in the process. Some organisations photocopy applications and send them to all shortlisters, with no control over their availability to others or restrictions on their use. It can be argued that this is to ensure that the process is open and above board and that the 'appropriate' people are involved.

From the applicant's point of view, this lack of respect gives no consideration to the individual's future relationships in the organisation. There are no promises made about the retention of the material, its future use or the method of destruction. Most employers retain applications for a period for record-keeping purposes (and they are also required to do so in case there is a claim to a Tribunal). Some organisations refer back to applications received earlier for similar posts and will contact individuals on the basis of their previous applications rather than a current expression of interest. Not all organisations destroy their old records, and some dump waste paper rather than shred confidential documents.

The traditional recruitment and selection practices found in the United Kingdom put the applicant in a weaker position than that of the employer. European practices reported by Iles and Robertson (1989) seem to have more concern for the vulnerability of the individual. This includes the rights of applicants and the use made of information they supply.

Unequal amounts of information

Employing organisations frequently sell themselves to potential applicants, painting a very positive picture of their current situation and future. Implicit, if not direct suggestions are made to applicants about career prospects and opportunities for growth. Organisations check the applicants' details, reputation and track record by using references with previous employers and others with relevant knowledge of the individuals. Applicants have few opportunities to test out the truth of the organisation's information without affecting their chances of success. Making contact with existing employees, unless they are known personally to the applicant, is not the 'done thing'.

The employing organisation also considers very carefully what information is to be sent to applicants. Information, which may prove sensitive or could give a competitive advantage to others tends not to be readily available, even though this may be the very material applicants need to help them decide whether they wish to apply and prepare their submission.

Domestic considerations

If the individual is applying for a job in another part of the country, decisions about lifestyle and non-work relationships need to be considered. Of course, personal decisions of this nature are outside the control of an employing organisation and may seem to be none of the employer's business. Yet they do have an effect. It is not uncommon for a successful applicant to turn down a job because their partner does not wish to move or cannot find work. Perhaps a worse scenario occurs when the appointee and family move home, only to find they cannot settle in the new area. Problems of commuting, the difficulties of selling the previous home and the problems of relocating can disrupt the new employee's first critical months.

Some organisations provide help with house moving. This varies from the repayment of costs, the provision of temporary accommodation and increasingly extensive aid packages. Even though these tend to be confined to executive, senior or other key posts, it is worth paying attention to the difficulties facing staff at other levels. Perhaps, when an employer is recruiting nationally, information about the locality, housing, its amenities and other job opportunities could be made available. This comparatively low-cost service can assist newly appointed employees settle into their new job more quickly by helping to alleviate some of the other sources of stress inherent in job change.

Uncertainty

Once an application has been submitted, the applicant enters a period of uncertainty. Research suggests that most applicants, currently in work, seek another post because they are dissatisfied in some way with their existing job rather than because they want the prospective job and employer. The submission of an application for another post can add to the disenchantment because the applicant sees the opportunity to leave coming closer and mentally prepares to go. This may lead individuals to take some actions that they would not otherwise have contemplated.

Susie Hunt was dissatisfied with the working relationship with her boss. The boss tolerated the other workers sitting with their feet up, chatting all day, while the work got further and further behind, and this was allowed to go on until the customers started to complain. Then everyone got told off and was expected to work overtime. This happened so often that Susie could not wait to get out. She had been watching the situations vacant columns for months and, at long last, a job appeared that matched her experience and skills. The application form was sent in and Susie was convinced that she stood a really good chance.

As the backlog mounted again Susie's anticipation of getting out increased. When the boss announced that overtime would be required, knowing that she was soon to leave, Susie could not resist the impulse of telling the boss what he could do with his overtime. The next day the letter of rejection arrived....

Recruitment consultants are able to approach individuals who are not necessarily discontented with their jobs, but for whom the invitation to apply for another post is flattering and inevitably contains prospects of enhancement and improvement. It also contains shades of the 'grass being greener'. If the individual agrees to consider the job, their current position is likely to be given closer scrutiny than is normal, and this examination may reveal features of the job that are satisfying and tempt the individual to stay. However, it may also reveal features that, once explored, become the source of dissatisfaction. If they had not been scrutinised they may have continued not to matter that much.

Lasting effects

The recruitment and selection process can have a long-lasting effect on applicants, especially those who are not successful. Some of the selection methods described in Chapter 6 can be invasive, and an individual's personal life, aspirations and aspects of their personality can be subjected to examination in ways that exceed those needed to assess an individual's abilities to perform the job.

Robin applied for a supervisor's job at the local factory. He had worked steadily since leaving school and had recently completed the relevant BTEC course successfully. He felt ready and qualified to take charge of a section of his own.

The job he applied for was with a large multinational organisation, although his previous employers had all been small companies. Even so, he was confident that his experience equipped him to work effectively and gain the respect he would need as the supervisor of a multi-trade work group. He was pleased to be called for an interview, expecting to meet perhaps one or two managers and someone from the personnel department. He was not prepared for what awaited him.

First, he was asked to complete a test to see if he was a suitable sort of person to be a supervisor. He was then asked to take part in a group task with other candidates. The task was a sort of game to see who could 'earn the most money'. This was not a pleasant experience. One of the other candidates was extremely aggressive and nasty to all the others. The people from the company just sat and watched as this person was rude to everyone. When the candidates had a private coffee break afterwards, they all agreed that the group task should have been stopped.

Each candidate was then interviewed by one of the managers. Robin came out feeling as though he had been grilled. He had been asked all sorts of questions about his personal life — what did he read, how did he spend his spare time, his aspirations for the rest of his life, and so on. He had been asked to prove that he was up to the job in a way that made him doubt his existing levels of proficiency and wonder if it was worth all the bother.

When he left the factory, he was not sure why he had exposed himself to such an experience and decided that he didn't want to be a supervisor after all. The company wrote offering him feedback, but he burnt the letter, not wanting to make himself vulnerable to them again.

The boxed example shows how selection activities can put candidates 'through the hoop' regardless of whether hoop-jumping is a requirement of the job. Another common example is the loading of selection events with stress to see if the candidates are 'up to it'. The whole recruitment and selection process is stressful enough, without adding any extra pressure — unless of course the job really does require high levels of resilience (in which case, perhaps the job should be redesigned anyway).

Sense of rejection

Herriot (1989a) states that, 'all too often rejection results in a loss of self-esteem. While one or two rejections can be attributed to the stupidity or poor selection procedures of organisations, more result in self-attribution for failure: I must be useless if everyone thinks so.' As well as feeling rejected just as workers, applicants can also feel rejected as people. If the application carried dreams and aspirations, the sense of rejection can damage self-esteem and lead to a reluctance to submit applications in future.

Post hoc rationalisation is another way in which rejection can be expressed. Individuals seek other reasons to explain why they have not been successful. This search may lead them to conclude that they have been treated unfairly or less equally than other applicants. Sometimes this is true and, in these circumstances, it is possible to seek redress from an Industrial Tribunal. But distinguishing between genuine grievance and disappointment can sometimes be difficult.

Discrimination

There is ample evidence to suggest that women and others from minority groups are still disadvantaged during the recruitment and selection process. Much research and investigation has been conducted in the USA into the equity of procedures, partly in response to their equal opportunities legislation and partly due to resulting litigation. During the 1970s and 1980s substantial action was taken to redress imbalances and ensure that minority groups were treated fairly, and some of these measures were intended to make sure that selection techniques related to job-relevant criteria. In this country, despite the Sex Discrimination Act 1975, the Race Relations Act 1976 and subsequent legislation, indirect (and some times direct) discrimination is still evident; 'An office supervisor with man management experience' is still seen in newspaper advertisements.

Statistical evidence

Statistics, proving the extent of imbalance and unequal treatment are published unrelentingly. The reality and depth of discrimination means that, sadly, even organisations actively pursuing equality of opportunity policies find it difficult to convince people from under-represented groups of the genuineness of their intent and their real wish to receive applications. Most explorations into the reasons for the low levels of application find ample evidence of perceived barriers. The 'Glass Ceiling' is perhaps the best known and most widely reported.

There is other evidence to demonstrate that the recruitment and selection process itself is disadvantageous to members of minority groups. Most of the reported research in British personnel and management texts focuses on the discrimination experienced by women, but this should not be taken to imply that people from black or other ethnic minorities are not disadvantaged in similar ways. Likewise, people with disabilities have little reason to be convinced that most employers really do want to provide them with the same work opportunities as their able-bodied counterparts. However, because women constitute over half the workforce, the impact of their unequal treatment has proportionately greater effect on both employers and individuals, and so will be considered in some detail.

Domestic responsibilities

There is significant evidence that women, in addition to work responsibilities shared with their male counterparts, have substantially heavier domestic responsibilities. Nicolson and West (1988) say that 'what every working woman needs is a wife'. They use the figures (see Table 7.1) to show the differences in home life between men and women in managerial jobs. Even though these figures are over 10 years old, the numbers of women in management and sociological patterns have not altered sufficiently to suggest that the figures are no longer valid.

Table 7.1   Married managers with and without children

	Females (%)	*Males (%)*
No children	48	11
One or more children	52	89

In addition, the number of men whose partners are at home or have part-time paid employment is considerably greater than women in similar posts. Marshall (1994) reports that she found, as part of her investigations into why women leave senior posts, that 'a linked theme was tiredness and wanting a rest'. One consequence is that women simply have less time and energy to devote to submitting applications. Women tend also to have less freedom of choice. They not only have care responsibilities for their own immediate family, but they also find themselves with commitments to their extended family (their own parents and those of their partner) and limitations imposed by their partner's career and job prospects. On these grounds alone, it is not surprising that less women than men submit applications, particularly for senior posts.

The 'Glass Ceiling'*

Another reason for the low level of applications is proposed by Alimo-Metcalfe (1994). She claims that 'Large British organisations now realise how much they need to attract and retain women, but I fear that without a serious and critical examination of their selection and assessment procedures little will change with respect to women's representation in either non-traditional female occupations or senior management positions.' She suggests that the criteria, the techniques and instruments, and the assessors used in the process all contain in-built bias that favour the status quo — ie dominance by men. Drawing from research evidence such as that conducted by Schein and Mueller (1990), Broverman et al (1975) and others, coupled with empirical data, Alimo-Metcalfe demonstrates that the underpinning assumptions about male and female behaviours are translated into the construction of selection activities, rating scales and profiles of effective behaviours. Women know that they are likely to be exposed to situations in which they will immediately find themselves disadvantaged, made to feel uncomfortable and have their failings and weakness paraded,

* This phrase was coined to describe the real, but invisible, barrier that prevents female managers reaching the top management levels.

and where the chances of obtaining a successful outcome are known to be slim. For even if the numerical odds are calculated, women understand that they face greater chances of failing because of the existence of barriers like the 'Glass Ceiling'. The odds are stacked against them.

Fear of failure

Very few people willingly go into situations where the chance of failure greatly outweighs the chance of success. Moreover, Deaux (1976) found that men tend to credit their own abilities for successes and blame external factors for their failures (see the 'Sense of rejection' section above), whereas women tend to do the reverse. This suggests that men will find fault in the process whereas women find fault with themselves. If this is so, the failure to be appointed or even shortlisted can have a greater negative impact on women than men.

Deaux (1976) also found that women are disinclined to 'sell' themselves. They credit past successes to the efforts of other people and engage in other self-deprecating activities. The researcher also identified that women will avoid the chance of success just as much as failure if they believe the outcome is likely to have a negative effect on them. A study conducted by Dale (1992) gave grounds for believing that success to women is not necessarily positive. The participants in the study expressed greater concern than comparable men about the undesirable outcomes success could have on the rest of their lives.

The fear of success also draws on a lack of faith in one's own skills and abilities. Men, it has been found, approach a new job believing they will be fully competent from day one. Women, on the other hand, believe that they will have to undergo a rapid learning curve. They tend not to apply for a job unless they are confident that they will be able to do all of it effectively. Women are more likely to recognise that they will need to learn and so apply knowing that there will be gaps between their current level of performance and that desired.

Double discrimination

People from ethnic minority groups are known to suffer discrimination at all stages of their education and employment. Statistics demonstrate their proportionately low level of participation in the labour market — and women especially so. This means that they do not get the chances to gain experience or participate in subsequent training and retraining. One reason for their difficulty in competing fairly for jobs is the discrimination and lack of resources experienced during schooling. This is changing but, according to a Department of Employment (1994) report, there is still a problem: 'The difference cannot be explained by different levels of qualifications or the increase in younger people among these groups. Even when qualifications held and age are taken into account, people from ethnic minorities are, according to the International Labour Organisation, more likely to be unemployed than white people.' This denial of opportunities is detrimental to employing organisations just as much as it is to the individuals who experience such disadvantage and discrimination.

On the organisation

Increasingly, management gurus, such as Charles Handy, are pointing to a future for organisations that will rely on the expertise of 'knowledge workers'. This expertise will not be based on technical knowledge acquired during initial education and training: rather, organisations will depend on their staff's abilities to learn and find solutions to new problems. Survival in a rapidly transforming and competitive world will require flexibility and the combination of different perspectives. The organisational model of the 'I'm in charge' manager will not suffice. Consequently, if this view of the future is realistic (and evidence suggests it is rapidly approaching as labour markets shift and working patterns alter), organisations will need to find ways of recruiting, selecting and retaining staff with different profiles. To succeed, stereotypes will need to be challenged, assumptions questioned and previously held beliefs contradicted. The use of job descriptions and person specifications, as described earlier, will be helpful but will not, in itself, ensure that the best candidate is attracted and engaged. Unless employing organisations fully appreciate the consequences of losing the best candidate, current practices will not be changed. Other traps also await the unwary selector. Some of the negative effects of poor recruitment and selection on employing organisations are discussed in the following sections.

Loss of talent

The dangers of recruiting more staff in the image of previously successful post occupants have been reported many times — initially by Belbin (1981). Cloning and replicating past patterns of behaviour ultimately leads to stagnation and failure to adapt. To preserve the status quo, an employing organisation finds itself selecting and deselecting applicants according to criteria other than those required for the effective performance of the job: the criteria focus more on 'fit' within existing groups and cultural norms rather than the skills, knowledge and expertise required for the job. In effect, the organisation discriminates either directly or indirectly against those who do not fit the traditional model.

Discrimination can have two effects on an organisation. The first, put simply, is prosecution. Direct discrimination on the grounds of gender, marital status or race has been illegal for 20 years, and an individual does not need to be employed by an organisation to have the right to complain to an Industrial Tribunal. The cost of defending a case and the associated damage to reputation can have serious effects on an organisation's well-being. The discrimination does not need to be institutionalised, and even employer organisations with well-developed equal opportunities policies and procedures are not free from risk. The failure of managers to follow laid down rules is no excuse and, if the case is proven, the organisation becomes culpable on two counts. First, it will have been found guilty of discrimination and, secondly, it will have failed to exercise proper control over its representatives' actions.

The risk of losing the best candidate is another negative outcome. Organisations need diversity. A team with exactly the same profile, same experiences and views is limited. Its horizons are constrained and it is unlikely to have the width of perspective needed to be able to respond rapidly to changing conditions. On the other hand, a team made up of individuals with different, complementary skills, knowledge and experience is able to view problems and new situations from a number of different perspectives, and can meld and synthesise new approaches by drawing on the broad range of its own resources. A manager, responsible for equipping the workforce for its future survival, needs to question the skills, knowledge and experience required for the job and the well-being of the team in the organisation, rather than relying on history.

Making the wrong appointment

Another consequence of using rules of thumbs, stereotypes and history is the appointment of the wrong person. This may be someone underqualified or overqualified for the needs of the job. It may be that the person is too different to fit or that they are not able to adapt to the organisation's culture. (We will discuss later how to deal with this situation.) Making the wrong appointment is damaging for the individual just as much as it is for the organisation.

The kinds of organisational damage resulting from a wrong appointment can vary from the predictable — failure to perform to the standards required — to the more subtle forms of damage such as that caused by the boredom of staff too well qualified for the posts they are occupying. Dealing with the individual who does not achieve the required standard or the desired outcomes can be straightforward. The criteria used for selection can be applied to monitor subsequent performance and used as evidence of lack of capability. However, the person who made the decision to appoint the individual needs evidence to support their initial judgement, for, even though it is known that selection methods are not necessarily perfect predictors and other factors influence performance, a manager can suffer considerable loss of face as a result of a poor appointment.

Over-recruitment (ie employing staff too well qualified or too experienced for the job) can in some ways be worse than appointing ill-equipped staff. In the latter case, the staff can be trained and provided with the necessary learning experiences, but overqualified staff cannot unlearn or forget their experience.

The town's largest employer, a mail order company, decided to relocate its head office. The consequences on employment took some time to make an impact. Most of the jobs lost were clerical, part time and low paid. The professional and specialist computer staff moved with the company. In the main, the other employers in the town were staffed by semi-skilled manual workers, engineering staff and service workers.

The mail order company had recruited school leavers and returners, trained them and then lost the more able to the other employers. After the relocation the schools and colleges advised their students to stay in education rather than seek employment. Consequently, it was two years before the company's move made an impact. Other employers began to find that their traditional pool of office and clerical juniors had dried up. Instead, to their initial delight, they found the applicants for their vacancies were more mature, better educated and capable of thinking for themselves. Two or three years later, delight changed to despair as their recruits found that the chances of career progression were limited and the jobs they were doing routine and unchallenging. Their abilities

> to question and look for stimulation had turned from being an attraction to being a nuisance.
>
> The town's doctors, solicitors, architects, estate agents, dentists and insurance brokers debated in the pubs and clubs what had happened to their willing juniors. They all found that they had a generation of rebellious, unsettled and dissatisfied office staff that they did not understand and did not know how to manage.

Some reference has already been made to the problems of recruiting staff similar to the existing profile. The results of this can take some time to become apparent. Initially, the employment of a person who seems to be a 'good fit' may seem a good appointment but, if the purpose of the job is to develop new approaches and move the organisation into different ways of working (and this is the purpose of many management appointments), employing a person with a background and profile that conforms to the status quo can lead eventually to decay. They may bring about some changes but the chances are that these will be more of the same. Inevitably we are all limited by our experience and learning, and if an employing organisation seeks radical changes, it needs to consider bringing in people whose experiences and views represent something new. This may be uncomfortable, but change and decay each bring their own sort of pain.

Being rejected

Offering a job to an individual, only for that person to reject the appointment, can cause quite a different set of problems. There are several possible reactions:

- **Consider the second runner**. This is rarely satisfactory. There will have been reasons why this person was not offered the job in the first place. These may not seem as important when revisited under different circumstances, but the areas of mismatch between the individual and the job requirements will not go away. In addition, the person will know that they were second choice and this is bound to have some impact on the way in which they see the job, the organisation and their own abilities in relation to both.
- **Re-examine the applications from people not shortlisted**. The same reservations apply. If the applicants had matched the person

specification (and providing the shortlisting had been rigorous) they would have been identified previously. Additionally, the people will have realised after the inevitable passage of time that they have not been successful in their application. They will have moved on — mentally and possibly physically. They may be flattered to be called in for the 'second round', but they may feel insulted.

• **Re-advertise the post**. While this option has some merit, it does tell the rest of the world that the first recruitment and selection process was not successful. It also takes nearly as long again. The delay may save salary costs, but what about the work not being done? Re-advertising can result in the post being vacant for six months or more.

In some organisations it is not uncommon for jobs to be covered by other staff. 'Acting up' schemes, temporary appointments and dividing the work between other staff are all common examples of cover arrangements. In the short term this may seem a good solution but, as time passes, problems can occur. The staff providing the cover may want to develop new approaches and try out ideas; but they may feel constrained, waiting for the new person to come. They can feel slighted and passed over and other staff can find it difficult to settle down, especially if the post vacant is that of the boss. The atmosphere of uncertainty will remain in the background.

The sense of rejection can affect everyone concerned — not just those involved in the selection process. The events are usually surrounded by interest and speculation on the part of the staff. There is a buzz of expectancy pending the announcement of who has been offered the job. To hear a few days later that the person has turned it down can be a big let down.

It will be necessary to explore why the applicant's initial interest in the job has changed. The usual reaction when this happens is to focus immediately on what the organisation has done to the individual to 'turn them off'. Did they not like what they saw or heard? Was the money not enough? (This is often seen as being the reason.) Was the job not what they were expecting? The rewards and challenges may have been too much or not enough for the individual to justify the upheaval of moving jobs.

While these are valid questions from the organisation's point of view, the real reasons may be intrinsic to the individual rather than the potential employer. Some individuals use the experience of going through a selection process as a way of exploring their current situation. This comparison can turn what seemed a problematic job into one that contains hidden benefits. Sometimes the current employer does not want to lose that individual and takes action to retain them. Moreover, domestic considerations, as discussed earlier, have to be given more attention as the possibility of being offered the job increases.

Finding out why some one turns down a job offer can be difficult. When staff know each other across organisations, getting one individual to articulate why they do not want to accept the offer of employment can be asking them to disclose confidences and express views they would prefer to keep to themselves. Enquiries are therefore likely to lead to anodyne responses.

Failing to appoint

Failing to appoint at the end of a selection process can be equally difficult for an employing organisation to manage as the rejection situation. After going through a lengthy and rigorous process, not being able to find a candidate of the calibre required to fit the job and the organisation can be embarrassing. More fundamentally, it leads to questions being asked about the search and selection criteria and processes. It would not be unusual for critics of the managers to say, 'They can't find what they want because they do not know'. If the steps suggested throughout this book had been followed, it should not be possible to make such an accusation. However, sometimes, no matter how careful the recruitment and selection processes have been, the candidates do not match the specification.

In these circumstances, it is possible to consider each of the candidates against the job requirements and person specification and ask the following questions:

- What are the gaps between the ideal candidate and the individual? (The answers should be expressed in terms of attainment, experiences, abilities and aptitudes.)
- Can these be filled by the individual in other ways? (Can the individual develop the missing criteria through training or a programme of development?)
- Can other people fill the gaps? (Was the job definition for a super-human? If so, is it possible to separate out parts to be filled by other people?)
- Do the criteria matter? (Can they be done without?)

Answering these questions, even though they may be hard, is comparatively straightforward. The more complex situation arises when it is believed that candidates will not fit the organisation. This occurs, for example, when the level of operation required is different from that offered by the candidates.

The post of catering manager required more than a good unit manager and cook. The restaurant needed to move into new markets because its current niche was far too cut-throat. The two fast food outlets in the town were beginning to move up market. They had both had recent refits that enabled them to retain their existing customers and attract new ones. Their volume allowed them to undercut prices and their ability to segment their markets into time slots meant that they could satisfy different types of clientele without then competing for space.

The applicants for the post were all extremely well qualified and, because of the nature of the industry, had a lot of experience of different types of outlets. However, none of them had the qualities the restaurant owners were seeking. They were looking for someone who could take on the competition — not on their own ground, but by offering a totally different type of eating experience. All the candidates, the owners felt, would have provided the town's restaurant goers with more of the same rather than the something different they would be prepared to pay just that little bit more for.

An example of such a mismatch would be when the value systems of all the candidates are quite different from the culture and values of the employing organisation. Effective leadership, for the sake of argument, can be defined by an organisation as the set of skills that result in staff being empowered to take responsibility for their own work, act on their own initiative and function effectively without close supervision. Some very capable managers would not agree with this view. They could argue that staff need precise instructions, regular follow-up, monitoring of performance and detailed feedback on where they need to improve. Both opinions may be equally valid but it is unlikely that they would be compatible. If the employing organisation subscribes to the first set of values and all the candidates for a key post to the second, the decision not to appoint would be understandable. In these circumstances, even though time is lost and more money spent, it would be better to start the recruitment process again rather than risk making a poor appointment.

HOW TO MAKE SOME IMPROVEMENTS

The chances of having a negative impact on the individual and the organisation can be significantly reduced by following the simple procedures outlined throughout this book. Nevertheless, recruitment and selection is a complex process, made up of several sub-processes that have to be put into operation by different people. They interact, have their own views on how procedures should be implemented, interpret rules and systems differently and, most importantly, form opinions about other people at all stages. Consequently action, over and above laying down a procedure and a set of rules, needs to be taken.

Responsibility

Who is responsible for the recruitment and selection process? At first this seems to be a simple question but, depending on the nature of the employing organisation, there may be several possibilities. For example:

- **The personnel department** will be responsible for the procedure and rules, and will endeavour to establish good practice. In some organisations, the personnel function carries out various tasks on behalf of the employing manager. However, unless it is clear who is doing what and why, there is plenty of scope for mistakes, blame and argument. In some organisations the personnel department will make selection decisions on behalf of managers. For example, with graduate trainee schemes, it is common for new starters to be appointed by a specific individual with responsibilities for recruiting and placing staff. However, care must be taken to ensure that this does not happen in isolation from the core business and the managers who will be ultimately responsible for the staff employed. Nevertheless there are legal reasons why the personnel department should issue the written statement of terms and conditions regarding the contract of employment.
- **The manager** to whom the postholder will report should be the person who is responsible for the appointment. After all, the success or failure of managers depends on the performance of the staff who work directly for them. In some organisations, the bureaucracy attempts to take away this responsibility. For example, in organisations that have trainee or job rotation schemes, staff are appointed centrally and then allocated to managers who are not involved in their selection. This situation can

provide managers with excuses if the appointee's subsequent performance is not satisfactory. One way of dealing with this is to find appropriate ways of involving managers, or at least their accepted representatives.

- **The employer's representative or agent**. Some organisations vest the authority to make appointment decisions in the hands of a limited number of individuals. There are convincing grounds for doing this, particularly if line managers are inexperienced in selection and employment matters. The binding nature of verbal offers of employment and contractual implications are explained more fully in Chapter 8. However, some managers may find it difficult to accept that they do not have the power to appoint their own staff.

Explanation and training is the way to eventually enable decision making to be delegated to those who will be responsible for the postholder's on-the-job performance. Until this state is reached, the limits and location of responsibilities should be clearly defined so that there is no scope for duplication, disagreement or avoidance.

Operation of the selection process

The way in which candidates experience selection events will have a major impact on them. It will affect the way in which they view themselves, their abilities in relation to the job and their aspirations and opinions in relation to the employing organisation. This latter point is important to organisations because candidates are likely to tell other people about their experiences after the event. If they report they have been well treated and feel as though they have been given a fair chance to demonstrate their abilities, the reputation of the organisation as an employer will be enhanced. Alternatively, if they are able to tell colleagues and peers how badly they have been treated, the organisation will suffer some damage to its reputation. These memories and perceptions are influenced by a range of factors outlined in the following sections.

Choice of method

The choice of selection methods to be used should be driven by need. How this can be done was described in Chapter 6, and reference was also made to the different forms of validity a selection activity should possess. Of these, content, construct, criterion and reliability validity are mainly of interest to the employing organisation. From the point of view of the individual being asked to take part in these activities, while these are important, the candidates will be more concerned about how the activity directly affects them. Face validity requires a method or activity to be acceptable to the candidate: ie is the method realistic and appropriate for the job in question? Impact validity is defined by Robertson and Smith (1988) as 'the extent to which a measuring instrument has an effect on a subject's psychological characteristics'. In addition, there are other aspects that affect the choice of method from the perspective of the participant.

Relevance

The selection method should be relevant to the job in question. The context of the organisation should be reflected and its core values incorporated into any activity. Sometimes, linkage between test content and the job can be difficult to demonstrate when 'off the shelf' activities are being used. However, their choice should be influenced by this need. The level and degree of difficulty should reflect the level of the job.

A branch manager employed by a finance company had been asked, as part of her selection process, to complete an exercise concerning share capital transactions. Even though she had not done very well in this particular mode of assessment, she had been appointed. She spent the next three years waiting, with some dread, for a customer to appear with a portfolio of shares.

Eventually, she plucked up courage to ask her regional manager why she had not been asked to sell or buy a share portfolio. The reply 'We don't trade in shares' both surprised and angered her.

Privacy

Candidates should not feel as though their privacy has been invaded. Some have been asked inappropriate questions or asked to reveal information concerning their personal lives that has nothing to do with their suitability for the job or employment, such as details about their domestic arrangements. Requiring individuals to participate in activities without giving them the power to refuse can also be invasive. Some activities, in themselves, take candidates into areas they would prefer not to go. For example, the use of Biodata may return an individual to an unhappy childhood.

Understandable technology

The selection method chosen should make use of technology that is understandable and challengeable — ie candidates should be told what they are using and why. 'Black boxes' can intimidate. It should be possible for a person of reasonable intelligence and the experience required for the particular post to make sense of the selection method, how it works and how it will be applied to him or her. The advances in computer-based tests and activities put this at risk because we tend to give undue power and authority to processes we do not understand.

Fairness and equity

Candidates should feel they have been treated fairly and with equity, and should not feel they have been subjected to any direct or indirect discrimination. Alimo-Metcalfe (1994) has expressed concern about the choice of activities that favour predominately male traits. She states:

> Assessment centre exercises reflect the commonly held 'espoused' views of managerial activity, portraying leadership more in terms of directing, controlling, decision making and informing, rather than Kotter's findings that some of the key characteristics (of successful managers) relate to interpersonal skills of creating co-operative networks, walking-the-patch, and seeking information rather than telling.

Other types of selection method can also indirectly favour tradition rather than reflecting accurately the needs of the job. Compare the following designs for the post of office manager:

1. An assessment centre comprising a group task in which participants were asked to compete for scarce resources, a mathematically based pen and paper exercise, a one-to-one interview asking for an explanation of a failure to meet targets and a battery of cognitive ability tests exploring mechanical and spatial abilities.
2. A series of work samples consisting of an in tray exercise, a one-to-one discussion about the approaches taken to the in tray, a written report

regarding the resolution of a staffing problem, the presentation to a group of 'staff' of a plan to cost and implement a computer software replacement programme, and a peer group meeting to discuss the problems of setting and maintaining performance standards.

Similarly, a series of activities involving a degree of knowledge that could only be gained by direct work experience in the particular organisation would appear to favour internal and disadvantage external candidates. These forms of built-in bias can be reduced by ensuring the job description and person specification have been drawn up from an analysis of the job, and the whole recruitment and selection process designed to find those people who match those requirements.

Conduct, preparation and operation of selection events

Conduct of staff

Usually, the people involved in the operation of a selection event are from the personnel department or are the support staff of the manager in charge of the appointment. Regardless, they should know what they are doing and appear to the candidates as competent and confident. The way in which the candidates are treated by these staff can have a major impact and can form a lasting impression. For example, if the staff are disorganised and surly, stand in corners chatting and giggling while candidates struggle to concentrate, and are unable to supply information or answer even the simplest of questions, not only is the validity of the selection activity brought into question, the professionalism of the organisation as an employer comes under scrutiny. If, on the other hand, the staff are well prepared and conduct themselves in a friendly, open and helpful manner, candidates will feel as though they have been professionally treated. This gives credibility to the process and helps to ensure that candidates go away feeling as though they have had a fair chance to display their abilities and their suitability for the post.

Paperwork

Likewise, the paperwork and organisation of the whole event should reflect thorough preparation and good administration. Candidates are not likely to have faith in the process if the paperwork contains inaccuracies, is poorly presented or is out of date. Rooms that are not ready, unclean and inadequately heated, lit or equipped are not going to stimulate peak performance.

Timetables

One of the worst failures often encountered is the inability to stick to the published timetable. Frequently, candidates are kept waiting as time is allowed to slip. Obviously rigid compliance is not possible nor desirable, but it is possible to prepare the timetable to take account of predictable slippage and build in time for contingencies which allows for some small over-runs. Candidates should always be kept informed about what is going on. Keeping them waiting and in the dark shows a lack of respect as well as a lack of organisation, planning and courtesy.

Power to refuse

Candidates should *feel* as though they are able to refuse to participate in a selection activity. Emphasis is given here because, in practice, candidates are usually compliant. If they refuse to carry out a task or an activity they will believe it is likely to reflect badly on them and will be taken to mean that they do not like carrying out instructions or are troublemakers. Even though it may remove a mode of assessment, candidates should be asked to agree to participate.

At the very least, candidates should be told as part of the invitation to attend that they will be asked to carry out some form of selection exercise but, overall, how much prior information should be given is debatable. Herriot (1989a) argues that selection should be seen as a process consisting of a series of on-going steps, and the commitment of candidates to proceed should be obtained at each stage. The reason behind this is the creation of a positive working relationship in which both parties trust the other. To achieve this, information needs to be exchanged as described in Chapter 4.

If candidates have been told that they are to be asked to participate in selection activities, there is the chance for them to discuss their personal circumstances privately beforehand. If they were then to decline, their decision would probably not be taken as an unwillingness to accommodate the organisation's procedures. However, if they are faced with a *fait accompli* on the day, they will have little information on which to base their response and little choice.

The assessors

Even though the textbooks say that assessors need to be carefully selected, trained and competent, in reality the choice of who is to be involved is often governed by other factors. The constraints, norms and priorities, not to mention the politics of the situation, often determine who is to participate. Normally, the manager to whom the postholder is to report should be responsible for the appointment and the decisions surrounding the selection procedure. Even in a matrix management system, the functional and project managers should be the people to make the joint decision, marrying their separate and shared concerns and priorities.

In addition, other people both from within and without the employing organisation can make valid contributions. They are able to examine the candidates against the predetermined criteria, but from different perspectives. The selection of these people should also be made against explicit criteria. For example:

- Who needs to be involved? (eg those with whom the postholder will need to work with closely.)
- Who can make a valuable contribution (eg those individuals able to offer specialist input such as representatives of professional bodies.)
- Who ought to be involved? (eg those upon whom the success of the appointment depends or whose status demand their involvement.)
- Who has to be involved? (eg those who need to give permission or authority for the appointment.)

Even if the inclusion of a certain individual is required rather than wanted, the reasons for their involvement should be known and explicit. If that individual is included for reasons of expediency, it is important that everyone knows their role, understands the criteria and is prepared to work within the agreed processes. There is little room for virtuosity and improvisation in recruitment and selection. Variation and deviation, once the process has started, can lead to unfair treatment of candidates and decisions being made on questionable grounds.

The assessors, once chosen, should be trained to apply the criteria and processes in accordance with the organisation's practice. It is not uncommon to face resistance to such training. Often managers and other staff, especially those with previous experience of recruiting and selecting staff, fail to appreciate why they should be systematically trained.

> Sara had been selecting staff for her employers since she didn't know when. She took pride in the fact that she had developed her questioning technique and the vast majority of the staff

she had appointed had proved to be good choices. Less experienced managers frequently asked for her guidance and help, and she was the personnel department's first choice as an assessor when special appointments were being made. Sadly, a reorganisation forced Sara to choose between relocation or redundancy. Due to family commitments, she chose the latter. With great relief, she quickly found another comparable job with a major employer in a neighbouring town.

Sara had been in the post for six months before she needed to appoint a new team member. She was shocked when she was told that she could not do so until she had been through the new employer's recruitment and selection skills workshop. Sara was understandably irritated but decided that it was too soon into her employment to rock the boat.

The next available course would be in four weeks time. Sara arrived at the workshop miffed and prepared to have her time wasted. She was pleasantly surprised at the professionalism and the quality of the trainer and so sat back comfortably to have her views and current practices confirmed. However, the first session contained some unpleasant surprises. The trainer outlined the results of research and findings of some Industrial Tribunals, and it was with some horror that Sara discovered that her previous company's practices, such as one-to-one interviews, obtaining character references via the telephone and not making or keeping notes, would have made her (personally) culpable if an individual applicant had felt aggrieved enough to lodge a complaint with a Tribunal. She had never heard of a person specification and, after some explanation and practice, found their use obvious. When the workshop ended, Sara left a changed and sobered person. She readily admitted that she had learnt a lot about appointing staff and saw the value of her new organisation's different approaches.

This need for training can pose an organisation wishing to use best practice some problems. How does one tell senior managers that they lack basic observational and interviewing skills? Apart from grasping the nettle and telling them, or finding excuses to exclude them, other ways to manage the incompetent but important person's involvement need to be found. The impact incompetent selection practices can have on candidates, their subsequent performance and the reputation of the employing organisation may be far more damaging than denting a senior manager's ego. Tactics, such as involving other managers to demonstrate ways of improving practices or using more systematic processes that limit the involvement of any one individual, can be helpful devices.

Making sure that even competent managers behave themselves during selection events can also be taxing — but bad behaviour does need to be tackled. It is not unknown for managers to giggle and gossip in the corner while candidates are completing difficult pen and paper exercises, and discussions about candidates within their earshot have also been observed. Candidates can sense what is happening around them and the way in which they are treated can have a direct impact on their performance.

Iles and Robertson (1989) have shown that if the candidates like the people acting as assessors and interviewers, the outcome of the selection process is likely to be more positive for both parties. Consequently, assessors and interviewers need to behave in a professional but sympathetic manner towards the candidates. Some managers find these roles stressful or believe they need to be remote, but there is no real reason for not being friendly and helpful. It is also important that existing employees, involved in the informal interactions and activities, are honest and open about their employer. There can be nothing worse for candidates than feeling that their performance is being judged by people who are hiding critical aspects of the organisation from them. Similarly, candidates are unlikely to be very positive about an organisation with employees who display hostility towards newcomers. They are more likely to choose to work for an organisation where their future colleagues are welcoming and helpful.

Decision making

Candidates should be told about the processes to be used for decision making, although there are different schools of thought about whether candidates should know the criteria used for selection. Some organisations publish person specifications and say how each component will be assessed. They also indicate what evidence is being sought. Other organisations are less inclined to be so open. One reason given for a lack of openness is the risk of prosecution, with some employers believing that providing too much detail will encourage complaints. This need not be the case, and providing that the agreed criteria are explicit and used consistently throughout the process, the employing organisation will have nothing to fear. Even if it is concluded that the criteria should remain confidential during the selection process, there is no reason why candidates should not be told the steps to be used and the timescale involved in making the decision.

Records

Adequate records should always be maintained. This means clear, accurate notes should be kept and judgements related to evidence. It should be possible to demonstrate that the decisions would be replicated at a later time and that the same outcome would result. This does not demand a forest of administrative paperwork; a simple decision matrix such as that described in Chapter 6 will suffice.

Operational practice

If the practice and operation of the selection method has been professional, overt and related to the needs of the job, candidates will be left with the impression of a good employer. It is even possible that they will have 'enjoyed' the process. The stress levels inherent in selection for all concerned are manageable and it is possible to create a climate that makes candidates feel that they are able to do their best. If this is achieved, they will feel that they have been assessed fairly in a way that is positive, helpful and informed. Overall this requires:

- the selection method to be administered by staff who are competent;
- a process organised professionally;
- the timetable to be followed;
- candidates to be informed of what is happening, when, why and with whom;
- candidates to be given some control and feel that they are able to say 'no'; and
- the stress of the situation to be realistic and irrelevant sources of pressure eliminated.

SUMMARY

This chapter has looked at how recruitment and selection can affect applicants. For people who are involved regularly with recruitment and selection, it is easy to forget how traumatic it can be for those who are not so familiar with the processes. This can apply just as much to managers as to applicants. The negative consequences can have lasting effects on the self-esteem and general well-being of applicants. It is worth remembering that they are applying for work, not psychoanalysis, and that employing organisations may have the right to gather relevant information about candidates, but they do not have the right to invade their private lives.

While selection methods should explore the required skills, abilities and aptitudes, they can add to the organisation's image. The methods need to reflect the content and context of the job in question and to be administered professionally and effectively. To achieve this, the assessors and other staff involved should be chosen on the basis of their contribution to the process, and be trained and briefed about the sort of conduct the candidates deserve to expect. Candidates do not like being played with — they like to know what is happening and why. (A basic rule is to treat them as you would want to be treated.)

The selection event needs to be planned and executed professionally. Even the best methods can easily be rendered invalid by sloppy administration. It is also important to ensure that adequate records are maintained so that, if anyone feels aggrieved enough to lodge a complaint, the grounds for the decision can be evidenced. As Iles and Robertson (1989) point out:

> Individuals who feel unfairly assessed by invalid techniques presented in ways that fail to include their active consent, participation or involvement may feel alienated from the organisation, uncommitted to it, think of leaving it and actively seek another job. Their work performance may also suffer if they feel insensitively treated and their future options closed off. On the other hand, if they are accurately and sensitively assessed and given constructive feedback, individuals may feel a rise in self-esteem, enhanced self-efficacy, a greater sense of personal agency, greater commitment to their organisation and greater motivation to undertake further training and work experience.

Even if they do not get the job for which they applied!

8

After the Offer

Once the excitement of the selection event has been completed, it would be easy to think that the vacancy has been filled and the recruitment and selection process has come to an end. This is not the case. Making an appointment decision should be seen as a distinct step in the process and, like all the other steps, it should be conducted in a planned and systematic fashion and records kept. When the decision has been finalised it needs to be communicated to the person to whom the offer of employment is to be made, and to the unsuccessful candidates. Many managers do not realise that the verbal offer constitutes a legally binding contract, so care and attention needs to be given to its form and content.

Similarly, the way in which the decision is communicated to the unsuccessful candidates needs consideration. Without due care and attention, damage can be caused and grounds given for complaints. These candidates, having vested energy and emotion into their application, will naturally be disappointed about its lack of success and will feel they have 'lost'. In this chapter we explore how making and announcing the appointment decision can be designed to create as much benefit as possible for all concerned. The process of making decisions in ways that produce information for subsequent use will be discussed. The information can be used to help the negotiations with the successful candidate regarding the terms and conditions of the contract of employment and be given to unsuccessful candidates as feedback. Giving feedback is not easy, particularly when sensitive issues are involved, and this chapter includes some guidance on how to be constructive in this specific situation. Feedback can help to reduce the disappointment because it can give unsuccessful candidates practical information about what to do differently in future applications and how to enhance their skills and experience. For the appointed candidate, it provides the beginning of their development in their new job.

MAKING WIN/WIN DECISIONS

The final decision to appoint or reject candidates is usually made after an interview. Even though interviews are known to be poor predictors of performance, the leading researchers have concluded that there is a legitimate place for them. Herriot (1989a) suggests that, at the later stages of selection, the social interaction between the candidates and the decision makers is important to the subsequent success of the appointment. This is the stage when details are verified, the final check between the individual and the job requirements is made, the degree of fit is established and negotiations regarding the contract are started.

The interview should be used in conjunction with other selection methods and structured in appropriate ways to ensure that all necessary aspects are covered. Chapter 6 suggests different ways of ensuring that the validity of the interview is enhanced. It is also advisable to have more than one person involved. Three is the ideal number, and the person responsible for the appointment and to whom the postholder is to report should be the one to make the decision, on the advice of the others. Three gives a breadth of views and the ability to examine the candidates from different perspectives. If only two people are involved in the final interview, it is possible that the divergence of opinion is too great to produce a clear decision, while more than three can add complexity and create a panel that is intimidating. It must be recognised, however, that the needs of some employing organisations require interview panels of far larger numbers. It is not uncommon for up to six panel members to be involved, and some organisations have been known to hold interviews for key or senior posts in front of committees of over 20!

The matrix, suggested earlier, can provide the basis for decision making. The information gathered throughout the previous selection activities can be collated to form a report on each candidate. This report (see Table 8.1) will include an assessment of each candidate against the predetermined selection criteria and recommend to members of the panel which aspects are in need of further exploration.

Table 8.1 Candidate assessment report

Criteria	Rating	Evidence
Understanding the organisation and its environment Recognises the impact opportunities and action have on other parts of the organisation, especially with regard to resource utilisation and cost		
Strategic approach Able to see ahead, determine priorities, devise plans and organise resources for their achievement		
Communication Able to express ideas and convey information clearly and concisely using appropriate media and checks to make sure the messages have been understood		
Budget management Understands the concepts relating to the application of funds and cash flow, can recognise how actions affect costs and acts to use resources economically, efficiently and effectively		
Involvement Can recognise when to involve others in a task, give them clear, precise instructions, set realistic deadlines, and provide the assistance needed to complete it in a way that contributes to the development of others		

Criteria	Rating	Evidence
Team working Able to work within a group without dominance and to influence its processes and group members in a positive way		
Resourceful Able to find other ways of doing things and to act on own initiative		
Role appreciation Able to balance several differing roles, assess the limits of authority each imposes and values the contributions made by others in different roles		
Social skills Able to develop and maintain constructive relationships with one or more people, demonstrating sensitivity to their moods and needs		
Recommendation		
Feedback comments		
Assessors		

However, this matrix should not dictate the format of the final interview. The needs of the job in the wider organisational context should set the agenda against which each candidate will be compared. Thus, the interview should be structured to provide consistency of treatment between the candidates and allow for the differences between them to be explored in full. This requires preparation and some discipline. Managers tend to find it very tempting to compare candidates with each other but, even at this last stage, they should be assessed against the criteria required for adequate performance of the job. This stricture can help an employing organisation withstand claims of unfair treatment as well as creating a framework for decision making.

The use of job-related criteria also provides the basis for the creation of records. It is absolutely essential that notes made during the final interview are kept in a form that makes sense and can be checked after the event:

- They should include the criteria set in the person specification and job description. The criteria should be clearly expressed in ways that are understandable to candidates and others outside the process who might have a legitimate interest in it.
- A separate record should be maintained for each candidate and authenticated by the person responsible for the appointment.
- Any other notes kept by members of the interview panel should be collated to form a complete record.
- Reasons for the rejection of an application should be recorded and evidenced against the criteria.
- Information for feedback to unsuccessful candidates, if they request it, should be noted.
- Reasons for offering the appointment to the selected candidate should be recorded against the criteria.
- Information for use in the individual's initial training and development should be noted.

A matrix such as the one shown in Figure 8.1 can be used both to record the interview and to aid the making of the decision.

Post title	Interview panel members	
Candidate		
Criteria	**Weighting**	**Evidence**
Attainment		
Experience		
Abilities		
Aptitudes		
Interests		
Circumstances		
Other factors		
Decision and reasons		

Figure 8.1 Interview record

The decision to offer a job to one individual is a judgement made by human beings, and it contains all the flaws of any human decision. Objectivity in recruitment and selection, it can be argued, is a myth. However, the use of aids such as the systematic collection of information from a number of sources (eg the application form or CV, selection tests and references), rating of performance during selection activities on the basis of evidence, and comparison against weighted factors can help to reduce some of the inherent errors and biases. Using an approach to structure decision making should help the members of the appointment panel conclude which candidate will be best able to meet the requirements of the job.

MAKING AN OFFER OF EMPLOYMENT

The most common way of conducting the last stages of selection is for the final interview panel to see each of the recommended or shortlisted candidates in turn, to make an assessment as each is interviewed and then, after all candidates have been seen, to make a decision. This decision can be made immediately after the interview or in the days following. Some employing organisations draw their conclusions and then seek confirmatory evidence from referees and carry out other checks such as security clearance, evidence of the achievements cited during the interview, and evidence of qualifications and registrations before deciding finally whether to make an offer of appointment.

Some candidates are asked to wait until the interviews have been concluded and the decision is announced to them as a group. Other employing organisations prefer to inform the chosen candidate by telephone and wait for the offer to be accepted before informing the others that their applications have not been successful. Another slower but safer way is to inform the candidates in writing. It is possible that the latter approach is less desirable in terms of fostering a working relationship but, because a verbal offer of employment constitutes a legally binding contract, some employing organisations prefer to ensure that the offer is made in a form that can be evidenced at a later date should a dispute arise. Others permit managers to inform the successful candidate that he or she will be made an offer by a properly authorised representative of the employer.

The contract is the agreement (the bond of trust) between the employee and employer. It creates the foundations for the legal rights and obligations, which are all two-way. It surprises some managers to discover that an employee does not have a legal right to a written contract. However, all employees now have the right — under the Trade Union Reform and Employment Rights Act 1993 (TURER) — to receive a written statement of terms and conditions within two months of commencing their employment or, for existing staff, within two months of a request being made to their employer. Acknowledgement of receipt of the written statement should itself be in writing.

The written terms and conditions constitute what is known as the explicit contract (ie the terms formally agreed and recorded). Under TURER, each employee is entitled to receive the following information within the two-month period:

1. The names of the employer and the employee.
2. The date when the employment began.
3. The date when the employee's period of continuous employment began.
4. The scale or rate of remuneration or method of calculating remuneration, including the method used for calculating commission or bonus payments if these are contractual entitlements.
5. The intervals at which the remuneration is paid.
6. Any terms and conditions relating to:
   — hours of work including compulsory overtime;
   — holiday entitlement (including paid and public holidays), with enough information to enable employees to calculate 'precisely' the accrued entitlement if they were to leave the employment;
   — any terms and conditions relating to sickness or injury, including sick pay and requirements regarding notification, certificates and submission to medical examination; and
   — pensions and pensions schemes.
7. The length of notice each party is required to give the other.
8. The title of the job or a brief description of the work for which the employee is employed.
9. Where the job is not permanent, the expected duration of the employment and the date of termination of a fixed-term contract.
10. The place of work or, if the employee is to work at various locations, a statement to this effect and the employer's address.
11. Any collective agreements which directly affect the terms and conditions of the employment, including (where the employee is not a party to those agreements) the persons by whom they were made.
12. Where the employee is required to work outside the UK for more than one month, certain particulars regarding the arrangements for working abroad (such as the duration, currency in which the salary will be paid,

additional remuneration or benefits and any conditions relating to
return to the UK).

13.   It is also expected that notes will be contained in the written statement
specifying disciplinary rules or references to a reasonably accessible
document containing them. The name of the person to whom appeal
can be made against any disciplinary decision or a grievance raised
must be included, as should the method of application and subsequent
procedures.

Most of the above will be brief details only, although item 11 could be quite
lengthy. The agreements referred to could include the rights and
responsibilities of employees relating to, for example, training and
development allowances, flexible working arrangements, special leave and
(of increasing importance) safe working practices. Regulations concerning
professional conduct, confidentiality, post-employment restrictions and
exclusivity may also be included. These latter clauses have become more
common because the ability to retain skilled staff can provide competitive
advantage. However, clauses forbidding an employee to work for a
competitor after the termination of the contract have not been easy to
enforce. The growth of short-term contracts and part-time working have
raised some ethical questions about many of these practices. For example,
is it reasonable to restrict the earning capacity of someone on a part-time
contract by trying to enforce an exclusivity clause forbidding the individual
to work in similar areas of employment?

Some organisations make use of staff handbooks to ensure that
employees (both existing and new) know about the conditions, practices
and rules of their employing organisation. There are a number of advantages
of such a handbook — for instance, consistency of interpretation between
managers in different parts of the organisation, and ensuring that staff have
just one source. (However, trying to make sure that every member of staff
keeps personal copies up to date is both unrealistic and costly.) Details
ancillary to employment but important features of the organisation can be
officially communicated and shared with all staff equally. Guidance on both
format and contents is given by Salthouse (1995).

The implicit terms and conditions of employment do not appear in writing
in the statement issued to new appointees. These implied terms are those
aspects of the contract that are understood to be part of the normally
accepted relationship between an employee and their employer. One
fundamental aspect of this understanding is that the employee will carry
out any reasonable request but that the employer will not ask the employee
to do anything that could be regarded as unreasonable or illegal.

Confidentiality and the duty of care are also aspects of the implicit contract. The need for mutual trust has been tested in court. It has been established that if an employer is able to demonstrate that the bond of trust has been eroded beyond repair, it is reasonable for the employer to conclude that the contract of employment has been broken and therefore the dismissal of the employee would be fair.

It follows that since the implicit terms are so important, understanding should not be assumed. Consequently, the more important aspects need to be discussed and agreed during the final stages of the appointment process. After all, they include some of the important expectations discussed earlier.

NEGOTIATIONS AFTER THE OFFER

Making an offer of employment to a candidate is not the end of the selection process. Increasingly, employers are introducing individually negotiated contracts, and this means that terms and conditions of employment can vary between individual members of staff. These types of contracts have been used to introduce changes to terms and conditions of employment, often to the disadvantage of existing staff. However, as staff learn that skill shortages and the scarcity of relevant experience changes the dynamics of job hunting, they become more confident about making demands of new employers and can negotiate contracts that are beneficial. Traditionally, salaries (unless they were laid down as a result of well established pay schemes such as those found in the public sector) were always open to some degree of discussion. Now, a whole range of benefits are subject to negotiation at the start of a contract of employment. Holiday allowances, sickness benefits and pensions have become part of the normally accepted 'perks', while cars, housing expenses, insurance, health schemes, shopping and preferential purchasing benefits, school fees and other benefits have been added to the 'basket'.

The time just after the offer of employment is made provides the opportunity to negotiate the terms and conditions of the employment contract, and it is also the time to clarify the role and expectations of the postholder. It is important that assumptions are checked and clarified. Negotiations can include, for example, access to and resources for training and development opportunities, standards of work practice and certainly should include key objectives and priorities. They may also cover other areas that can easily lead to misunderstandings and possible conflict. These tend to concern acceptable behaviour and the underpinning values of the organisation — those unique features of a particular organisation's culture that everyone within in it take for granted but which may not be obvious to those from outside.

At Freda's previous employer, because taking work home was accepted practice, there was never a problem borrowing equipment such as the office's lap-top computer for the weekend. And, as the machine was at home, there was no reason why the children should not use it to help with their home work and for the occasional game.

When Freda moved companies she expected this attitude to exist in the new company. She was somewhat embarrassed to find herself summoned by the boss to explain why she had taken a lap-top from the office. Even though the organisation knew staff took work home, borrowing machinery and equipment was regarded as misuse of property.

It is important that newly appointed staff be given information about the organisation's accepted behaviour and culture as early as possible. This should be more than the usual standards of performance and rules about official conduct. Other aspects of behaviour are embedded in an employing organisation's culture, like how staff treat each other. The attention given in recent years to inappropriate behaviour, manifested as sexual and racial harassment, has now been extended to include bullying.

Arthur had just the sort of industrial and academic background the Research Institute needed, and he was a 'red hot' find. The director could not wait for him to start, looking forward to the new contracts Arthur would be able to win for them. Arthur's credibility with his industrial colleagues was very high, his knowledge of up-to-date applications was extensive and he had brilliant ideas for future developments. His writing skills were a bit wanting, but that would not be a problem. The research students would do most of the drafting of articles for publication.

Everything seemed to augur well for the Institute and Arthur — until he hit his first problem, at which point he really showed his temper. He shouted at the secretaries, told the technician he was incompetent and threatened to sack the researcher. The director was floored. He had never seen a member of staff behave so outrageously. When he challenged Arthur, the latter was genuinely puzzled. 'Why', he said 'in my last organisation that was nothing special. You should have seen Tom when he got mad.' The director struggled to explain that a less emotional expression of dissatisfaction was the norm in the Institute and began to wonder if the appointment was 'red hot' in the way he had originally believed. Would Arthur be able to make the changes to his behaviour the Institute demanded?

The time spent at the negotiation stage can prevent later misunderstanding and lay the groundwork for the induction phase that starts when the new employee begins work. Induction and initial training and development are discussed in Chapter 9, but the point to make here is that research demonstrates the more good quality information that is obtained by the successful candidate early in employment, the more successful the employment is likely to be.

TREATING UNSUCCESSFUL CANDIDATES WELL

Unsuccessful candidates might find it hard to believe that they can get a positive result by failing to obtain a job they really wanted. The process of submitting an application requires the commitment of time, at the very least, and most applicants invest some emotion. When the application proceeds into the selection phase, this emotional investment is increased. Consequently, failing at the last hurdle will be disappointing. Even if the unsuccessful candidate has decided independently that they would not accept the job if it were to be offered, there is still a slight sense of rejection and let down.

Individuals are vulnerable after an application has not been successful and they deserve sensitive treatment. If the process has been regarded from the outset as an opportunity for learning and development, and candidates have been told that this will be the case, the chances of all candidates obtaining a positive outcome can be increased. Experience of running assessment centres and senior selection events has shown that if candidates are treated with respect and consideration throughout the process, even though they may not be progressed to the final stages of the appointment, they generally say that they feel that they have had a fair chance and have gained some additional insight and learning.

However, this approach is different from that normally found in organisations and requires the employing organisation's selectors to be skilful. It starts at the very beginning of the recruitment phase. It has been found that if applicants are given information about the selection processes as well as the job for which they are applying and the employing organisation, then they are able to prepare themselves for what is to come. This means that they are prepared for the offer of feedback. Research carried out by Mabey and Iles (1991) has shown that candidates tend to prefer procedures that are forward-looking rather than those that concern only the past. Some of the other initial considerations are reported in Dale and Iles (1992).

A sensitive approach is especially important when internal candidates are involved. Mishandling internal candidates can have long-term consequences on their morale and that of others. There is little point in letting them (and helping them) lose their commitment to their employer by reducing their motivation. The way internal candidates are treated is also witnessed by their colleagues and friends within the organisation, and if it is perceived that they have not been treated well, this will be seen as a manifestation of the organisation's attitude to its staff in general and can feed other sources of discontent. Some simple measures can be taken that both enrich the recruitment and selection process and help the unsuccessful candidate retain their self-esteem and dignity. They also demonstrate to the workforce as a whole that the organisation is able to act on its commitments to good employment policies and practices. This is achieved by making sure that:

- the methods and criteria to be used are explicit and open;
- the candidates are treated with consideration and respect throughout;
- the candidates are kept fully informed at every stage and the reasons for taking particular approaches are explained;
- the assessment is seen as a diagnostic, not a pejorative, process;
- decision making is used to inform action planning to help longer-term learning and subsequent growth;
- feedback is given constructively and confidentially; and
- action results and follow-up takes place.

A number of career-grade librarians had been recruited during a period of expansion. They were very much of an age and possessed similar qualifications. However, their interests were very different, as were their motivations for advancement. After a period of low staff turnover, a section head post fell vacant. Because of the specialist nature of the section and the different levels of ambition in the group, only two members of staff applied.

This was obviously a difficult situation to handle. Only one could be promoted and that person would have to provide day-to-day supervision of the other. The selection process was carefully planned to be thorough and sensitive, and the debriefing and feedback sessions were seen as being critical to the successful implementation of the appointment decision. For not only did the employer have to select the best candidate, that decision had to be open and acceptable, and regarded by all concerned as fair and seen to be fair to both candidates and other members of staff.

Before the selection decision was made, both candidates were seen jointly by the department manager. The selection process was outlined to both, the criteria described and the means of assessment explained. They were told that the unsuccessful candidate would be expected to meet a careers counsellor after the event.

Peter was promoted and Dennis was not. Naturally Dennis was very disappointed, felt extremely devalued and didn't really want to see the careers counsellor (the meeting had been scheduled for 10 days after the final interview). As the meeting approached, Dennis wished he could forget the whole business. Peter was being very careful and the rest of the staff were keeping well away; they seemed afraid of hurting him.

When Dennis met the counsellor he was pleasantly surprised. The meeting was not the non-event he was expecting. The counsellor took a very practical and focused approach. There was no beating about the bush, and Dennis was asked about his feelings and encouraged to express his anger and disappointment. Then the counsellor asked him to examine the criteria, consider the feedback and explain why he thought his application had not been successful. He was not asked to compare himself with Peter in any way (which was something he had been dreading because they had previously been very good friends). The counsellor encouraged Dennis to stand back and focus on the areas of mismatch between the criteria and his skills and, once that had been done, they moved on to what Dennis wanted from a job.

Several meetings were held between the two of them, and gradually Dennis came to realise that he did not really want to be a manager. His skills were professional rather than those required for management, and his weaknesses lay in the very areas needed for effective management. He was good at finding information, relating to service users and organising events, and his job satisfaction came from pleasing people. He did not enjoy dealing with conflict, planning workloads or dealing with the routine paperwork needed for the smooth running of the library.

Dennis finally decided that his future lay in librarianship rather than management, so he applied to take a further course of study which would lead to a post-graduate qualification. The course was based on action research and would support an application for Fellowship of the Library Association. He also turned his attention to producing articles for the professional journals. Over the next few years, his reputation grew and increasingly he was invited to present his work to his colleagues at conferences.

Meanwhile, Peter became more and more removed from his professional role. Even though he was enjoying his job, he was getting bogged down in the paperwork and was having to work longer and longer hours to keep on top.

Who was the most successful applicant in this example?

GIVING FEEDBACK

Giving feedback is increasingly seen as part of the contract between organisations and applicants for jobs. As selection methods become more sophisticated and probing, candidates expect to be told about the 'results' of tests and the findings of assessors. However, the term 'giving feedback' is the wrong way round; candidates should be offered feedback *if they so wish*. Forcing feedback on to unwilling listeners is likely to do more harm than good. Reference has been made earlier to the vulnerability of candidates after selection and the power imbalance between employing organisations and candidates during the recruitment and selection process. Often people feel obliged to take up the offer of feedback, and this is particularly so when the appointment has been internal to the organisation and everyone else is getting feedback.

During the recruitment and selection process applicants will have raised their hopes and aspirations. They will have considered the likely impact of success on their personal lives and may have discussed the implications with family and friends. Very few people when psyching themselves up for a job prepare for failure. They are busy 'going for it', preparing themselves for the interview, considering the possible questions and situations they will be asked to face and thinking themselves into the new job. It is not common for people to think how they will react if they do not get the job. Even if asked, they will probably only say 'carry on as before'. They do not prepare themselves for disappointment and the sense of failure.

For some people, not getting the job will come as a shock. Likely responses include denial, rationalisation and allocating blame to the process. The tasks were unrepresentative, they were too hard/easy, the process was not valid, the assessors were unfair and behaved badly, the whole thing was too much like a game, and so on. While some of these post-selection responses may be justified, they are really examples of post hoc rationalisation. Imposing feedback on to people in this psychological state can be damaging to their self-esteem. In effect, the information can serve to destroy the candidates' psychological defences at a time when it may be important for them to protect themselves and rationalise any sense of disappointment and failure. Consequently, it is far better to let candidates know they may have feedback, if they request it. They should not be forced to listen to feedback when they do not want it.

If the appointment has been an entirely internal affair within an organisation, it is likely that feedback will become the norm. But perhaps not everyone will want the information at that particular time. The person charged with the task of providing individuals with information about performance should be sensitive to the possibility of peer group pressure and give individuals the opportunity to change their minds without any loss of face. Respecting the individual's privacy and their right to refuse feedback is a key to success.

Detailed advice outlining ways of providing feedback to aid development is given in Dale (1993). Lord (1994) also gives very practical and sensible advice on ways of feeding back test results. There are some slight differences between normal feedback on performance and that given after recruitment and selection that need to be taken into account. A main consideration is the individual's perception of their lack of success after the investment of time and emotion. The other is the imbalance of power. This is particularly so if psychometric instruments have been administered.

During recruitment and selection applicants are 'processed'. They are asked to expose their abilities, experience, attainments and personality to external scrutiny, and they are asked to explain and justify their actions and to demonstrate their future potential for an unknown job often to unknown people in an unknown organisation. Even if care has been taken to give candidates choice in the process, they are still very much in the hands of the employing organisation. The use of instruments, methods and techniques that are administered by experts and have a scientific basis gives the results and outcomes high credibility, and they can appear to contain the whole truth (and nothing but the truth) about an individual.

Usually this form of information is given to the selectors before the candidate knows what the tests have revealed and therefore it is virtually impossible for the candidate to deny or explain the outcome. If the information is used as part of the final interview to probe certain aspects of likely performance, individuals may find themselves on the defensive and unsure of their position. It is better for the results of such tests to be communicated to the candidates before the final interview so they are able to discuss on an equal basis the implications of the findings in relation to the job.

However, when providing feedback after the use of these instruments, great care is needed to ensure that the recipient understands the context and the meaning of the results. Usually organisations that use the instruments ensure that only trained and qualified practitioners provide feedback, and the British Psychological Society, recognising the potential for damage to individuals, has introduced levels of competence in an attempt to improve practice. Even so, there are organisations that do not comply with acknowledged good practice as outlined by the BPS and set out in the Institute of Personnel and Development codes of practice.

The recent rapid expansion in the use of IT has made psychometric instruments more accessible and simpler to administer. Some of the computer-based tests are very easy to obtain. (One example is a version of the Myers-Briggs test obtained through shareware.) However, even though these packages may be based on well-known tests, they are simplistic and, at the very best, can only been seen as indicative. One basic rule is that whenever feeding back the results of psychometric instruments, candidates should be told the validity of the instrument in terms they can understand. The following checklist provides some more tips:

- **Let the candidate ask for feedback**. Offer the opportunity and encourage candidates to take it up, but do not force them. The likely impact on candidates' well-being should be the uppermost concern.
- **The timing of when the feedback is to be given should be under the control of the applicant**. Consider that most often the candidate will have returned to their normal environment and job. Ringing up and offering to give feedback may constitute an breach of confidentiality. If the candidate has not told anyone of their application before the selection process, having another organisation contact them after the event could make public a fact the individual would have preferred to keep private. This would constitute an invasion of privacy and may be an unwelcome reminder of failure and unrealised ambitions.
- **If feedback is wanted, begin by asking the candidates to reflect on their own performance**. Encourage them to identify gaps against the person specification for themselves. Most people are aware of their own strengths and weaknesses and only need them to be put into the context of the requirements of the job and organisation. They do not want their failings paraded before them. Rather they would prefer guidance on how to improve. The use of exploratory questions can help candidates reflect both on their weaknesses, but also on their strengths. Please do not tell candidates where they went wrong.
- **Judge the amount of detail to provide**. Some candidates will be very disappointed and will try to prove that the employing organisation made the wrong decision. If too much detail is given, it is possible that the feedback session will become a fight back session and not be useful for anyone. The way to avoid this happening is for the person providing the feedback to move gradually, testing how much information the individual is able to accept. Remember the reason for providing feedback is to help the candidate move forward, not to tell them where

they failed.

- **Provide indications of what was being sought**. If it is felt to be appropriate for the individual concerned, make the person specification contents and the job description requirements explicit and give practical examples of the sorts of skills, behaviour and standards being sought.

- **Focus on behaviour that can be changed**. This can be done by providing evidence and offering examples of alternative approaches, and by suggesting ways in which improvements could be achieved. However, in considering the above point, make sure any evidence presented is factually accurate and demonstrable.

- **Try to avoid passing judgement**. The use of adjectives, such as 'poor', 'good' or 'better' are comparative and are difficult to substantiate. What may be good in one context could be awful in the opinion of another employer.

- **The amount of feedback given should be limited**. There is no point in overloading candidates with detail. They should be given broad indications of areas of mismatch with the job requirements and where improvement would have increased the chance of them being successful in their application.

- **Make use of the positive**. Make sure the candidates understand that they have strengths as well as shortcomings. Remember that another employer will possibly think they are by far the best candidate for their job.

- **Remember the candidates have the right to disagree and not accept the feedback**. After all, they decided to submit an application for a job; they did not ask for an in-depth analysis of their personality and its shortcomings.

- **Leave the candidates with a sense of the future**. No one is unemployable. Give positive indications and offer suggestions about ways in which, in your opinion, they could improve their chances of gaining a job in their chosen area. But remember your opinion may differ from that of other employers — and the candidate.

Above all, it must be remembered that the feedback should relate to the demonstration of skills against the job requirements at the time of the assessment. If the candidate did not do very well in the eyes of the assessors for one particular organisation, it does not necessarily mean that the individual is not able to perform to the standard required for another employer. All that can be said, in the circumstances and at the time, is that the selectors were given no or little indication of that individual's abilities.

Providing feedback to internal candidates is of critical importance if their employing organisation wishes to maintain their commitment and contribute to their continuing development. While it is vital that the candidates' right to refuse feedback is respected, there may be a need to help them over any disappointment. The use of sensitively provided feedback in this situation can change what could be a negative experience into very positive learning that can make a significant contribution to the individual's development. It can indicate areas where support would be mutually beneficial and could stimulate the individual to review the direction of their career. The assessment of weaknesses may enable them to be seen, in a different context, as strengths.

The Housing Association decided to invite its district managers to apply for the vacant post of regional manager. The selection process was in three phases — a technical interview focusing on housing law and practice; a personality inventory; and an assessment centre concentrating on management skills. Following the assessments, three of the ten applicants were invited to a final interview. One of these was Gillian, the 'hot favourite'. Gillian was highly respected by her colleagues, staff and residents. It was generally felt that she would be promoted. She was intelligent, articulate, sensitive and paid attention to detail. But she did not get the job.

The general manager arranged to meet Gillian to discuss her present and future. Naturally she was disappointed, but not as much as she had expected. This she could not understand. In the discussion the general manager told Gillian that she had been the strongest candidate after the technical interview. None of the other managers could match her knowledge and grasp of the issues facing housing management. The psychometric inventory showed that her preferred styles were those congruent with the desired profile. However, the level of her management skills was her weakness. Gillian readily agreed. She found the day-to-day grind of resolving problems, monitoring performance, keeping on top of the budget, paperwork and the like, the least enjoyable part of the job. Yet she agreed that those were essential parts of the regional manager's role. She enjoyed planning special projects, meeting with people, and dealing with one-off situations that she could get stuck into.

When she reflected on these contradictory aspects of her preferred work, she began to realise that she did not want a career in management; she wanted a career in research and project planning. The general manager had come to a similar conclusion.

As the Housing Association was growing rapidly, there was an emerging need for someone to lead developments. Gillian was the ideal person. When asked, she happily agreed to leave her management role and concentrate on the work she was good at and enjoyed.

CORRECTING MISTAKES

Not all selection events avoid appointing the wrong person to the wrong job. Even when the processes have been very carefully designed and executed, it is possible that the decisions made during the final stages are no good. Improving the processes used to aid human decision making can only help to minimise some of the known inherent flaws and errors in judgement, and perfect decision making is a dream, not a reality. As we have seen, even the very best predictors only achieve a validity coefficient of just about 0.6. Therefore there will be occasions when the wrong person is offered a contract of employment and mistakenly accept it.

While it is important to understand how this occurred, it is more important to work out what to do about the situation. Regrettably, many poor appointments are accepted, and the employees concerned may either continue in blind ignorance of their failure to match up to expectations or find themselves stuck, uncomfortably, in a job they do not like. Failure to tackle this situation is an example of poor management, yet dealing with such appointments is not straightforward. Assuming everything reasonable has been done to match expectations and clarify objectives and standards of performance, the first step to take to correct a poor appointment is the admission of a mistake. Not many managers relish this, but once the step has been taken it is possible to devise suitable action to rectify or at least improve the situation.

The developmental approach

If the employing organisation makes use of performance appraisal or a development review scheme as part of its human resource management practices, and has used the results of the selection assessment to feed the early stages of development planning, it can be comparatively easy to pick up any shortfall in performance. Selection criteria will have been explicit and behaviourally defined, while the selection events will have provided information and feedback. The basis will have thus been created from which to review subsequent performance.

Stephan was appointed as product development manager in July 1993. The employing organisation had found filling the post difficult. The first round of advertising had failed to provide a strong field and so a second trawl was attempted. The applicants seemed better and six were shortlisted. The general manager had decided to go ahead with the selection event with the strict proviso that if none of the candidates met the criteria no appointment was to be made. This instruction had created a certain amount of tension, and the continuing vacancy was hampering other elements of the organisation's business plans.

During the selection event, one candidate stood out from the rest, four were obviously not suitable, one was marginal and Stephan seemed fine. The two were recommended for final interview. There were some areas of doubt about Stephan's performance but, considering the circumstances, the assessors felt confident in their recommendation to the interviewing panel.

Stephan was duly appointed and given feedback. The assessors had been concerned about his abilities to forward plan and pull resources together to enact those plans. They felt that while he was very good at detail and interpersonal relationships, he could get bogged down. These concerns were included in his early development plan and a note made for his manager to check on progress at the first appraisal meeting which would be held in January 1994.

This example demonstrates how areas of concern highlighted during selection can be used as benchmarks from which to review initial performance and provide a means of addressing any areas of perceived shortfall. Appropriate action can be identified and plans implemented to address specific issues. Stephan could have, as predicted, got bogged down in the detail of his new job and failed to address the longer-term issues. If this were the case, his manager could have, say, pulled him out for a day a week, or given a deadline for the creation of a development plan. Alternatively, if Stephan did not know how to plan, action could be taken to fill this gap.

The important point is the need to face up to any problems early in the appointment. Performance problems do not go away if they are ignored — they hide, fester and get bigger and, as they get older, they change. This makes it difficult to get to their root cause. Other people get involved and the whole situation eventually becomes such a mess that it is nearly impossible to untangle. If the issues are addressed early they can be dealt with and resolved.

Job redesign

If a developmental approach has been tried and training has proved not to be the answer to the problem, there are other measures that can be taken to resolve a poor appointment. First, it is possible that even if the measures outlined in Chapter 2 have been taken, the job could have been constructed in such a way that inhibits rather than facilitates achievement. This can happen in two ways — separately or combined. The job may be:

- too big (ie too many disparate activities to complete);
- too complex (ie the context may be changing rapidly, with too many external factors impinging on the postholder's performance);
- dependent on others who do not deliver;
- impossible (ie has objectives that are not attainable).

Alternatively, the job could have demanded a range of skills that cannot be possessed by one human being.

Stephan was finding his new job more difficult than he anticipated. He knew there would be two aspects to it that could cause conflict, but he did not expect the demands to be so contradictory. He understood that the main purpose of the job was to lead the development of products, liaising with R&D, production and marketing. To do this he had a small team of engineers and was, as part of his job, supposed to manage them. Technically these engineers were meant to act as project managers but, instead, Stephan discovered that they were involving themselves in the detail of the production processes.

Stephan had decided that he would need to win their trust and respect before attempting to move them back into their proper roles. However, this meant that he too had found himself involved in inappropriate detail. He had found it difficult to get the support he needed to resist these pressures and began to realise that one reason for the engineers' involvement in production was due to a lack of co-operation from the R&D scientists.

Redeployment

There are occasions when it is the individual, not the design of the job, that is the problem. In these circumstances action more akin to discipline than initial training is needed. The first steps in any disciplinary action should be designed to help the job holder correct performance that is not up to the standards expected or in accordance with the employing organisation's procedures. However, if all reasonable remedial measures have been taken to help the individual achieve the standards or objectives required, other measures can be implemented as part of informal disciplinary procedures. The first of these is redeployment.

Stephan had discussed his early difficulties with his line manager during their first appraisal meeting. The manager shared his views. Together they had agreed a plan of campaign to deal with the problems Stephan had identified and that would enable him to move more into the planning work expected by his manager. They set a date to meet again three months on.

In April, when they met, Stephan's manager expressed his disappointment about the progress made. Stephan had not done anything to build bridges with the R&D department and his staff were still mainly involved in production issues. The development plan Stephan had promised to implement was still in its initial draft. The reasons for non-achievement were thin, to say the least. The manager agreed to give Stephan another three months to get the plan into action.

By the time of the next progress meeting, Stephan's manager was beginning to wonder if the reasons given in January had really been excuses. He decided to start thinking about what other possibilities might account for Stephan's poor performance on these aspects. The manager was torn. Stephan certainly possessed qualities the organisation could use and some of his work had been really good, but the problem was that it was the wrong work. He began to think about other parts of the organisation that might be able to make better use of Stephan's talents.

Redeployment is one option an employing organisation can take, with the employee's agreement, if the original post is proving to be unsatisfactory. In this sense, asking an employee to move into another post should not be seen as an easy alternative to formal disciplinary action. Nor should it be seen as a way of parking the problem. The move should be to another similar job at a similar level and the process should be handled discretely. It should be designed to enable both the employee and the employing organisation to form a new working relationship that is mutually beneficial.

The danger for the employing organisation of this approach is that the individual could attempt to claim constructive dismissal. To do this, however, the employee would have to resign and then demonstrate that the actions of the employing organisation had broken the contract of employment, or that it was no longer possible for the individual to do the job for which they were employed. According to Selwyn (1988):

Making unilateral changes in employment terms, such as a change in the job, a lowering of earnings or change in location, providing there are no contractual rights to do so, would entitle an employee to resign. However, it must be borne in mind that although this may amount to a dismissal in law, whether the dismissal is fair or unfair has still to be determined by the facts of the case and whether or not the employer has acted reasonably.

Therefore, if feedback on the areas of performance causing concern had been given, action taken to help the individual make improvements, time support and resources made available and a further review undertaken, the individual would have a hard time convincing a Tribunal.

Demotion

This step is serious and should be taken only after other measures have been tried and failed. Asking an individual to move to a post at a lower salary and lower status is formal disciplinary action and therefore must be allowed for in the employing organisation's disciplinary procedures. These procedures should accompany the written statement of terms and conditions given to all new employees at the start of their employment (or reference made to their location).

In February 1995 the general manager was asked to meet Stephan's current manager and his former manager to discuss the problem of Stephan's non-achievement. In August 1994, Stephan had been asked to move into the post of administration manager. The previous occupant had been forced unexpectedly to take ill health retirement. To Stephan's manager, this seemed to be a God-sent opportunity for both the organisation and Stephan. The job demanded someone who was able to pay attention to detail and yet be able to marry a number of conflicting demands. Stephan's qualities, during the time he had been with the organisation, were seen as his abilities to get on well with people at all levels, produce reports to tight deadlines and deal effectively with matters that demanded high levels of accuracy.

> Stephan had fitted in well with the organisation. He had played a useful role in re-establishing the Staff Association that had been floundering and was generally liked. Since there was a job that needed to be done, the general manager had agreed to the move. Now she was wondering if she had been wise.
>
> Stephan was still not achieving the objectives set for him. He was burying himself even more in detail, seemingly relishing the minutiae, while the staff seemed to be doing their own thing. Stephan was popular, but this was more because he was 'one of the gang' rather than respected as a manager and leader.

Dismissal

If it is not possible to remedy poor performance or the failure to meet objectives or standards agreed through training and development, redeployment or demotion, it may ultimately be that the employing organisation decides that the best course of action is to dismiss the employee. This is a regrettable state to have reached for all concerned, but sometimes, rather than prolong the situation, it is better to make a clean break.

If this step is decided upon, it is essential that the employing organisation makes the decision to dismiss fairly and properly. To safeguard employees from draconian measures the employment laws, laid down in the 1970s and subsequently amended, make it quite clear what should happen. The following comments are not legal guidance and, if an employer does decide to dismiss an employee, professional advice should be sought and the employee concerned should be made aware of their rights to independent guidance and advice.

An employer can legally dismiss an employee providing the grounds are fair and the proper procedures are followed. Conversely, an employee can claim to have been unfairly or wrongly dismissed if specified steps have not been taken before and during the dismissal. However, to be able to make such a claim, the employee must have been in the employment of the employing organisation for at least two years. (Staff employed on fixed-term and some temporary contracts will have been asked to waive the right of recourse to an Industrial Tribunal when the terms of the contract were agreed. This waiver however does not usually include the termination of a contract before its expiry date. The terms and condition of these types of contracts are complex and are outside the scope of this book.)

For a lawful dismissal to occur, it needs to be fair. The Employment Protection (Consolidation) Act 1978 lays down five grounds:

- a reason relating to the capability or qualifications of the employee for performing the work of the kind for which the employee was employed by the employing organisation;
- a reason relating to the conduct of the employee;
- the redundancy of the employee;
- because the employee could not continue to work in the position without contravention of a restriction or duty imposed by or under a statute; or
- some other substantial reason such as to justify the dismissal of an employee.

The failure of an employee to perform the job to the standard required could fall into one or several of the above categories, depending on the circumstances. The most common, however, would be the first, if the employee demonstrably was not achieving the desired output: 'capable' can include 'any assessment by reference to skill, aptitude, health or other physical or mental quality' and 'qualifications' mean 'any degree, diploma or other academic, technical or professional qualification relevant to the position which the employee holds.'

If an employing organisation concludes that a place cannot be kept for the employee — because the appointment was not successful or that the employee's standard of work has deteriorated — the proper procedures (based on professional advice) should then be followed. This applies whether the individual had achieved two years service or not. The reason for ensuring that the proposed steps be taken is not just to safeguard the employing organisation against Tribunal action. Wrongful and unfair dismissal will reflect badly on the organisation, damage its reputation as a good employer and harm its ability to recruit good quality staff in the future. It will also harm the individual. Getting dismissal right is not difficult, and all that is required is that individuals are given:

- feedback and information regarding their inadequate performance;
- the chance to state their perspective;
- several fair chances to improve or rectify inadequate performance;
- support and further feedback;
- warnings of the consequences;
- rights of appeal; and
- the right to be accompanied.

In April 1995 the general manager decided to act. Stephan would be offered a lower-paid post comparable to his level of performance. If this was not acceptable, he would be given formal warnings in accordance with the company's disciplinary procedure. The personnel manager was duly consulted and a meeting arranged with Stephan and, if he wished, a 'friend'. The meeting was intended to state the company's position and ask Stephan to explain his continued inadequate performance. Depending on his responses, the company's options would be presented.

Stephan would be given two days to think about the situation. It was expected that he would either reject the company's position, make an alternative set of proposals to enable him to continue in his present post or accept the offer of a lower-paid post. The general manager rehearsed each possibility with the personnel manager and planned appropriate responses.

Sometimes, obviously depending on the particular circumstances, it is better for everyone to wind up the contract. This enables the individual employee to leave the organisation quickly, with little public exposure of the problem. A clean break approach like this can save face for both the employer and employee as it is tantamount to an acceptance on both sides of a genuine mistake. Demotion and dismissal contain elements of blaming the employee, but when a poor appointment leads to inadequate performance, it is rarely anyone's fault. Instead, it tends to be a combination of unfortunate circumstances that would have been difficult to foresee. Even if there were hints in the initial assessment, the employing organisation failed by not taking heed, just as much as the employee overestimated his or her own abilities.

Settling up could mean one of several different things. It could be pay in lieu of notice, compensation for loss of earnings while the employee finds new work, the retention of certain benefits (such as a car, computer or personal healthcare plans) or even an out of court settlement. This payment tends to be made when an employing organisation decides that the consequences of retaining the employee or following time-consuming procedures would be more costly than the payment. This is not a course of action to be counselled, nor should it be taken without proper professional advice. It can be expensive, lead to acrimony and jeopardise everyone's reputation.

Again depending on the circumstances, if the employee is unwell or approaching retirement age, it is possible to make arrangements with pension funds or obtain a long-term assessment of the individual's health which would enable them to leave their employment with dignity and a suitable settlement.

It was July by the time the various formal meetings had been held and the final conclusion reached. Stephan was not going to accept demotion and he refused to agree that he was not doing the job to the standard for which he had been employed. He had argued that the action taken since his first appraisal had been intended throughout and that he had reached most of the targets set. Where there had been failures, this was due to the fault of others, not him.

The general manager had not been able to reach any common ground and had finally decided that she would end Stephan's employment. She was dismayed to find that Stephan had two years service and was worried that it had taken the organisation so long to deal with the problem. Because Stephan had been so difficult, she wondered what the consequences of giving him notice would be.

The matter was discussed with the personnel director and together they concluded that it was more than likely that Stephan would claim unfair dismissal. They agreed they did not want to face the time, costs and publicity of attending a Tribunal and so decided to recommend to the finance director that if Stephan did file a claim, discussions should be opened to see if a suitable settlement could be found.

Termination by mutual agreement

There are occasions when employees themselves realise that an appointment has been a failure. They will want to find a route out that will maintain their dignity and self-respect, and they will also want to safeguard their chances of finding alternative, suitable employment. Ending a contract of employment on mutually agreeable terms is perhaps the best solution to an unsatisfactory situation. The integrity of both parties can be preserved and a 'no come back' agreement reached.

> The general manager arranged to see Stephan at the beginning of August 1995 to give him his notice of dismissal. She was surprised when he came in to announce he wanted to leave. He had suspected what was coming but couldn't find a way to admit that he had been wrong to apply for the job in the first place. He told the GM that he had been under a lot of pressure to earn more money and had been really surprised when he had done so well at the selection event. The first few months had been a real struggle for him, but he had not been happy and now wanted a way out.
>
> It did not take long to find a suitable formula that Stephan felt would tide him over, and the organisation was prepared to pay to solve the problem and avoid possible embarrassment.

WORDS OF CAUTION

Not keeping adequate records and providing poor quality feedback to unsuccessful candidates, as well as being poor practice, can be risky. It can lay the organisation open to accusations of unfair treatment. The phenomenon of post hoc rationalisation discussed above shows how someone who feels rejected may be inclined to find an external source to blame. If the selection process has not been conducted professionally and feedback given in a clumsy, unskilled way, individuals are more likely to blame the employing organisation for not letting them display their abilities rather than examining, critically, their degree of fit with the organisational requirements. In these circumstances, an individual may express their dissatisfaction formally.

Muriel was a very experienced personnel professional who, for a number of years and in several organisations, had worked in the areas of policy development and implementation, organisational development and the management of change. She applied for a new post with a major local employer, believing that she had demonstrated her abilities against the published person specification, and was surprised to find that she had not been shortlisted. When she took up the invitation to receive feedback, she was even more surprised to be told that she did not have experience in change management and policy formulation. The person giving the feedback seemed a little vague and was not able to give any specific examples. When Muriel pointed to parts of her application that demonstrated her skills and expertise in those areas, the employer's representative agreed, admitted to being puzzled, and wondered why she had not been shortlisted. He promised to look at her application again. Muriel heard nothing more and finally, after a few weeks, assumed that she would not do so. She was not surprised to hear later that the internal candidate was appointed.

Was Muriel lacking when compared to the person specification, or was the process a fix?

Sometimes the process is flawed and unlawful bias is used as the basis for decision making. In the UK the anti-discrimination legislation describes what should not be done, whereas elsewhere laws encourage affirmative action to redress imbalance and previous inequalities. The American system, for example, has used targeting and quotas, and this has led to backlash, litigation, counter-claim and the development of recruitment and selection practices that are demonstrably fair. In this country, practices are more concerned with avoiding prosecution rather than complying with the spirit of the law by encouraging improvements to practice and widening opportunities. Even in organisations claiming to be committed to equal opportunities, practices are deficient. Examples of discriminatory advertisements are still common — 'An experienced man-manager' is often wanted. Managers fail to follow internal procedures and do not keep records despite organisations adopting equal opportunities policies and codes of practice.

Any applicant or candidate who feels that they have been subjected to discrimination or unfair treatment has the right of recourse to an Industrial Tribunal. This right is not limited to people from black or ethnic minority groups and women: men and white people have the same access to the Tribunal if they believe they have been discriminated against on any of the grounds laid out in the relevant Acts. Examples of discriminatory practice can include the selection of a member of one ethnic group in preference to members of another on grounds unrelated to the needs of the job, or the denial of employment to men in a mainly female work group.

SUMMARY

This chapter has outlined how to make the final stages of the selection process beneficial for all candidates, regardless of whether their application had been successful or not. Taking a developmental approach from the outset can foster a climate that prepares the unsuccessful candidate to receive constructive feedback and to move on positively. Not taking this approach to selection can lead to disappointment, a sense of rejection and loss of confidence, post hoc rationalisation and complaint. Turning the process into a win/win situation is not difficult providing the sensitivities of the individuals involved are respected.

After the decision has been made, contractual terms need to be agreed and the terms and conditions of the employment, both explicit and implicit, need to be clarified. Unsuccessful candidates need to be offered feedback and treated in such a way that enables them to retain their sense of self-worth. There are ways which, if followed, make the provision of feedback a positive experience. However, crass handling of people after they have been turned down can cause a lot of unnecessary pain and even damage.

Sometimes, even though good practice has been followed and correct steps taken, a poor decision is made. Once the new employee has started work it can be difficult to rectify a poor appointment. Often the fault for the mistake cannot be attributed to one side or the other: both the employer and the employee will have played some part in the poor decision. It is possible to remedy a situation that tends to be unsatisfactory for all concerned. However, admitting to the existence of this position requires an uncommon degree of honesty. Nevertheless, this first step is essential if the other measures are to be applied.

Depending on the nature of the particular situation, there are several things that can be done. All require confidence on the part of the manager, compliance with proper procedures and the use of professional advice. Once a contract has been made, both parties have rights and obligations that are enforceable by law. Failure to follow procedures, accepted good practice and statute can lead an employing organisation into an Industrial Tribunal.

An employer has nothing at all to fear from complaints, providing:

- A good quality job description and person specification have been prepared.
- The advertisement, other announcements and supporting information reflect the needs of the job and the organisation and do not make use of characteristics that are directly or indirectly discriminatory.
- The shortlisting is carried out against the job requirements and person specification.
- The reasons for rejection have been evidenced and recorded.
- Factual information that can be checked and evidenced is available for applicants if they ask why they have not been shortlisted. Any feedback is related to the criteria used for selection.
- Selection activities are designed to elicit required behaviours.
- Decisions are based on evidence and are recorded.
- Candidates are informed firmly of the decision and are given access to feedback if they so wish.
- Feedback is factual and is based on evidence. Developmental advice, if given, is separated and it is made clear that any subsequent advice proffered is not related to the decision.
- The person giving feedback does not express their personal opinion or feelings and respects the feelings of the candidate.
- Records are kept accurately and maintained in a form that, after the event, enables the reasons for the decision to be recognised against the criteria.

If these steps are taken and a complaint is lodged, the employing organisation should be able refute the allegations. However, it is far better to make sure that candidates do not feel badly treated in the first place.

On a more positive note, the next chapter moves on to look at the early days of the employment of the best candidate.

9

Induction and Welcome

It is generally believed that if the recruitment process has attracted a large and strong field and the selection activities have resulted in the best candidate being appointed, then everything is set for a rosy future. Nothing could be less true. So many good appointments have been turned into poor employees because the induction phase has been ignored. In this chapter we examine the various stages of induction and consider how some simple actions can make sure that new employees feel welcomed, are introduced to their new role and quickly become familiar with the culture of the organisation.

Research and experience has shown that, if the early stages are got right, the chances of the appointment being successful (ie the employee working productively and happily for a useful period) are greater than if the new starter is thrown in at the deep end. Most organisations believe that they welcome their new staff very well. However, when their systems are examined they find that they pay attention to only some of the needs of the new employees. This is because, on the surface, these needs seem to be straightforward: 'If the new starters are told what will be expected from them in terms of performance, the layout of their workspace, the location of facilities such as toilets, cloakroom and kitchen, and the employer's rules and health and safety requirements are explained, what more could be reasonably expected?'

NEEDS OF NEW EMPLOYEES

Starting a new job is a strange time. Stresses and emotions interplay in ways that are unpredictable even for the practised job mover. This is because they are influenced by other people and the circumstances of the time, and needs and emotions are unique to each individual. It is also likely that new employees will not know what they need to help them perform in their new organisation and new job quickly. Consider the recent experiences of a new member of staff:

- The decision to apply for another job has been made.
- The application has been submitted and the self-examination that this entails carried out.
- A period of uncertainty has been experienced. This might have consisted of high expectations and ambition, and doubts about personal ability to be successful in both the application and the job.
- The selection process has been gone through with the associated stress.
- A decision to relocate may have to be considered and the possible effects on other people (eg the rest of the family) taken into account.
- The existing job and colleagues have to be left and a period of 'bereavement' lived through (even if the job was hateful, a sense of loss can be expected).
- The existing home perhaps has to be sold and friends and routines abandoned.
- The new job has to be started and again the sense of uncertainty and doubts about abilities have to be overcome.
- New people have to be met, assessed, new friendships formed and decisions made about who and who not to trust.
- A phase of learning is started where a great deal is unknown.

There is little wonder that moving jobs is recognised as a common cause of stress. The factors noted above can make the new employee very uncertain and lacking in self-confidence at a time when the opposite could be expected. Why should new appointees need special care and reinforcement of self-worth? The only answer to this question is that they often do. Sensitive employers will recognise that new staff experience these feelings and, as a consequence, are prepared to take action to prevent them inhibiting the individual's performance. Steps in addition to those listed in the personnel text books (for example Armstrong, 1991) are required to induct employees effectively into the organisation.

STARTING WITH RECRUITMENT

Normally, induction is seen as one of the training needs of a new employee, but an alternative view is proposed here. The value of seeing induction within the overall recruitment and selection process has already been mentioned and, if this holistic approach is taken, the needs of new recruits is given primary consideration throughout.

Sadly, the pressures on organisations have led some to recruit staff with the experience and skills required to enable them to 'hit the ground running'. It is not unknown for these people to fall flat on their faces because they have not fitted into the organisation. Adequate planning, preparation and briefing for the new start is required if competent staff are to make use of their abilities quickly and effectively. This planning starts right at the beginning of the recruitment and selection process. When working out a schedule of dates for each of the stages (see Table 9.1), it is possible to anticipate the likely start date.

Table 9.1   A recruitment and selection schedule

Week	Action
1	Agree job descriptions, person specification and recruitment process
2	Prepare advertisement and additional information
3	Place advertisement
4	Respond to enquiries
5	Receive applications
	Closing date
6	Shortlist
	Invite candidates to selection event
8	Selection event
	Obtain references and make other checks
9	Negotiate terms and conditions
10	Written contracts exchanged
	Pre-appointment meetings and visits
14/18*	**Start day**
	Agree initial training and meetings schedule
	Start scheduled training, meetings and discussions
15/19	Start work on initial assignment
16/20	Progress review
	Feedback from selection process included in the training plan
	Schedule of second round of training, meetings and discussions
17/21	Additional assignments
18/22	Progress review
	Agree initial targets, key objectives and development plan
20/24	Progress review against job description, person specification and development plan
24/28	Repeat week 24 every 4 weeks

* Depends on the notice to be given to the former employer.

This form of planning may seem mechanistic but, allowing for slippage, it can ensure that the new starter is brought into the organisation efficiently.

But this sort of programme cannot succeed if material and people are not adequately prepared. For example, the job description has to be written in such a way that facilitates the identification and agreement of targets and key objectives. The person specification has to be phrased to enable the assessment of performance on the job as well as during the recruitment and selection process. The assessment process during selection needs to be rigorous enough to provide information to help the formulation of a development plan. The workload of the section needs to be planned and tasks allocated to allow a build up that reflects the new employee's early progress and growth in confidence. Immediate colleagues also need to know what is happening and why, so that they do not make unreasonable demands or believe that the new starter is being given special privileges.

Fiona was appointed as the quality control manager. The post had been vacant for several months before she started and, in that time, some jobs had moved from being pressing to urgent. Nevertheless, even though the MD had every faith in her abilities, he resisted the temptation of asking her to clear the backlog. He planned her first month with the finance director thus:

- **Week 1**
Day 1	Introductions to the new team then the rest of the day to be spent shadowing the MD
Day 2	The finance director
Day 3	The company secretary
Day 4	The works manager
Day 5	The sales and marketing manager

- **Week 2**
Day 1	The MD and works manager
Day 2–4	The quality team on assignment 1 and familiarisation
Day 5	The sales and marketing manager at a customers conference

- **Week 3**
Day 1–2	The quality team on assignment 1 and familiarisation with procedures
Day 3	Computer system briefing

Day 4   Quality team on assignment 1 and
           familiarisation with procedures
Day 5   Progress review with MD and explanation of
           assignment 2
• **Week 4**
Day 1–4   Assignments 1 and 2
Day 5   Progress review with MD and agreement of
           key targets, objectives and development
           plan

The MD justified the objections from the quality team by assuring them that their new manager's planned assimilation into the company would enable her to become effective more quickly than the more normal approach to induction. In the long run, he assured them, they would all gain. Fiona was also anxious to get going with her real work but agreed with the plan. At the end of the four weeks she felt as though she had been with the company for several months rather than just one. Everyone agreed that she certainly knew her way around the organisation and its ways of working.

Effective induction, as will be explained, is more than just ensuring the new employee has pens, paper, a desk and a phone. The way in which the new person is received and introduced to the organisation can have a direct effect on their long-term success, productivity and happiness. Garratt (1987) draws attention to two distinct processes that occur during a new employee's early days. These he calls induction and inclusion. The former is when 'people are introduced to their new organisation or job, the people with whom they will be working and given some clues as to what is expected of them in terms of the technical side of their jobs'. The latter 'is about building up rapport, trust and credibility so that we can be accepted by and work with our fellows. Most organisations assume that Inclusion will happen somehow and put little energy or time into ensuring that it is effective.'

INDUCTION METHODS

Despite the assertion by Garratt (1987) to the contrary, in the main employers do not organise the induction of new staff very well. Most are welcomed to their desk and effectively are abandoned, left to make sense of their new world the best way they can. When induction is organised, it is usually a series of visits and meetings and the newcomer is bombarded with vast amounts of information. The common outcome is a new member of staff who has forgotten much of what he or she has been told and who has a confused and partial picture of their employer and its world. The very best employers provide a structure to enable new members assimilate information at a rate they can absorb. They are provided with memory aids and sources of reference to enable them to access what they need to know but cannot reasonably be expected to remember.

CHECKLISTS AND HANDBOOKS

There is a real dilemma at the start of any employment. A large amount of information with differing degrees of importance has to be transmitted by the employer to the new employee. Newcomers need at least two forms of information — what they have to know and what they want to know — and the sheer quantity of information can lead to mental overload. Also, the stress inherent in starting a new job makes it very difficult for the recruit to sort out the peripheral from the important information and remember any of it. A practical approach to overcoming these difficulties is the use of a checklist supported by a handbook or guide. The value of staff handbooks and their presentation is described in Salthouse (1995) and their role in relation to the written statement of terms and conditions was discussed in Chapter 8.

A checklist can ensure the whole range of topics a new starter should be told about — the rules that need to be explained, places and facilities to be shown and people to be met — are covered. The guide or handbook will provide the written back-up and supplementary information.

In addition, an employer may wish to explain to new (and existing) employees the organisation's vision, its core business, strategic priorities, markets and values. A handbook provides the opportunity to give new employees a written guide to help them find their way around the organisation. This is of particular value when the organisation is large, has several outlets, locations or sites, or has a range of activities in its operational portfolio. The handbook can also include or summarise policies and formalised procedures. Many organisations make use of manuals but it would be unreasonable to expect every employee to have their own copy;

however, they should know what those key policies cover and where to find them.

Induction checklists help line managers make sure nothing is missed and indicates to the new starter what will be covered. The list serves as a reminder of what the individual has been told and can provide space for private notes. It can also form a record to demonstrate that the employee has been told about certain rules and regulations. While this should not be the primary motivation for the use of a checklist, its existence can be of value if, for any reason, the employer wishes to demonstrate that the employee has received information, has been trained to work to the desired standard or has been made aware of rules.

An induction checklist might begin by listing the action needed before the start date. For example:

1. Decide who is going to induct the new employee. If several people are to be involved, be sure each knows what they are covering and who is going to be the main 'inductor'.
2. Ensure that the new employee knows where and when to report, who to meet and what to bring (for example, documents to be checked, refreshments, safety clothing, etc).
3. Make sure the main inductor is ready and prepared to meet the new employee.
4. Make sure that the necessary facilities (eg desk, telephone, parking place, keys, etc) are arranged and ready.

Table 9.2 comprises a list of possible topics that might usefully to be covered. It shows how the induction can be scheduled and refers to documents or other sources of reference. Space is provided for each item to be signed off once it has been explained to the new recruit.

Table 9.2 An induction checklist

Topic	Point of Reference	Initials starter	Initials inductor	Date
Day 1 Introduce the inductors and explain the nature of their relationship to the new employee				

Topic	Point of Reference	Initials starter	Initials inductor	Date
The Job Check the new start has a copy of the job description and understands:				
• Their duties and responsibilities				
• The expected results and standards				
• The reporting lines and other relationships with key others				
• General issues that affect the job				
• Possible early problems and how to deal with them				
• Details of protective or special clothing	*Safety Handbook*			
• Rules about safe working practice and conduct	*Safety Handbook*			
• Arrangements for	*Staff Handbook*			
— working hours and overtime	*Forms available*			
— time sheets	*available*			
— sickness, holidays and other absences	*from office*			
— meal times				
— leaving the workplace				
• Storage and use of personal property				
• Social rules of the work place (eg tea clubs)				
Contract of employment Check understanding of terms and conditions and period of probation, notice and main procedures	*Personnel Office Staff Handbook*			

Topic	Point of Reference	Initials starter	Initials inductor	Date
Payment Complete necessary forms for payroll, tax and pensions. Explain arrangements for pay and layout of payslip	*Personnel Office*			
The workplace Make sure the new starter is shown around and knows the location of: • entrances, exits and emergency assembly points • cloakrooms and toilets • cooking facilities • rest room • first aid facilities and fire fighting equipment • notice boards • supplies • telephones and their availability for private calls • car parking	*Safety manual*			
Key others Introduce to immediate colleagues. Explain who the important others are and why. Make arrangements for initial meetings and visits.	*Organisation structure in Staff Handbook*			
First week • Tour of main site(s) • Explain how the work of the individual fits into the work of the section	*Business Plan*			

Topic	Point of Reference	Initials starter	Initials inductor	Date
• Explain how the work of the section fits into the work of the organisation and contributes to its primary purpose	*Strategic Plan and Annual Report*			
• Who are the main internal customers of the section	*Telephone Directory*			
• What services are provided for them				
• What quality standards exist	*Quality procedures*			
• What performance indicators are used				
• How complaints and feedback are handled	*Complaints procedure*			
Checks Check understanding of: • individuals' expectations of their job, boss and employer • lines of communication • job purpose • priorities • standards of work • reporting relationships • working relationships • main policies, procedures and operating rules • working arrangements, hours, conduct and safe practice • source and use of forms Does the new employee know how to discuss problems and with whom?				

Topic	Point of Reference	Initials starter	Initials inductor	Date
Within first month • Relationships and memberships • Organisational structures • Key relationships between the postholder and the rest of the organisation • Social clubs • Staff associations • Trade unions Organisational communications • Formal • Newsletters • Notice boards • Meetings • Others • Informal • Reliability • Main sources of gossip • Sources of information • Formal decisions • Procedures • Employment matters • Pay matters • Personal advice Employment conditions • Training opportunities. • Location of terms and conditions of employment and sources of advice.	*Staff Handbook* *Training Plan Staff Handbook*			

Many employing organisations have lists like the one in the table — largely unused. One reason for this is due to lack of knowledge on the part of the line manager and main inductor. Most trainers can point to well-produced but seldom used guides for managers explaining how to make sure new staff are welcomed and assimilated into the workplace quickly and easily, but horror stories abound. Take the new employee who found she had no desk because the previous postholder had not left (and had not been told that he was being replaced). Another had to wait six weeks for a key to the office building and was forced to wait outside every day. Worse still was the newcomer allocated a private office and a phone, and who was told by the boss to 'get on with it'; new colleagues introduced themselves as they passed in the corridor. Welcoming of this quality is unlikely to produce enthusiastic employees who feel a high level of commitment to their employer.

Checklists, such as in Table 9.2, are certainly helpful, but their real value is dependent on the way in which they are used. In general, it is the line manager who is responsible for inducting new members of staff. Sometimes, however, even though the boss should always welcome the new start, it is more appropriate for another member of staff to carry out the detail of the induction. For good reasons, the manager may not know, for example, all the details of how the tea club works or the communication methods used by the trade union. Some aspects of employment are better dealt with by others in the organisation — for example, getting the details of pay and the contract right are too important to be left to the vagueness of an uncertain manager. Health and safety rules also need to be communicated accurately. Even though the line manager should know and endorse safety rules, the fire officer may be the best person to explain evacuation procedures and an experienced work colleague perhaps the most effective demonstrator of safe working practices.

Buddying

Some organisations make use of the 'buddy' system. New employees are allocated a buddy who, in effect, befriends them. The buddy is an experienced worker who understands how the organisation functions, and is willing and able to be of assistance and provide a good role model. While there is little point in asking the worst cynic to welcome new staff, there is likewise little point in glossing over problems. The new person will find out the truth soon enough.

Under this system the new start shadows the buddy for the first few days. Thus they have ready access to someone who knows their way around. The new starter gets to know the job and find out what it is like to work for the employing organisation. The induction checklist provides a link between the line manager, the buddy and appropriate others. It ensures that everything the new employee needs to know will have been explained satisfactorily or at least steps taken to help them find out. (Finding out also can be of benefit to those carrying out the induction.) As the new employee becomes more confident and is able to take charge of their learning about the new employer, workplace and colleagues, their dependence on the buddy can decline. Even so, if the relationship has been productive, the new starter will have acquired a 'sympathetic ear' for future use.

Mentoring

A similar but different approach rapidly gaining in popularity is mentoring. A mentor is usually a more experienced employee who is able to help new members of staff learn about their jobs and the organisation they are working for. The mentor also encourages the new starter to learn by reflecting on experiences and considering the appropriateness and effectiveness of work practices. More commonly found among professional groups and managers, a mentor scheme can be a powerful developmental tool with benefits lasting long beyond the induction phase of employment. The role of a mentor is described more fully in Dale (1993).

INCLUSION

According to Garratt (1987): 'Most organisations assume that inclusion will happen somehow and put little energy or time into ensuring that it is effective. I believe that it is an important developmental state which needs managing because, without it, it is impossible to become competent in an organisation or job.'

Prem was the first management accountant the organisation had employed. The other professional staff in the finance department were qualified chartered accountants. Prem's appointment signalled that the change in accounting methods, discussed for months, was about to take place. Some people viewed the change with excitement; others believed it was a recipe for disaster and were suspicious of Prem. The finance manager was nervous yet hopeful. She expected Prem's appointment to be successful even though she knew that some obstacles would have to be overcome. Prem was very well qualified, enthusiastic and seemed to appreciate some of the problems he was likely to encounter.

For the first few weeks everything seemed to be going well and the finance manager started to relax. Then the first indications of problems began to emerge. Staff, including those who were initially supportive, began to complain about Prem's attitude to his work. They said he was not fitting in and was slow. The boss was puzzled. Prem's work seemed to suggest that he was getting to grips with the organisation and had some good early ideas. She decided to ignore the moans and hope that they would go away. They did not. Prem, despite his cheerful attitude, was becoming more isolated. The staff were excluding him not just from the social chit chat of the office, but were failing to give him the business information he needed to do his job.

Eventually the finance manager felt the situation had deteriorated far enough. She asked Prem what was going on. Prem said that he was very unhappy and did not understand why his colleagues were failing to accept him. He had tried, he said, to be sociable and to make friends in his early days. At first he thought he was succeeding and had started to build a productive relationship with one person in particular, but suddenly that person had started to back off. The lunchtime walks they had begun to share, stopped abruptly. Prem had not felt able to question his colleague about what had happened, but from then things had become steadily worse.

The finance manager asked to see Michael, the colleague in question. At first Michael was hesitant and said that he was not aware of any problem, but the finance manager pressed on. Eventually Michael blushed and began to tell his manager what had happened. Prem never washed up. One or two heavy hints had been dropped but Prem had not taken any notice. His failure to follow office customs had become the favourite topic of conversation and one or two of the staff had made some outrageous racist remarks (Prem was of Asian origin).

> A very bitter argument had followed, the atmosphere in the office was tense and Prem was seen by most people as the cause. Even those, like Michael himself who did not approve of what was happening, had decided the best course of action was to stay away from the source of the trouble.
>
> The finance manager was faced with a very difficult situation to resolve. All caused by the fact that no-one had told Prem, properly, about the office's normal customs.

As can be seen from the boxed example, including a new member of staff requires more than hints and time. New colleagues need to gain the acceptance of existing staff if they are all to work productively together. Ways to involve staff in the various stages of the recruitment and selection process were described earlier. Involvement and appropriate participation can help to achieve successful inclusions and acceptance of a new member of staff. However, other supplementary action is needed to make sure that this important aspect of induction is not left to chance. The use of buddies and mentors can help considerably, but only if they know how important it is to make explicit some of the more vital but often unspoken rules and rituals inherent in the organisation's culture.

Socialisation

Any new member of a group goes through a period of initial socialisation. It is a normal part of group formation and development. The consequences of non-acceptance are known to lead to withdrawal, rebellion or rejection. The example of Prem demonstrated the first and the last of these phenomena. Rebellion occurs when the new but non-accepted group member begins to disrupt the work and life of the group. The processes of socialisation aim to bring conformity to the group's existing culture. They strive to reinforce existing behaviours and ensure that the new member adopts the assumptions that underpin the group's working methods, practices and value systems. These processes are subtle and strong. Refusal to consider alternatives, resistance to change and peer group pressure are some examples of the ways in which groups impose conformity on new members.

Thus, a newcomer who wants to share experiences from previous work settings may be told, 'Yes, that might have worked there but it won't here because Mary in customer accounts won't accept it' or 'because our systems are more complicated'. Resistance can take the form of 'We are too busy this week, but we will try next...' or 'Have a go if you want (but we won't help you)' or 'It won't work'. Peer group pressure includes flattery and special treatment, allocation or withdrawal of privileges, and exclusion.

When appointing a new member of staff with the intention of bringing about change, an organisation needs to consider the power of socialisation, the social dynamics of the work group and the need for inclusion and acceptance. All new employees needs to be able to understand the culture of their employing organisation to be able to work effectively within it, but if the reason for appointing that particular individual is to bring about change to that very culture, the organisation needs to consider how best to manage the inclusion phase.

Talking about promoting individuals to the role of director, Garratt (1987) points out:

> There seems to be an implicit assumption in organisations that the very act of declaring someone a director or general manager somehow bestows on them omniscience. Suddenly they are expected to be able to understand and advise upon all matters regardless of specialist discipline. They are expected to be able to interpret political nuances in the external world in areas which have been positively banned to them before and to understand the cultural aspects of their international relationships even when their previous career has been insular in the extreme.

Even though most appointments are not to this level of seniority, the effect is similar. Situations where it was felt possible to induct and include new members without drawing them completely into the existing culture occurred in the public sector in the 1980s. There was a trend in favour of introducing private sector business methods as a way of increasing efficiency and effectiveness, but repeatedly appointments failed to live up to expectations. The new appointees often encountered frustration and opposition, and many left their jobs after comparatively brief periods. Others introduced inappropriate methods, hoping to translate working practices from one culture to the other. There have been occasions when the transfer between sectors has been very positive, but they are not as well known or apparent as the failures. It is possible to attribute some of the lack of success to the poor quality of the induction and inclusion programmes used by the employing organisation, rather than to the problem of cross-sector employment.

CELEBRATING THE NEWCOMER'S APPOINTMENT

In most organisations, a new employee just starts work. After all, it is almost an everyday event, especially in large organisations. But everyday for whom? Certainly not the new employee. Starting a new job is a new beginning, a new way of life, a make or break opportunity and the beginning of new relationships. In other words, a major life event. Even if the employee only expects to stay in the job for five years, in most working lives the 'first day experience' will only happen perhaps eight or nine times, so starting a new job is something to celebrate.

There are various ways in which this can occur. Some organisations report starters and leavers to their major decision making body such as the board of directors, but this is usually done as numbers not names. If names are reported at all, it is normally confined to senior appointments. Another medium for the public announcement of appointments is the organisation's staff newsletter. Photographs of new employees may augment brief biographies and details posted on notice boards with words of welcome appended.

Some organisations arrange receptions at suitable points in the year to enable the new staff to meet 'important' people such as the chief executive or the managing director. Similarly, if the organisation is large enough and recruits enough new starts to merit induction courses, the presence of a senior member of staff to welcome new employees and to outline the organisation's priorities can be beneficial. These help new staff to fit themselves and their jobs into the wider context and to appreciate the priorities of their employer.

Ideas such as these may seem out of place in the days of temporary contracts and high staff turnover, but if the point of good quality induction is to achieve rapid assimilation into the employing organisation and high affiliation with its aims, perhaps the productivity gains outweigh the cost. Moreover, actions such as those described above demonstrate a greater commitment to staff than do bland words in the *Annual Report* about 'caring employment practices'.

PROBATION AND TEMPORARY CONTRACTS

At one time, after a minimum of six months in employment, all employees on permanent contracts had the right to appeal to an Industrial Tribunal if they considered their contract to have been ended unfairly or wrongly. The minimum time period for this right was increased in the 1980s to the current two years. Many employers found that the original regime facilitated the use of probationary periods. The new employee was, in effect, on trial and confirmation of their permanent post was given when the probationary period had been completed satisfactorily. The best employers had safeguards to make sure that the trial was conducted properly and not used to avoid giving staff enough service to gain the right of appeal to the Tribunals.

Mary started work with a major retailer on 4 January 1978 and for her first two months she was placed with a manager in the customer sales and invoice office. On 4 March, the manager asked to see her to review formally her first two months with the organisation. She was asked to reflect on what had gone well and what not so well, and was given feedback and advice about which areas of her work to concentrate on improving. Her next two months were spent on the shop floor. At the end of this period her work was again reviewed, this time by the merchandising manager. She was also required to complete a self-assessment form.

A discussion was then held between Mary and the stores personnel and training manager to decide whether she should go on to the training scheme, whether she needed more general office experience or whether she needed to spend more time on the shop floor. A move on to the training scheme suggested that initial progress had been satisfactory. More time in either the office or on the shop floor indicated a cause for concern. If Mary did not achieve a satisfactory report at the end of a further month, she knew she would not be confirmed as a permanent employee. If she was confirmed she would join the training scheme.

The changes in the employment protection legislation have reduced the use of probationary periods, which now tend to be restricted to jobs such as nursing or teaching, where professional training and an assessment of competence to practice are certified. Meanwhile, the use of temporary contracts has increased considerably. The main reasons for this trend are to provide employing organisations with increased flexibility and to avoid giving staff their full employment rights. To quote Torrington and Hall (1991):

> Firms are developing flexibility in their approach to employment and these are inducing changes in labour market mechanisms: firms have found themselves under pressure to find more flexible ways of manning.... They have put a premium on achieving a workforce which can respond quickly, easily and cheaply to unforeseen changes, which may need to contract as smoothly as it expands, in which worked time precisely matches job requirements, and in which unit costs can be held down.

He goes on to identify 'core employees who form the primary labour market' and then two other groups – 'first those who have skills that are needed but not specific to a particular firm, like typing and word processing' and 'those enjoying even less security, as they have contracts of employment that are limited, either to a short-term or to a part-time attachment.' He also suggests, 'An alternative or additional means toward this flexibility is to contract out the work that has to be done, either by employing temporary personnel from agencies or by sub-contracting the entire operation, as has happened so extensively in office cleaning and catering...'

To most people it may be an unwelcome development as it provides few safe havens for people seeking security. For others, however, it provides the attraction of being one's own boss, having a variety of work experiences and being able to organise one's life to accommodate, for instance, periods of several months away from work to take a long holiday, renovate the house, update skills or simply to have a break. Posts in the peripheral group of jobs appear more suitable for, and maybe more attractive to, married women, many of whom adopt a lifestyle that has been called 'portfolio living', maintaining a mix of activities without the single-minded preoccupation with one job that is more common among men. The recent increase in the number of part-time jobs has been almost entirely filled by women. Whether this is providing them with the sorts of opportunity they are seeking, or exploiting the workforce as a whole by providing the sorts of jobs that only women will accept because of their limited employment opportunities is a matter of opinion.

The flexibility, in reality, means that employers are (or at least were) able to staff their operations to cope with peaks and then to lay off employees without having to make redundancy payments. Until 1994, employees employed for between 5 and 16 hours per week had to complete 5 years continuous service before having rights to claim wrongful or unfair dismissal at an Industrial Tribunal. Staff working less than 5 hours never attained such rights. However, in 1994 the House of Lords decided that this was contrary to European Union legislation and gave the same rights to all permanent employees, and this was confirmed by the government at the end of the year. Thus, all staff with a contract of employment will obtain full statutory rights after two years employment. How this will affect the pattern of employment will be interesting. Some commentators believe that the opportunities for female part-time employment will decrease as employers no longer gain advantage from using staff in this way. Alternatively, the unification of rights may make part-time working less risky and so more attractive to men.

Some employers have found the use of temporary contracts a valid way of placing staff on probation. Indeed, some of the Government training schemes aimed at reducing youth unemployment and training them for jobs last this amount of time. Work samples and job trials are regarded as the best predictor of subsequent performance: both Cook (1988) and Smith, Gregg and Andrews (1989) give them a predictive validity of over 0.5. One would hope that work samples and trials lasting this length of time would achieve a better coefficient.

INITIAL TRAINING

If it is rare for induction to be seen as part of the recruitment and selection process, it is even less common for initial training to be linked. Yet there are two reasons why this phase of training should be seen as an integral part of recruitment and selection.

First, when devising the job description and assessing the basic person specification criteria, consideration should be given to which elements would need to be competently performed immediately (ie what skills and knowledge are absolutely essential for effective performance) and which could be acquired or developed later. These latter aspects of the job could be tasks of secondary importance and skills and knowledge that could be obtained later or in other ways. The absolutely essential criteria should not include organisation-specific items unless the post in question was being filled internally. If rapid acquisition of specific knowledge or skills is necessary, these too should be covered in the early training programme.

Secondly, the recruitment and selection process subjects an individual to rigorous scrutiny and a detailed assessment of their attainments, experience, skills and aptitudes. When else does this occur to such a depth, with so many other people involved? The assessment provides a wonderful opportunity for using the outcomes to inform an initial training and longer-term development programme.

If the recruitment and selection process is viewed as a matching process which enables individuals' experiences and capabilities to be assessed against the requirements of the organisation and the job, the type of punitive judgements that detract from learning can be avoided. Rather, the process can be used to identify gaps in skill, experience and competence. This alternative view of recruitment and selection is of particular importance and value when internal appointments are being made. This approach should not, and need not be the preserve of large employers. On the contrary, smaller organisations depend just as much, if not more so, on the goodwill and continued commitment of their staff. Thus, using the full range of available opportunities to contribute to their development and invest in their future will be of benefit to all concerned.

The assessment can give unsuccessful candidates valuable information about what to do differently to aid their future career prospects, in two respects. First, their profile in comparison with the job description, person specification and other job requirements can be considered.

> The post of site manager, when it came vacant, had been seen as the golden opportunity for all the engineering managers employed in the Production Plant. Staff turnover was low and so chances to apply for promotion had been thin on the ground. The managing director and personnel manager were very aware of what could happen, unless they handled the process very carefully. Competition already existed between the sections and they felt that if the vacancy was presented as a point-scoring exercise several undesirable outcomes could result.
>
> They were also fearful of the negative aspects of competition that might develop between the applicants, such as growing rivalries as each applicant attracted their own team of

supporters. They felt that the criteria for selection used by the workforce would not match those of the management, and that, after the event, whoever was appointed would be nobody's first choice. They would then find themselves in an almost impossible position with the difficult task of trying to heal the schisms that had been created by the vacancy.

They planned a normal recruitment and selection process and then considered how it could be changed into a total team development programme. They saw this as the chance to upgrade overall management skills available by influencing management processes and increasing the skills of the individual engineering managers. Their solution was:

1. To create a person specification that would reflect the needs of the job as a manager and as a leader of the engineers. While it included attainment and educational requirements, the skills were more tightly defined to ensure that the level of the job could be assessed and distinct competencies identified. Thus leadership (guiding, directing and enabling), communication skills, negotiating, dealing with conflict and teambuilding were weighted more heavily than other skills (for example, customer and market relations, business skills and strategic planning abilities) normally expected of a post at this level.
2. No advertisement was published. Instead staff were asked to register their interest by agreeing to participate in a diagnostic process. After this process, those who wished to become candidates would be asked to submit formal applications in a more traditional fashion.
3. It was made clear that everyone who expressed interest would come out of the process with a personal assessment that would inform a development plan. They would be expected to agree to a learning contract with the managing director and the newly appointed site manager.
4. The diagnostic process was designed by the personnel manager and managing director with assistance from a specialist management consultant. The MD also decided

to invite the chief executive of a friendly competitor to be an assessor and ultimately to act as a mentor for the site manager. The diagnostic process was a battery of activities comprising:

— A series of work-based activities drawn from the job description and designed to elicit the skills outlined in the person specification.

— A self-assessment questionnaire designed on the basis of a repertory grid and using elements of the job description. The engineering managers were asked to enter their constructs describing the features of the most effective and least effective postholder and to weight the others in comparison. The results were analysed and contrasted to those of the managing director and personnel director.

— The staff in each of the engineering sections were asked to give confidential feedback about their managers' performance against the relevant criteria.

— The main customers (internal and external) were asked to provide evidence in specified areas demonstrating the quality of service received from, and their experience of the manager in question.

(This number of information sources may seem excessive but the MD believed that the recruitment process was more than just investing £0.5 million plus for at least 5 years. The opportunity was seen as a chance to upgrade the human management resource and, consequently, the MD wanted to gather information in the same way as would be done for any other significant investment decision. The appointment also was being made in a climate in which development was seen as a critical part of assuring the quality of Production Plant's work and output.)

5. The information was analysed by the management consultant (to ensure impartiality) and was fed back first to the individual. This was to demonstrate that the managers had control over the information and the chance to add any comments and explanations about why they

behaved in a particular way. (The possibility of post hoc rationalisation was acknowledged but it was felt that the managers should have the right to discharge any feelings before the next stage of the process.)

6. On the basis of the feedback and reports, the managers were asked to declare if they wished to make a formal application. Out of the group of 15 engineering managers, only 3 decided that they wanted to go on to the next stage. The remaining 12 agreed that they wanted to concentrate on developing their skills in their current positions. The challenges this would present them, they all agreed, would provide them with enough career advancement for the time being.

7. The formal applications were made in the form of a presentation to members of the company's board. The candidates had been asked to 'sell' themselves as if they were a service, which would allow board members to make the decision in exactly the same way as if they were deciding to invest in a new piece of equipment. The MD and personnel manager were conscious that the board members knew some of the engineering managers personally and so wanted to remove, as much as possible, any halo effect. It was also thought that taking this approach would help the unsuccessful candidates feel less rejected.

8. Throughout the whole process, everyone on the site was kept fully informed of what was happening via the bulletin boards.

9. The final appointment was announced in an atmosphere of celebration:

   — There was general sympathy for the candidates but a recognition that the process had been open, fair and testing.
   — The non-appointed managers had 'won' from the experience and their learning contracts.
   — Because of the use of very specific criteria, the two unsuccessful candidates could see very clearly the differences between their performance and that of the person appointed.

> — They could not claim they had not been given a fair and full opportunity and, even though they were disappointed, they knew they had the chance to make a different sort of impression on the members of the company's board. In addition, they had learning contracts that were qualitatively different from the rest of their colleagues.
> — A new management process had been introduced and the learning culture had been reinforced throughout the firm.

Secondly, the individual's application and behaviour throughout the selection process can provide useful information that can be used as feedback during a debriefing.

One of the candidates for site manager, Maurice, gave a really disappointing presentation. The managing director had predicted that he would be the best but, on the day, Maurice did not deliver. Perhaps it was nerves, but more likely he had misjudged the situation.

His presentation had not been professional and he had not interpreted the brief correctly. He had seen the opportunity as a chance to tell the board what he had done throughout his career — in effect, presenting a verbal CV. Also, Maurice had used the audio-visual aids poorly, again seeing the presentation as a projection of the person rather than as a sales event. The overhead projector slides, therefore, had been produced by his secretary as typed lists. The focus was totally historic, concentrating of past achievements. There was only a passing reference to what Maurice intended to do in the future.

The managing director debriefed Maurice after the appointment had been made. He opened the session by asking Maurice how he had seen the presentation and what he thought the board had been looking for. This approach was chosen to enable the MD to make sure that Maurice was ready to receive some stark messages. The main mistake he had made was not to think himself into the position of his audience. Maurice had thought merely about what *he* wanted to tell the appointment panel. He had not considered what they wanted to hear, and he had missed totally the point of selling a service to a board making an investment decision. This had been taken as a reflection on his abilities to relate to his customers and markets and to plan strategically.

At the end of the debriefing the MD arranged, as part of Maurice's learning contract (which included presentation skills), for him to spend some time in the company's main marketing and business planning departments.

The assessment carried out during recruitment and selection need not be limited to unsuccessful candidates. The chances of making a perfect appointment are slim. It is far more likely that the person appointed will have some gaps between their current performance levels when compared to the person specification. The opportunities presented by this rigorous examination of an individual's skills, experience and capabilities can be used to indicate which areas:

- need initial work following the appointment of the successful candidates;
- would benefit from longer-term development; and
- need to be guarded against as sources of concern or weakness.

Bruce was delighted when he was appointed to the post of site manager. He had worked really hard throughout the appointment process and felt as though he had earned his achievement. Nevertheless, he was somewhat daunted by what he knew faced him in the coming years. The plant's future was far from secure. Competition was hotting up and the need to keep costs and prices down would be even more critical. The workforce was good and a high spirit of co-operation existed, but Bruce knew that some hard and perhaps bitter decisions would have to be taken.

The managing director debriefed him after the presentation to the board. Bruce was told that the board felt he would be a good appointment and his popularity with the other managers and workforce would be a positive help in the future. As they sat back to consider what was to come and Bruce's learning contract, the MD asked what aspects of the job Bruce felt would cause him the most difficulty. Bruce initially identified internal communications. The presentation itself had not been easy for him. He was not used to public speaking and felt that his performance could be improved. Skills in this area would be essential if he was to make an early impact on the works council meetings. The MD readily agreed to Bruce's suggestion that he should receive some training and support in this area.

Bruce went on to think about how he would manage the team. He recognised the value of the shared experience the managers all had gone through as part of the process. A real team spirit had developed. However, even though he wanted to continue in this vein, he was not sure how to do it. This, he felt, was not an immediate development need because the benefits of the selection and the learning contracts approach would last some time, but he did not want the gains to slip. Bruce and the MD, therefore, agreed that teambuilding and development would be part of his longer-term plan.

'But', asked the MD, 'what will you do if you find yourself faced by opposition from members of the team?' This question took Bruce by surprise. He had not really considered that any one of his colleagues and friends would disagree with him. The MD explained that the board was a little worried about Bruce's ability to deal with conflict because they simply did not know how he would react. Bruce accepted that he did not know either, and they both agreed to keep this in mind as the future unrolled. If such a situation arose and if Bruce did not feel as though he had the abilities to handle direct conflict, he and the MD would have to take action to manage the problem in other ways.

The example shows how the recruitment and selection process can be used to provide some tangible spin off for those who are not appointed. This can take the form of structured and informed feedback which can include recognition of strengths as well as weaknesses against the person specification and job requirements. The feedback can also give the applicants good quality evidence about how they can take action themselves to improve their performance in both their job-related skills and experience and the abilities needed for use when submitting applications.

The assessment of skills also provides information for the person appointed. It would be a mistake for anyone to sit back after a success of this nature and think that it was the end of their learning. New jobs will always present new challenges and even if the person appointed is superbly qualified and equipped there are bound to be some areas where learning is needed. Seeing the assessment as an opportunity to obtain some good quality information can speed up the assimilation into the new job and increase the chances of long-term success.

DEVELOPMENT

In the above example, the immediate need was concerned with the skills required in making presentations. More significant for the long-term success of the appointment would be Bruce's abilities to keep the team together during difficult times. Both these needs can be addressed through the creation of development plans with key objectives against which progress can be assessed and further needs identified.

The days following an appointment tend to be euphoric and optimistic, especially if the successful candidate is a popular choice. One or two people may have axes to grind or scores to settle, but these tend to be held in abeyance as those who consider themselves to be the 'losers' wait to see how the new appointment shapes up. The postholder is full of enthusiasm, energy and commitment, ready to make changes and get going. A wise person takes some, but not too much time to take stock and plan their programme of change. Part of this programme should include consideration of how to gain commitment and take everyone along willingly, including the 'losers'.

Bruce's management programme for the Production Plant included improvements to stock management, purchasing and waste control, energy efficiency and changes to the employment conditions of supervisory staff. The last was known to be sensitive and probably the most difficult to achieve, especially since Bruce suspected that not all the engineering managers agreed with the need to make the changes. He decided this would merit discussion with his mentor.

During their next meeting, Bruce broached the topic. The mentor agreed with Bruce's diagnosis and saw the problem as an initial test of Bruce's teambuilding skills. Team leadership is easy when times are good, but not so when hard choices have to be made. The mentor suggested Bruce should use a force-field analysis to explore the problem in greater depth. He asked Bruce to list the forces in favour of the change and those opposing it (these forces should include circumstantial factors as well as people). He was then asked to consider how best to mobilise the forces in favour and to deal with the opposing forces.

At a subsequent meeting they discussed the results of Bruce's deliberations about the forces, and the mentor had some additions to suggest and some ideas about the tactics Bruce could use to make progress.

Bruce was maintaining a portfolio of his learning. At the moment this took the form of a document wallet containing his learning contract, copies of the notes he was producing as his early plans for the Production Plant were being developed and a notebook containing his thoughts and reflections on his experiences. Even after only three months the records of his plans were showing interesting evidence of how he was making progress. His thinking was becoming clearer and his understanding of the plant's market was deepening. When he read back through the papers he could also see indications of where he was not so confident. The same sort of difficulty was presenting itself time and again

> — he hadn't got to grips with the inconsistent flow of information from the external sales force.
>
> His notebook was the most valuable part of his portfolio. This was where he jotted down the ideas and insights he was gaining. Gradually the picture was making sense to him. No one knew exactly what went into the book, but its existence had been noticed. He was getting into the habit of getting it out of his wallet and making the odd jotting now and again. Bruce's 'red book' was becoming the centre of jovial speculation, and some of the other managers had started to copy him.

The development programme identified as part of recruitment and selection can be used to inform subsequent progress and performance reviews. If the initial performance objectives were derived from the job description and the person specification listed the basis of the skills and experiences needed to achieve those objectives, it makes sense for the work of the postholder to be focused towards the realisation of these. Thus, the review of performance should concern the progress made towards them and the development of the individual's abilities. The identification of areas in need of further development stem from them. Any initial training programme drawn up from the selection process should reflect the needs of the job and the organisation as well as those of the individual. The longer-term development programme should do likewise, yet be contingent enough to allow for future change. If this approach is taken, the early months will automatically prepare for subsequent performance reviews and appraisals.

> Six months after Bruce's appointment the managing director arranged for a formal review of progress. The agenda contained the following items:
>
> - **business plan;**
>   - current conditions
>   - market share
>   - financial performance
>   - current and planned production volume
> - **business development;**
>   - current customers

> — new markets
> — competitors
> • **internal management**;
> — health and safety
> — operational state of plant and equipment
> — stock levels and work in progress
> — energy utilisation
> • **human resource management**;
> — morale
> — skill levels
> — internal communications
> • **team development**; and
> • **Bruce's development**.

While the above may seem a lengthy agenda, it focuses on all aspects of the business and areas directly within Bruce's zone of influence and control. In effect, the areas are all his responsibility as defined by the job description and person specification. The factors identified during the selection process can be seen in the context of the whole and their relevancy highlighted. This demonstrates the importance of ensuring that selection activities are chosen and designed to be relevant to the job and the skills and experiences required for its effective performance. If 'games' or irrelevant techniques are chosen the potential of the whole process is sadly reduced. Using recruitment and selection as an integral part of human resource and personal development can be a very powerful way of managing the growth of an organisation and the people within it.

SUMMARY

This chapter has covered an area of employment most commonly regarded as being a training activity rather than a part of the recruitment and selection process. The reason for its discussion here has been to demonstrate that, if the need for effective induction and inclusion is considered early, it is possible to integrate all aspects into an holistic approach to human resource development.

Any new employee, if they are to use their skills and abilities effectively and quickly and develop their potential in the context of their employing organisation, needs to be seen as an individual. Beginning a new job contains stresses and pressures that are often ignored in the euphoria of a new start. Some of these have been listed, but it must also be remembered that the needs of any one person will be unique. It is even possible that they will experience some lack of confidence despite their success. Planning to deal with the initial learning needs can be built into the phasing of the recruitment and selection schedule.

Most people take a new job because it presents some challenges. It is highly unlikely that the individual appointed will be fully competent in every area of the job. And even if they were to be able to 'hit the ground running' inevitably there will be some things to be learnt. Effective induction makes sure the individual knows the necessary details concerning their employment and the organisation. An induction checklist, such as the one described, can help the manager provide a 'route map' for the new employee, act as a source of reference and provide a record evidencing what was covered. The latter can facilitate other processes such as probation and subsequent performance measurement.

Inclusion is part of socialisation into the organisation. To be totally effective, an individual needs to be competent at the job, but they also need to 'fit'. Even if the appointment was made in order to challenge and change the organisation's culture, the individual needs some insight into the rules, customs and underpinning assumptions. Often the importance of this phase goes unrecognised. Many promising appointments fail due to the lack of understanding, acceptance or failing to fit.

Inclusion can be assisted if the appointment is seen as a reason for celebration by the organisation and new employees are feted in some appropriate ways. At its very simplest level, a formal welcome from an 'important' person can make a new person feel part of the employing organisation. Even when this person is only temporary, the organisation is dependent on the quality of the work done. Efforts made to ensure that new employees understand the priorities of the organisation and its key policies can be time well spent. This is especially important if temporary employment contracts are seen as extended work samples and trials that frequently lead to the permanent employment of individuals.

The rigour of the assessments carried out during recruitment and selection often get left behind once the person has accepted the contract of employment. Yet, it is very seldom that the assessment of an individual's skills and abilities is carried out in such depth. If the assessment has been made against criteria drawn from the job description and person specification, it is possible to use the results to provide high quality feedback and inform a development plan. The latter will include information about initial training and development needs, and will also feed into longer-term plans and contribute to performance review.

The development plan need not be confined to the successful candidate. The people not appointed have the right to be offered feedback. If these people are current employees of the organisation, it is in the employer's long-term interest to offer developmental action. People not selected are, in reality, rejected, and have every right to feel that way. If the employing organisation wishes to retain their commitment and motivation, some positive action is required to prevent them feeling as though they are 'losers'. A learning contract and development plan are ways of turning the process from win/lose into win/win.

The recruitment and selection process is too expensive to finish once the person is in post. It consumes considerable time, resources and money, yet, often, what happens within the process goes unchallenged. It is one of the many management processes that just happens. The validity of the selection methods has been researched, but the overall effectiveness of the other stages are rarely questioned. Making use of the information gathered during the assessment phase is one way of maximising the activity, but how else can the process be judged and improved? The final chapter considers this question.

10

Evaluating the Decision

The theme of this book has concerned the ways and means of getting the best person into the right job. Ways of describing the best person and how best to recruit and select them have been discussed. But how do we decide, after the event, whether the best person has been appointed? After the offer of employment has been made, the contracts signed and exchanged and the person starts work, definitions might change. Who decides if the best person was employed? The person themselves, the employer (and in the case of large organisations, who is this?), the people who work with the new person, the customer, etc?

Even if it is clear who judges whether the best person has been appointed, how is this decided if all the other people who could have been appointed if they had applied are taken into account? How does an organisation know that it has not rejected the best person when that person was not given the chance to demonstrate their abilities? How can the employer be sure that its definition of the job requirements and person specification were accurate in the first place?

Some of these questions are rhetorical and, as such, are impossible to answer with any degree of accuracy. For it must be remembered that conditions are changing and even the very fastest recruitment and selection process takes some weeks and, during that time, something will have changed that will have altered the definition of 'best'. This chapter explores rather than answers these questions. It also considers how to judge the meaning of 'best', and some ways of evaluating the effectiveness of the whole recruitment and selection process are suggested.

MEASURES OF SUCCESS

In Chapter 4, some of the flaws in the processes of human decision making were described. People making judgements about other people do not make dispassionate assessments; decisions are made on the basis of errors, prejudgements and erroneous assumptions. Nevertheless, there is a compelling desire to demonstrate that these decisions are objective. Many organisations operate on the assumption that rational and logical decisions are made and therefore their efficacy can be evaluated scientifically and their results counted. While this may be true for many areas of business (the importance of accounts, statistics and ratios as performance indicators demonstrates this) human resource management does not lend itself to the use of numerical values to judge achievement. However, the reality of organisational life must be appreciated. It is not good enough to say that everything to do with human performance needs to be assessed in qualitative terms. Some genuine efforts are needed to evaluate the recruitment and selection process in a quantifiable way. As Herriot (1989a) says, evaluation can be assessed against two dimensions:

- **effectiveness** — 'selection procedures should yield the right type of information and lead to correct decisions'; and
- **efficiency** — 'every step taken within a selection procedure and any instrument used may add to the procedure's utility as well as its cost'.

Mike Smith (Smith, Gregg and Andrews, 1989) is perhaps the main researcher active in this country in assessing the worth and value of human resource methods in a quantitative way. He, too, bases his estimation on two main quantifiers — validity and utility. How these two measures can be used to assess the efficiency of recruitment and selection will be briefly described before ways of assessing effectiveness are explored.

Validity

We considered the main types of validity in Chapter 6. These can be summarised as:

- **Face validity** — do the techniques and methods appear to be appropriate to those involved?
- **Content validity** — are the contents of the process appropriate for the job in question?
- **Construct validity** — do the methods and techniques examine relevant aspects of behaviour for the job and organisation?
- **Criterion validity** — do the methods and techniques do what they claim to do and nothing more?
- **Reliable validity** — do the techniques and methods do the same job every time they are used?
- **Impact validity** — is the effect on the people involved beneficial?

However, before one even starts to assess the validity of the techniques used, it may be appropriate to ask if engaging in a recruitment and selection process is a valid course of action.

The managing director concluded that enough was enough. She was tired of the production manager and the marketing manager squabbling. After-sales advice, she now decided, belonged to neither. They had already been given what they had wanted. A training room had been set up and a member of the production department had been freed to train customers' engineering staff to maintain the products supplied by the company. The move was beginning to pay off. The time spent by the company's engineers on site had been reduced because mistakes and misdiagnosis had decreased as the accuracy of fault analysis by the customers' own staff had improved. Customer satisfaction had increased and working relationship improved. The training service was paying its way and was proving to be a real boost.

When the MD reviewed progress at the end of the first quarter, a different picture emerged. The managers argued still. The production manager was being awkward, while the engineer, who had been released to become the trainer, was not being allowed enough time to prepare, and the training room was being used by other staff for everyday jobs. The other engineers were leaving the room in a mess and were not being very co-operative. The marketing manager was being supportive but the trainer was not able to get the engineers to clear up or take messages from customers.

The MD decided to put an end to the conflict once and for all by reorganising and appointing a customer training manager. The trainer was disappointed. The marketing manager argued that the appointment would not make any difference and, in any case, the income gained from the training service would not be enough to cover the additional salary costs. The service manager sulked.

A recruitment consultancy was engaged to find the right person. Within two months a superb appointment was made. The training manager was well qualified and very skilled. He stayed a year, leaving after becoming very frustrated at the lack of co-operation from most of the engineers and the production manager. Meanwhile the trainer had also left to take a better paid job in the local college.

The decision to appoint a training manager rather than deal with the real problem had cost a total of £31,000 (£21,000 for the salary plus £10,000 for the consultant's fees) and the company's capacity to provide training to customers had been lost.

Was the decision to engage in recruitment and selection a valid one to take?

Utility

Utility is defined as 'the condition of being useful or profitable'. In the context of recruitment and selection it is generally used to calculate the robustness and comparative worth of various recruitment and selection techniques. The findings are used to support the case for changing and improving practices. The analysis of utility can also provide some indicators to judge the overall value of the process. Smith, Gregg and Andrews (1989) argue that: 'investment in selection procedures has been shown to be one of the best investments an organisation can make ... utility analysis has now developed to the point where different strategies of selection can be compared and an informed choice of the most effective strategy can be taken.' They demonstrate how utility is calculated:

- **Estimating the selection ratio** — how many applications are received for every job (if this is 10 per job the ratio is 0.1, if it is 50 the ratio is 0.5).
- **Applying the validity coefficient** — this is an estimate of the predictive validity of the particular technique being scrutinised (as described in Chapter 6).
- **Estimating the percentage of applicants who can adequately perform the job** (for example if the job is easy perhaps 50 per cent of

the applicants could be expected to do it; if it is complex and requires a lot of specific knowledge, this might be 3 per cent).

This approach relies on the use of complex formulae and calculation and is limited to estimating the inputs (ie qualified applicants and validity of techniques) rather than estimating the worth of the outcome (ie the value of the end result).

The managing director wanted a new secretary. The personnel manager predicted that the advertisement would attract an excessive response unless care was taken to build very tight screens into it. In the event, 66 applications were received.

The MD insisted that the new employee should be able to take fast, accurate dictation and produce a finished copy ready to go out without any further checking, but did not want to be bothered with any fussy selection activities. He would know the best person for the job from an interview. The personnel manager, on the other hand, argued that for only a small extra cost and effort, the use of a work sample would be a more effective way to assess the shortlisted candidates.

Creating the shortlist would not be a problem as the personnel manager anticipated that only 30 per cent of the applicants would meet the requirements of the person specification. Using these parameters and a mathematical formula, the personnel manager was able to calculate the comparative effectiveness of the two selection methods in relation to the actual cost and salary investment. Because the results of the calculations were presented in the sort of numeric terms the MD was used to, the personnel manager was able to convince him that the fuss was worth the effort.

Cascio (1987) takes this approach further and makes use of decision theory to include other factors that affect the process. He says 'the utility of a selection device is the degree to which its use improves the quality of the individuals selected beyond what would have occurred had that device not been used. Quality may be defined in terms of:

- the proportion of individuals in the selected group who are considered "successful";
- the average standard score on the criterion for the selected group; and
- the pay-off to the organisation resulting from the use of a particular selection procedure.'

To obtain a reliable result from these calculations, extensive investigations are required to determine the monetary equivalents of the individual parameters used. The methods proposed are very similar to the work study procedures that were used once to determine efficiency levels and fix productivity pay. For the findings and results to be valid and robust, a large sample from the target population is needed to form the database. Also, a degree of stability is required so that the findings can be repeated and checked, and some measure of subsequent job performance also needs to be developed and agreed. Inevitably the results of the investigations are based on historic data. Moreover, the effort needed to gather and test the data is considerable, requiring the outlay of expertise and time and access to a large number of employees and managers. This means that these techniques are most valuable to very large organisations that engage in the recruitment of large numbers of people to very similar jobs. They are less useful for small organisations, or when conditions are changing rapidly.

Nevertheless, the thinking underpinning utility analysis has some value. It provides a way of estimating benefit and providing numeric values to enable comparison between otherwise incomparable processes. However, the technique does not tell the manager how effective the recruitment and selection process has been. This can only be achieved, after the event, by assessing the accuracy of the process and the quality of its outcome against a number of predetermined criteria. Cost is one of these factors, and the effect filling the post has had on the rest of the organisation is another. But the performance and achievement of the postholder must be also figure as a main source of evidence about the quality and effectiveness of the recruitment and selection process.

EFFECTIVENESS OF THE APPOINTMENT

How the assessment opportunities presented by recruitment and selection can be used to aid induction, initial training and longer-term development was described in Chapter 8. The same can be applied when deciding whether the person appointed was the 'best' person for the job providing the basis for this assessment are the job description and person specification. If they have been well and carefully written at the outset they provide an enduring means to evaluate the quality of the outcome of the process.

When the job description and person specification are used to assess performance in the job, the changes that will have inevitably occurred after the appointment has been made will need to be taken into account. There will have been changes within the organisation and in the context in which is operating. Markets change as do customers, competitors, and suppliers. The people within an organisation also change, almost continuously. People acquire skills, knowledge and experience, their level of motivation and job satisfaction vary, their personal circumstances influence their attitude to work and working relationships shift. Also, the person appointed makes an impact. They will affect the dynamics of the work group, their output will contribute to the work of the team and should add to the achievement of the organisation. The individual will have made the new job their own by focusing on different aspects of the job description and encompassing their priorities into the key objectives agreed with their line manager. A well-written job description will have taken account of this by building in flexibility.

The quality of an appointment may be assessed using a number of measures in addition to the criteria contained in the job description and person specification, plus the assessment of the utility of the process. These methods are discussed in the following sections.

Trainability

Factors here are:

- How quickly can the individual progress up the learning curve to attain the status of a competent employee? This will depend on prior skills, knowledge and the relevance and applicability of previous experience.
- How steep is their learning curve? This will be influenced by the individual's ability to assimilate information and comprehend the new job and its environment. The environmental factors must not be taken lightly. Take, for example, the individual who has always worked in a closely regimented environment. When they move into one in which individuals are given targets and expected to organise their own work, the newcomer will need time to adjust. This should to be taken into account when assessing their speed of progress up the learning curve.
- Level of attainment: some people's learning curve flattens out before

others. Even though the prediction of ultimate performance should be part of the selection decision, estimating what that will actually be is far from straightforward. (Remember the frailty of the best predictive validity coefficient.)

Performance

The performance of individual employees is assessed all the time, and one reason for systematising the process of appraisal is to give proper recognition to this. Formal appraisal also helps to ensure that judgements are made against explicit factors rather than the private, idiosyncratic prejudices of a particular line manager.

If a systematic approach has been taken to the operation of the recruitment and selection process, such appraisals can be based on the content of a job. It is easier to assess performance if the job is built up of elements that can be counted, such as sales made, widgets built or customers served. Nevertheless, it is possible to use the same form of assessment for less tangible tasks, so long as good quality objectives have been agreed and account taken of how achievement is to be assessed.

The level of performance can also be assessed by comparing performance against the behavioural criteria laid down in the person specification. Again, allowances must be made for changes that have occurred since the appointment. These will have occurred in the organisation, the work of the individual and other people who have an influence. Some insight into the processes of attribution can be helpful to provide an understanding of how we view other people's achievement. When we see or experience an individual's behaviour, we attribute the cause of that behaviour to one or more of three sources: the individual (the actor); the target of the behaviour (the entity); and the circumstances. To be able to decide which is the real cause, information is needed to explain the behaviour as witnessed. In the following example, it will be seen that more explanation is required to answer the question 'why?'

Belinda does not talk to her co-workers — why?

- *Belinda is moody and anti-social.*
- *Belinda's co-workers are offensive.*
- *The organisation in which Belinda works for does not encourage social interaction.*

Even though the root cause of behaviour is usually a combination of factors, we tend to regard the actor as being responsible. This tendency is known as the fundamental attribution error and is thought to be generally pervasive. The value of this theory here is that it acts as a warning to those appraising the behaviour of others. When there is little experience of that person (for example a new employee) there is likely to be a tendency to focus on the individual and see them as the cause of events and to ignore or minimise the importance of other factors. Weiner (1974) has developed a 'two by two' model to demonstrate how the factors can influence an individual's level of performance (see Table 10.1).

Table 10.1   How factors influence an individual's level of performance
(Weiner, 1974)

	Temporary behaviour (likely to change)	*Stable behaviour (unlikely to change)*
Internal to the individual	Effort, mood, fatigue	Ability, intelligence, physical characteristics
External to the individual	Luck, chance, opportunity	Task difficulty, environmental barriers

Thus, the dangers of making judgements without allowing for other causes are evident. Proper appraisal designed to involve the 'actor' fully is the simplest way of ensuring that the effects of biases and assumptions are reduced. The individual can be involved in the assessment and diagnosis of reasons using shared and explicit criteria. Thus the *assessments* made during recruitment and selection form a basis for a *development plan* which was drawn up in way that fully involved the individual and was designed to address the *key objectives* as outlined in the job description to provide a fair basis for *performance review*.

If a rating scale is used to inform assessments, this too can contribute to later performance review. Care, however, should be exercised to ensure that subsequent reappraisal takes into account the changes and other causal factors, as outlined above, that may have influenced the individual's performance. This is especially important if the rating scale was numeric and based on absolutes. Bald numbers tend to have a permanency about them which, in reality, is fallacious. What was seen as 'excellent' performance in the context of a selection event may seem ordinary in the cold light of day. For example, if an individual achieved a rating of four for communications during the selection exercises, one would reasonably expect that individual to maintain or increase the rating as a result of increased exposure to the job and additional experience. A subsequent performance review rating of three or less would make any manager wonder what was happening.

An alternative to simple numerical rating scales is to use behaviourally anchored rating scales. These use numbers to symbolise a statement describing a level of performance. Thus, if the individual's rating was 'skills used with positive impact some but not all of the time (development is needed in some but not all aspects)', the subsequent review allows greater opportunity to explore which aspects of the individual's communication behaviour and skills had improved and which still required attention.

If the performance review and assessment of progress are being used to reward performance by giving additional pay or access to training schemes, permanent employment or other opportunities, extra care needs to be taken to ensure both fair treatment and that unreasonable sources of bias are reduced.

Fit into the organisation

If, during the selection decision, the quality of 'fit' was given consideration, this can be a useful dimension against which to evaluate the quality of the recruitment and selection process. An assessment of the individual's likely fit should be taken into account when deciding whether they are the best person for the job. The dilemma of appointing someone who will be easily assimilated into the existing culture of the organisation against someone who would challenge it has been discussed in Chapter 8. Of course, how well an individual fits into the organisation is partly within their own control but is also dependent on the quality of the induction process and the attitude of significant others. Even so, it is reasonable to expect that if the various phases of recruitment and selection process have been effective it will be possible to judge whether the individual is able to work productively within the organisation after a reasonable period of time in post.

Achievement

Productivity by definition implies some measures of achievement are available to calculate actual against desired output. Achievement depends on the clarity of the job or role purpose and agreement of key objectives. The recruitment process is intended to attract individuals who are able to perform the job to the standards required and in the special conditions of the organisation. The selection process is to discriminate between those who, the organisation believes, will match the criteria and those, it believes, are not likely to be able to do the job. During the course of both recruitment and selection, information is supplied to candidates about the role and organisation. This enables them to decide whether the job is one they want to, and feel able to do. If these processes have been effective, the individual and the organisation, as represented by its managers, should have attained a high level of understanding about the nature, key aspects of the job and the purpose of the role. This understanding should have included agreement on the key objectives, the comparative priorities and the desired level of achievement.

Considering the amount of effort that goes into these processes to attain a good level of understanding, it makes sense to use the achievement of the agreed objectives and tasks as the main measure to judge the effectiveness of the recruitment and selection process, as well as the performance of the individual. If the desired levels of achievement are not being obtained, a well-planned and documented recruitment and selection process should make it possible to track back to ascertain the reasons for non-achievement and identify where remedial action is needed. And, again, remembering the fundamental attribution error, these reasons may not be the responsibility of the individual appointed.

During the assessment centre, Jackson was by far the best of the candidates. Depending on the judgement of the final interview panel and references, the assessors believed that it was more than likely he would be offered the post.

The assessment centre, however, had not been entirely satisfactory. The candidates had misinterpreted the topic for the group exercise and had pitched the level of their discussion on operational, local issues rather than seeing the strategic implications. This meant that the assessors had found no evidence on which to assess the strategic thinking skills of any of the candidates. Even though Jackson's performance in the group was better than the others, he had not acquitted himself particularly well in the two other exercises designed to explore this dimension. Notes of these weaknesses were made in the overall report submitted to the selectors. However, the need to get someone in post was urgent, none of the other candidates seemed as good, and it was felt that this weakness (if it actually was present) could be addressed as part of Jackson's development plan.

Jackson started work and quickly found himself immersed in the operational demands of the job. His development plan had been agreed but good reasons were found for not completing its various stages. As time passed, his manager became more and more worried about Jackson's performance. While he was good at the detail, he was not planning ahead — his lack of foresight was beginning to show and he was not reading the signs around him. Even though procedurally the section was working well, a sense of impending crisis was beginning to reduce productivity and effectiveness.

Jackson's manager decided to review his performance formally after nine months rather than waiting for the full first year to be completed. His personnel file was retrieved and the comments of the assessors made sense in the light of actual performance. The manager saw, with hindsight, that more directive action should have been taken to ensure that the perceived weakness in strategic thinking skills should have been addressed. The organisation of Jackson's work should also have been more tightly planned so that the development needs could not have been so easily sidelined. Rather than blame Jackson, wisely she saw her part in his poor level of performance. She decided to restructure the work of the section, on a temporary basis, and to take away long-term planning until Jackson's abilities had increased sufficiently for it to be returned. A schedule of work was arranged to include regular meetings. During these, Jackson's manager agreed with him to act as a coach, using the planning aspects of the job as vehicles for learning. While, initially, the manager would take responsibility for this area of work, the gradual transfer back to Jackson would be facilitated, providing he made satisfactory progress.

Moreover, the manager was aware that if Jackson did not achieve the desired level of progress, she was doing everything right to start formal proceedings towards dismissal on the grounds of lack of capability. Jackson too was aware that unless he made the required effort and changed his behaviour, he would need to start looking for another job that better suited his abilities.

Even though the full implications of predictions made during the recruitment and selection process are not always seen until later, they need not always be negative. Sometimes, people outstrip the assessment of their abilities and flower under the conditions offered by a new job. The opportunities for growth can unleash potential and start an exponential learning curve. The adage 'nothing succeeds like success' can be very true in employment. Achievement leads to growth in confidence which encourages the individual to try more difficult or complex tasks and learn new skills. The halo effect also favours them as others increase their trust in the individual and allow them to take more risks. This phenomenon does not happen that often, but when it does it gives those involved in the appointment a reason for their own satisfaction and a sense of achievement.

ACHIEVEMENT OF OUTCOMES

The aim of recruitment and selection is to appoint the best person for the job, in a cost-effective way that suits the organisation's standards and values. Deciding whether this has been achieved requires the application of value and qualitative judgements. Some aspects of the process can be counted. For example:

- How many suitably qualified applicants expressed their interest, at what cost?
- Were all the vacant posts filled?
- How long did it take to fill the post(s)?
- How much did the selection process cost?
- Did the selection methods provide enough information to support decision making?
- Was the person appointed at a cost (in terms of salary and other benefits) that the organisation wanted to pay?

But these measures are more concerned with quantifying the inputs rather than assessing the quality of the outcomes. For the most part, deciding whether the process produced the desired outcome (ie the 'best' person for the job), gave value for money and was of the overall standard desired requires the application of less tangible measures. The evaluation of these is an assessment of quality. Quality is defined as 'fit for purpose' and this, therefore, must beg the questions:

- Who decides?
- Whose purpose?
- Using which measures?

Some attempt will be made to answer these questions from the standpoint of the key stakeholders involved in the process.

The postholder

This person is often forgotten in the evaluation of the success of the recruitment and selection process (except as the object of the evaluation). The most common measures used are those discussed above:

- Is the person trainable?
- Do they perform to the desired standard and achieve their objectives?
- Do they stay long enough (but not too long) in the post, etc?

How frequently do organisations assess the quality of the recruitment process from the postholder's perspective? Is it assumed that because they were successful, their view of the process will be seen through a haze of glory? And because the organisation was generous enough to offer them a post, they will not have (nor have the right to have) any criticisms.

In fact, the person appointed will possess a great deal of information regarding the quality of the process, based on their own real experience, that will help the employing organisation with its evaluation. The sorts of questions that could be posed include, for example:

- Was the information supplied relevant, accurate and realistic?
  — do the work conditions match those contained in the glossy brochure?
  — are training opportunities provided?
  — are on-target earnings really obtainable?
  — does the postholder actually have the authority to decide and freedom to act?
- are working relationships as good as suggested, etc?
- Were the initial impressions created confirmed by later experiences?

- Were the expectations created in the mind of the applicant about the nature of the job and the role made real after the appointment?
- Does the job offer realistic opportunities for obtaining the achievement of the postholder's desired outcomes (for example money, status, job satisfaction, further progress)?

Asking newly appointed staff during induction about their experiences can be revealing. It can be better if these questions are asked by someone outside line management or not connected with the process, because this helps the new staff to be open and more honest than perhaps they would be with the people who were responsible for the appointment.

The personnel function

The personnel function has several areas of interest regarding the effectiveness of recruitment and selection. For example:

- The costs of the various stages, such as consultants' fees, the size of the advertisement, printing costs and the number of people involved.
- The quality of the outcome — did adequate (not too many and not too few) suitably qualified applicants come forward?
- Was the person appointed the best, or was the appointment made because there was no one better at the time?
- The validity of the different stages and their contribution to the overall quality of the process — how did each stage fit into the cohesiveness of the whole? Did they make sense separately and yet combine to add value to the information being exchanged and the final decisions of those involved?
- The cost-effectiveness — could the same result have been achieved in ways that were easier, simpler, cheaper or faster?
- What was the contribution made by the process to the human resource management function and the achievement of the organisation's overall goals?
- Did the process aid the implementation of other policies such as equal opportunities, skill enhancement, strategic achievement and change?

It is very easy for each of the different aspects of personnel management to be seen as stand alone functions and for them to be separated out. Alternatively, they can be integrated to achieve a greater good, additional to the benefits supplied by specialisation. Evaluation of recruitment campaigns and selection events in the light of the organisation's strategic needs and business plans can be a valuable way of improving the integrated functioning of the personnel section as well as adding to the quality of recruitment and selection.

The employer

More and more organisations are engaging in strategic planning and the use of business plans to inform their decision making and actions. A key part of drawing up such plans is the SWOT analysis performed on the organisation's environment, its operations and resources. The strengths and weaknesses of the organisation's human resources base have a direct bearing on its ability to achieve its goals and ambitions. Recruitment and selection, even if the post in question is the most junior, should be aimed at minimising the weaknesses and augmenting the organisation's strengths. The evaluation of the process, from the employer's perspective, should concern the contribution it has made to organisational performance:

- Will the processes used and the person appointed help with the achievement of the desired performance/business outcomes? Can clear links be seen between the skills, as outlined on the person specification, and the role, as defined in the job description, and those needed for the achievement of business and strategic plans?
- Have the process and appointment avoided creating new problems and helped to resolve old ones? Some appointments can cause more damage than benefit and if the process is handled badly, the resentment caused can lower productivity.
- Have the organisation's ethical considerations been taken into account and has the organisation been helped to discharge its social responsibilities? The way in which recruitment and selection decisions are made can be at odds with the organisation's espoused values. For example, an organisation that prides itself on openness is not being consistent if the appointment process is conducted in secret. Commitment to improving job prospects in the locality is not fully discharged if local people are appointed only to lower-paid posts and the better-paid ones filled by people attracted from elsewhere.
- Has the organisation's reputation been enhanced? Recruitment and selection is normally carried out in public. Discriminatory advertisements, poorly produced, inaccurate information, mistakes in letters, breaches of confidentiality, badly organised selection events and absence of feedback or follow-up information are all known examples

of poor practice. None of these help paint a picture of a professional or business-like organisation.

The manager

Most managers want to fill the vacant post quickly with the least disruption to their existing staff and with a minimum amount of effort and cost. They hope the person appointed will be effective and no trouble. Most seem to realise that they are taking a risk, but few appreciate the size of the risk nor how proper planning can help to reduce it. The following questions might be part of their assessment of the process:

- Was it easier to get the vacancy advertised than expected?
- Did the advertisement result in an application from someone who could be appointed immediately?
- Did the expected disagreements fail to materialise?
- Did that one person 'hit the ground running'?
- Did everyone approve of the appointment?
- Did the person appointed solve all the problems in their first month in post and turn the organisation around in the second, without making any waves?

Perhaps these are extremes, but most personnel practitioners would recognise these motivators and the, perhaps, unexpressed fears of managers. The anxiety and stress levels of candidates are recognised and taken into account (for example, it is common to hear assessors comment about how nervous the candidates were), but how often is acknowledgement given to the anxieties of managers and assessors? The chances of getting an appointment wrong have been discussed earlier. The failure to get it right (whatever this might mean) also lies with the manager, and the consequences of having to unpick an unsuccessful appointment can be enough to cause most managers some concern. Therefore it is no wonder that most view having to fill a vacant post with some trepidation. Even though their own success depends on the effective recruitment and selection of staff, how often does any one manager have to fill a post? Perhaps more account should be taken of managers' stress levels as they go through the process, and perhaps they should be guided and supported more rather than being expected to know how to do it and left to get on with it.

Colleagues

Much of the success of the appointed individual depends on their abilities to build good working relationships with their new peers and colleagues. This is two way. Most people coming into a new job are filled with enthusiasm and wish to make a good impression. Very few people start a period of employment with the intent of making enemies. However, not all existing staff view their new colleague with the same degree of enthusiasm. Part of the manager's responsibilities after an appointment has been made is to prepare the team.

Any group of people naturally view a new member with suspicion. The status quo is being disrupted and the new person will inevitably challenge custom and practice. The existing staff will want someone who will fit in and who will make a positive contribution to both the work of the unit and the life of the team. How this positive contribution is defined will vary considerably from team to team and should have been taken into account during the preparation of the person specification and the recruitment process.

From the point of view of colleagues, the best way of finding out whether an appointment will be successful is to ask them what they expect the outcome to be. It is also worth asking them what constitutes a successful recruitment and selection process from their perspective. Anticipated responses might include:

- Transparency of the process to all concerned.
- Openness and clarity of the selection criteria.
- Fairness and reasonable treatment of the candidates.
- Opportunities to be involved — appropriately. This does not necessarily mean being involved in the decision making; just the opportunity to show the work place to candidates may be sufficient.
- Speed of decision making — no one likes not knowing for long periods of time.
- Appropriate communication of the results — white puffs of smoke from the board room are not really adequate ways of telling existing staff about a major investment decision.
- Good quality feedback to the unsuccessful candidates with some benefit accruing to them.

From the newly appointed colleague, existing staff would be justified in expecting someone who is willing to contribute from their previous experiences and knowledge while learning about the organisation's history and current ways of working. 'New brooms' might sweep clean but they are seldom very popular, whereas someone who is prepared to listen, learn and then share is more likely to be well received. However, the best way of finding out how colleagues will decide if the best person for the job has been picked is to ask them — before the event.

Customers and suppliers

The proponents of total quality management stress the importance of working closely with customers and suppliers. The degree of involvement varies considerably. Some organisations (especially those in service and care businesses) see the customers as being integral to the organisation and want to involve them in decision making. Student representatives on the boards of governors in educational establishments, residents' associations, tenants groups, fan clubs and car owners' groups are all examples of the customer groups who get involved in the decision making of their supplier organisations. These valued customers may have views on the success or otherwise of the recruitment and selection process. They will have their own individual criteria and expectations about the appropriate level of involvement. Similarly, the employing organisation and its managers will have views on how much involvement from these groups in the recruitment and selection of new staff would be appropriate.

Regardless, the customers' and suppliers' acceptance of the new postholder will have a positive or detrimental effect on that person's ability to perform their duties effectively. Again, it is worth considering, and asking, at the beginning of the recruitment and selection process, what criteria will be used by these and other key stakeholders to evaluate the end-product.

Recruitment consultant, advertising agency

Recruitment and other agencies have different criteria to the other stakeholders. Their reputation and the possibility of repeat business depends on reaching a satisfactory outcome. However, this satisfactory outcome may be very different from that desired by the employing organisation. The following example demonstrates how easy it is for different agendas to influence the quality of the outcome.

Philip's earnings in the agency were determined by the number of posts filled. His job was to find clients, find candidates, make a match and achieve an appointment. His on-target earnings were set in terms of completed assignments. The agency's client base was made up of large organisations and its' particular speciality was senior management and board level appointments. Consequently, the chances of repeat business were slim. Most clients had a single post to fill and came to the agency as a result of seeing advertisements for similar vacancies to their own in the press, or as a result of word of mouth. The agency's reputation was built on two factors — speed and confidentiality.

What was important to Philip was that he got someone in post — fast. If they did not stay in the job for very long, it did not really matter. Appointment 'failures' were usually seen as the responsibility of the employing organisation (for example, they had not inducted the person properly or they had made a bad decision) or the individual (the new appointment had not transferred well or they had interviewed well but could not deliver). Rarely was it seen as the fault of the agency for putting forward low quality candidates. In any case, if the postholder left quickly, there was always the chance of repeat business, especially if the process had appeared to be smooth and professional.

Most reputable recruitment agencies follow up with both the clients and the people appointed because they realise that business is not built on quick fixes alone. Nevertheless, when commissioning consultants, it is worth discussing at the start of the assignment what constitutes a satisfactory outcome for all parties and building evaluation into the contract.

Advertising agencies are usually anonymous. Their work appears under the banner of the employing organisation and their reputations exist in their own industry more than in their market, Nevertheless, they have distinctive styles that can be recognised by those who watch the situations vacant columns. Their desired outcome, unlike some recruitment consultants, is the establishment of long-term working relationships with the client. Short-term gains, such as oversizing advertisements, not passing on commissions obtained from publishers and poor quality control tend to work against the renewal of contracts and so are counter-productive in the long run. Employing organisations usually place contracts with agencies after a process of tenders and presentations, examples of work and are followed by contractual negotiations. Perhaps it would be worth agreeing how to evaluate the success of recruitment and selection activities at the time of agreeing the initial contract.

A strategic opportunity

The only real measure of success must be the contribution the process and appointment make to achievement of the employing organisation's strategic plans and operational imperatives. There is little point in doing something that does not add value to its operations and takes the organisation closer to realising its ambitions. The size of the investment in a post, even at the most junior level, has been described earlier. The recruitment and selection process should thus be paralleled with any other investment decision, except that, because it directly affects the lives of people, it must be seen as having more serious consequences.

The steps described below indicate the distinct stages in the process. If these guidelines are followed, they can help to ensure that the process contributes to strategic achievement. They also take into account the needs of the people involved in the operation of the process and those being processed:

1. Define and design the job to be done.
2. Identify the skills, knowledge and experience required to:
   — achieve the organisation's objectives;
   — meet needs — fill gaps, enhance strengths, minimise weaknesses;
   — carry out the tasks comprising the job; and
   — contribute to the organisation's well-being.
3. Develop a profile of a competent performer (ie the idealised person who is performing the whole range of duties at a level above that deemed to be satisfactory).
4. Attract candidates cost-effectively (ie applications are received from an adequate number of suitably qualified individuals to enable a selection to be made).
5. Supply candidates with good quality information so they are able to form a realistic picture of the organisation and its requirements.

6. Devise a selection process that obtains enough accurate information to enable all parties to make the best decision.
7. Assess the skills, knowledge and experience of candidates against the criteria and job requirements so that potential performance may be predicted and development needs identified.
8. Provide information to support the negotiations about the explicit contract of employment and clarify the expectations contained in the implicit terms.
9. Draw up an induction orientation and initial training programme to enable the appointed candidate to become effective quickly.
10. Inform the early stages of the development programme needed to help the appointee move from adequate to competent and beyond.
11. Complement the initial induction with inclusion activities to help the existing team assimilate its new member quickly and to regain and enhance the level of the whole team's performance.

SUMMARY

Throughout this book attempts have been made to combine the disparate and sometimes conflicting needs of the employing organisation, the line manager, colleagues and the person to be appointed to a job. The requirements of the organisation for its long-term success must be paramount because without its continued existence, no one can be employed within it. Nevertheless, this does not relegate the needs of the people involved nor should it provide excuses for sloppy practice.

The decisions taken during the recruitment and selection process lay the foundations for the success or failure of any appointment. Once an offer of employment has been made and accepted, it is difficult to change the explicit terms and conditions of the contract. It is even more difficult to alter the understanding and operation of the implicit terms. It is during the recruitment and selection process when these terms are communicated and their meanings begin to be understood, or misunderstood.

There is no excuse for creating misunderstandings. Clear expression of job requirements and the creation of explicit criteria in the job description and person specification make the other stages of the process straightforward. If fundamental mistakes are made in the initial stages, the repercussions can be difficult and stressful for all concerned. Getting the process right can be fun. It can provide the opportunity to let people demonstrate their abilities, assess them against useful criteria and provide them with some very helpful feedback. It can lay the foundations for good quality learning contracts and development plans, and it can give people chances to grow and realise potential they did not know they possessed.

Recruitment and selection is a major investment, that affects the employing organisation's ability to succeed and implement its strategic plans, it is also a series of decisions made by people that influence the quality of the lives of others. The processes used to make those decisions are known to be flawed and imperfect but, even so, the decisions can be made in ways that reduce the negative effect of these errors and biases (although not eliminated) and improve their overall quality.

This book has outlined some of the ways in which these improvements can be put into practice and has demonstrated how quality can be enhanced. There have been examples and checklists to help managers implement the suggestions and develop their own practice. The final words of guidance recognise that assessing the performance of others and being assessed is stressful and demanding. Getting the initial stages right and setting up good quality criteria and processes make the assessments more straightforward. Planning the processes in advance and allowing time makes it easier to give the details the attention they need. But above all, if the process is designed to ensure that the right people are matched to the right job in the right organisation, there is a chance that all involved will gain and learn from the experience.

References

Alban-Metcalf, B and Nicholson, N (1984) *The Career Development of British Managers*, BIM, London.

Alimo-Metcalfe, B (1994) 'Waiting for fish to grow feet', in Tanton, M (ed) (1994).

Armstrong, M (1991) *A Handbook of Personnel Management Practice, 4th edn*, Kogan Page, London.

Bazerman, M H (1994) *Judgement in Managerial Decision Making, 3rd edn*, Wiley, Chichester.

Belbin, R M (1981) *Management Teams: Why They Succeed or Fail*, Heinemann, London.

Boyatzis, R E (1982) *The Competent Manager*, Wiley, Chichester.

Broverman, I K, Vogel, S R, Broverman, D M, Clarkson, F E and Rosenkrantz, P S (1975) 'Sex-role stereotypes: A current appraisal', in Schuch Mednick, M T, Tangri, S S and Hoffman, L W (eds) *Women and Achievement: Social and Motivational Analyses*, Hemisphere Publishing, New York.

Cascio, W F (1987) *Applied Psychology in Personnel Management*, Prentice Hall, Englewood Cliffs.

Child, J (1984) *Organisation: A Guide to problems and Practice, 2nd edn*, Harper & Row, London.

Cook, M (1988) *Personnel Selection and Productivity, 2nd edn*, Wiley, Bath.

Dainty, P (1987) 'Work motivation and job design: Is progress over?', *Journal of Occupational Psychology*, (28), p 59–78.

Dale, M (1992) 'Why do women decide not to submit applications for management jobs?', Dissertation for the MSc in *The Analysis of Decision Processes*, Huddersfield Polytechnic.

Dale, M (1993) *Developing Management Skills*, Kogan Page, London.

Dale, M and Iles, P (1992) *Assessing Management Skills*, Kogan Page, London.

Deaux, K (1976) *The Behaviour of Women and Men*, Brooks/Cole Publishing Co.

Department of Employment (1994) *Labour Market and Skill Trends 1995/96*, Skills and Enterprise Network, Nottingham.

De Witte, K (1989) 'Recruiting and advertising', in Herriot, P (ed) (1989).

Fyock, C D (1993) *Get the Best: How to Recruit the People You Want*, Business One Irwin, Homewood, Illinois.

Garratt, B (1987) *The Learning Organisation*, Fontana, London.

Hackman, J R and Oldham, G R (1980) *Work Design*, Addison-Wesley, Reading, MA.

Handy, C (1985) *Understanding Organisations, 2nd edn*, Penguin, Harmondsworth.

Handy, C (1989) *Age of Unreason*, Arrow, London.

Handy, C (1994) *Empty Raincoat*, Hutchinson, London.

Herriot, P (1989a) *Recruitment in the 90s*, IPM, London.

Herriot, P (ed) (1989b) *Assessment and Selection in Organisations: Methods and Practice for Recruitment and Appraisal*, Wiley, Chichester.

Hertzberg, F, Mausner, B and Snyderman, B (1959) *The Motivation to Work*, Wiley, Chichester.

Hunter, J E and Hunter, R F (1984) 'Validity and utility: Alternative predictors of job performance', *Psychology Bulletin* 96, pp 72–98.

Iles, P A and Robertson, I T (1989) 'The impact of personnel selection procedures on candidates', in Herriot, P (ed) (1989b).

Kakabadse, A, Ludlow, R and Vinnicombe, S (1987) *Working in Organisations*, Gower Press, Aldershot.

Kelly, G A (1955) *A Theory of Personality: The Psychology of Personal Constructs*, Norton, New York.

Lord, W (1994) 'The face behind the figures', *Personnel Management*, December.

Mabey, C and Iles, P (1991) 'HRM from the other side of the fence', *Personnel Management*, February.

Makin, P J (1989) 'Selection of professional groups', in Herriot, P (ed) (1989b).

Marshall J (1994) 'Why women leave senior management jobs', in Tanton, M (ed) (1994).

Maslow, A (1954) *Motivation and Personality*, Harper & Row, New York.

McClelland, D C (1953) *The Achievement Motive*, Appleton-Century-Crofts, New York.

Nicholson, N & West, M (1988) *Managerial Job Changes: Men and Women in Transition*, Cambridge University Press, Cambridge.

Pedler, M J and Boydell, T H (1985) *Managing Yourself*, Fontana, London.

Robertson, I T and Smith J M (1988) 'Personnel selection methods', in Herriot, P (ed) (1989b).

Roe, R A (1989) 'Designing selection procedures', in Herriot, P (ed) (1989b).

Salthouse, M (1995) *A Guide to Staff Handbooks*, Croner, Kingston-on-Thames.

Schein, V E and Mueller, R (1990) 'Sex role stereotyping and requisite management characteristics: A cross-cultural look', Paper presented to the 22nd International Congress of Applied Psychology, Kyoto, Japan.

Schmidt, F L and Hunter, J E (1977) 'Development of a general solution to the problem of validity generalisation', *Journal of Applied Psychology* 62, pp 529–40.

Selwyn, N M (1988) *Law of Employment, 6th edn*, Butterworths, London.

Smith, M, Clegg, M and Andrews, D (1989) *Selection and Assessment: A New Appraisal*, Pitman, London.

Sternberg, R J (1988) 'Sketch of componential sub-theory of human intelligence', *Behavioural and Brain Sciences* 3, pp 573–584.

Tanton, M (ed) (1994) *Women in Management: A Developing Presence*, Routledge, London.

Taylor, F W (1911) *The Principles of Scientific Management*, Harper & Row, New York.

Torrington, D and Hall L (1991) *Personnel Management: A New Approach, 2nd edn*, Prentice Hall, Hemel Hempstead.

Weiner, B (ed) (1974) *Achievement Motivation and Attribution Theory*, General Learning Press, Morristown, NJ.

ADDITIONAL READING

Armstrong, M (ed) (1994) *Human Resources Management Yearbook*, AP Information Services, London.

British Qualifications 25th ed (1994) Kogan Page, London.

Chandler, P (1995) *An A–Z of Employment Law*, Kogan Page, London.

Christopher, E M and Smith, L E (1995) *Managing Recruitment, Training and Development: A Source Book of Activities*, Kogan Page, London.

Conlow, R (1994) *Excellence in Management*, Kogan Page, London.

Corfield, R (1990) *Preparing Your Own CV*, Kogan Page, London.

Corfield, R (1992) *How You Can Get That Job: Application Forms and Letters Made Easy*, Kogan Page, London.

Edenborough, R (1994) *Using Psychometrics*, Kogan Page, London.

Farbey, D (1994) *How to Produce Successful Advertising*, Kogan Page, London.

Fletcher, J (1995) *Effective Interviewing*, Kogan Page, London.

Greenwood, D (1994) *The Job Hunter's Handbook*, Kogan Page, London.

Jackson, J and Ansari, N K (1994) *Managing Cultural Diversity at Work*, Kogan Page, London.

Leighton, P (ed) (1990) *The Daily Telegraph Recruitment Handbook*, Kogan Page, London.

Lewis, C (1985) *Employee Selection*, Hutchinson, London.

Lunn, T (1992) *The Talent Factor: Key Strategies for Recruiting, Rewarding and Retaining Top Performers*, Kogan Page, London.

Malone, M (1993) *Discrimination Law: A Practical Guide for Management*, Kogan Page, London.

Mitrani, A Dalziel, M M and Fitt, D (1992) *Competency Based Human Resource Management: Value-driven Strategies for Recruitment*, Kogan Page, London.

Obeng, E and Crainer, S (1994) *Making Re-engineering Happen*, Pitman, London.

Parkinson, M (1994) *Interviews Made Easy*, Kogan Page, London.

Ryan, C (1994) *The Master Marketer: How to Combine Tried and Tested Techniques with the Latest Ideas To Achieve Spectacular Marketing Success*, Kogan Page, London.

Sadler, P (1994) *Designing Organisations: The Foundation for Excellence*, Kogan Page, London.

Singer, M (1993) *Fairness in Personnel Selection: An Organisational Justice Perspective*, Avebury, Hampshire.

Skeats, J (1991) *Successful Induction: How to Get the Most From Your New Employees*, Kogan Page, London.

Smith, P (1993) *Marketing Communications: An Integrated Approach*, Kogan Page, London.

Waud, C (1994) *Employment Law 1994–95: The Practical Guide for Personnel Managers, Trade Union Officials, Employers, Employees and Lawyers*, Kogan Page, London.

Yate, M J (1992) *Great Answers to Tough Interview Questions: How to Get the Job You Want*, Kogan Page, London.

SOURCES OF INFORMATION

Rather than risk giving outdated information, only the titles and location towns of organisations are given below. Current addresses and telephone numbers may be obtained from local reference libraries or directory enquiries.

Association of Search and Selection Consultants, Ashbourne, Derbyshire.
British Institute of Graphologists, Weybridge, Surrey.
British Psychological Society, Leicester.
Campaign Against Age Discrimination in Employment, Altrincham, Cheshire.
Commission for Racial Equality, London.
Equal Opportunities Commission, Manchester.
Executive Recruitment Association, London.
Federation of Recruitment and Employment Services, London.
Institute of Employment Consultants, Woking, Surrey.
Institute of Employment Studies, Brighton, Sussex.
Institute of Personnel and Development, London.
New Ways to Work, London.

TRAINING MATERIAL

Effective Interviewing (audio cassette) based on the book by John Fletcher, (1991), Kogan Page, London.
Lowe, P (1993) *Recruitment and Interviewing Skills*, (workshop package), Kogan Page, London.
Meighan, M (1991) *How to Design and Deliver Induction Training Programmes*, Kogan Page, London.
Video Arts series of training videos and brief case booklets.

The major producers of psychometric instruments and tests (Saville and Holdsworth, The Psychological Corporation, ASE for example) provide training and information.

REFERENCE SOURCES

Local reference libraries will maintain an up-to-date section containing information on employment law and recent judgments. The most comprehensive service is published by Croner Information Services and includes reference books for employers, such as *Employment Law*, *Industrial Relations Law* and *Employment Law Line*.

Index